The POETRY of EVERYDAY LIFE

BOOKS BY STEVE ZEITLIN

A Celebration of American Family Folklore: Tales and Traditions from the Smithsonian Collection, with Amy Kotkin and Holly Cutting Baker

City Play, with Amanda Dargan

While Standing on One Foot: Puzzle Stories and Wisdom Tales from Jewish Tradition, with Nina Jaffe

Cow of No Color: Justice Stories from around the World, with Nina Jaffe

Because God Loves Stories: An Anthology of Jewish Storytelling

The Four Corners of the Sky: Creation Stories and Cosmologies from around the World

I Hear America Singing in the Rain: Poems, 1968–2002

Giving a Voice to Sorrow: Personal Responses to Death and Mourning, with Ilana Harlow

Hidden New York: A Guide to Places that Matter, with Marci Reaven

Steve Zeitlin

The POETRY of EVERYDAY LIFE

Storytelling and the Art of Awareness

With a Foreword by Bob Holman

Cornell University Press *Ithaca and London*

Permissions may be found at the end of the book.

First published 2016 by Cornell University Press

Printed in the United States of America

Library of Congress Cataloging-in-Publication Data

Names: Zeitlin, Steven J., author.
Title: The poetry of everyday life : storytelling and the art of awareness / Steve Zeitlin.
Description: Ithaca : Cornell University Press, 2016. | Includes bibliographical references and index.
Identifiers: LCCN 2016017477 | ISBN 9781501702358 (cloth : alk. paper)
Subjects: LCSH: Storytelling—United States. | Folklore—United States. | Folk-poetry, American—Themes, motives.
Classification: LCC GR72.5 .Z45 2016 | DDC 398.20973—dc23
LC record available at https://lccn.loc.gov/2016017477

Cloth printing   10 9 8 7 6 5 4 3 2 1

For my beautiful wife, Amanda,
with whom I've shared the poetry and
prose of everyday life

By poet, I mean every inventor, be he big or small, every discoverer, be he strong or weak, every creator, be he great or humble . . . and everyone who stands in awe before the day and the night, be he a philosopher or a guard at a vineyard.

—Kahlil Gibran

. . . As we beheld her striding there alone,
[We] knew that there never was a world for her
Except the one she sang and, singing, made.

—Wallace Stevens, "The Idea of Order at Key West"

I believe that creativity makes the world better: that if we are able, all of us, to figure out a way to reach into our deepest selves, to draw upon the unknown, to go below the surface of what we must do to live and to survive, to examine, with as much honesty as we can, what we believe, what we know to be true, and what we must do to be on that path, that the world is thereby improved. But nothing is easy. Really nothing.

—Esther Cohen

CONTENTS

FOREWORD

The Poetry of Everyday Life is a how-to book for everyone.

This is a book where language itself becomes a way of life, where poetry, so often thought of as obscure or elitist, takes its rightful place as the essence of language.

The Poetry of Everyday Life acknowledges and respects as "real" art what has come to be known as "folk" art, which is what Steve Zeitlin does for his day job as founding director of City Lore, the urban folklore center in New York. Since there's precious little basket weaving and pottery making going on in the mean streets of New York City, Zeitlin finds art in the words of the everyday citizens, tales told by real people, the characters and denizens who give the city its true story—its poetry. Although they are generally not poets, "real" poets do show up here, from Whitman to Tennyson to Shel Silverstein. On one page is Zeitlin's friend from elementary school Alex Pludwinsky, on another Billy Collins. Read just the poems in this book and you've got a great anthology. You know poetry—the sections where the lines are indented and the words don't go to the end of the page, poetry itself being as non-regularized as the cornucopia of characters living in these pages.

This book is a folklorist's contact list come to life, right before your eyes, spouting wisdom and truths that, as Zeitlin sees it, are actual poems. And after he points this out to you, then you see them that way, too. *The Poetry of Everyday Life* takes the black and white of a printed book and pours color in. We're Dorothy, arriving in Oz, not in Kansas anymore.

Every quote gets credited with the speaker's name. And then every name is ID'd, as Zeitlin seeks to credit each scrap of wisdom that came his way as a folklorist and a human being. The point is that acknowledging who spoke or wrote the words is crucial to understanding the content of what is said or written. In this way, Zeitlin is true to the impulse of the oral tradition. It's all genealogy, someone begetting someone who begets someone else. Except here it's words that do the begetting. It's the memories of your grandparents that are the poems, and when you lose that human connection, you lose the poetry.

And then there's the way that *The Poetry of Everyday Life* finds real poetry in real events. Whether it's the city reacting to 9/11, a sideshow barker inviting you into the tent, or two people inventing love, human happenstance not only provides an opportunity for a poem but is in itself a poem. In this way he reminds me of the griots, the West African poet-musicians, keepers of the oral tradition. There's not an event that can happen in tribal life in much of West Africa unless there's a griot there to announce it, to sing it into existence accompanied by the twenty-one-string kora, to pronounce to one and all that there's going to be a wedding now! or a naming ceremony, or a funeral.

Folks! Dear readers! One and all! Step right up! Direct your eyes to these pages, aka the Eighth Wonder of the World! For herein Steve Zeitlin pitches poetry the way a carny barker does, the way a good preacher/rabbi/swami does. In fact, he considers these talkers *poets*. His weekly Ping-Pong co-combatants turn out to be poets. His father, the Jewish atheist, just happens to be a poet. The man who lives in the subway tunnel? You got it. Listen to him long enough, you may come to believe, as he does, that

You are a poet!

(I like the pullout quotes spread through the chapters. If you want a shortcut to being a poet, just use them as a to-do list.)

The *Poetry of Everyday Life*, with its folkloric take on poetry, is in fact part of a new, diversifying definition of poetry in the United States, one that is developing its own history, often from ancient lineages. Hip hop is an example. Zeitlin sees the graffiti artists writing on trains as taking risks far different from the dictums you learn when your creative writing professor urges you to "take risks!" with your writing. I think of the visionaries, the precursors of hip hop, poets like proto-rappers Abiodun Oyewole and Umar Bin Hassan of The Last Poets and Gil Scott-Heron.

And there's the poetry slam, the mock-competitive poetry event invented by poet–construction worker Marc Smith, which is among the most vital grassroots art movements of the last fifty years. Smith sees slam as a wellspring for community, and the movement is still growing thirty years after the first hastily improvised slam (yes, he called it that from the start) at the Get Me High bar in Chicago.

Zeitlin also follows in the footsteps of a couple of other poets who helped popularize the art toward the end of the twentieth century. Piri Thomas (1928–2011), the Nuyorican (New York–Puerto Rican) poet, also took on the idea of the universality of poetry. There's a documentary film of his life named after words he often spoke, words that could have been Zeitlin's: *Every Child Is Born a Poet*. The film moves from El Barrio (Spanish Harlem), where Piri was born and raised, his coming-of-age via gangs, drugs, and crime, through his years in prison, to the writing of his autobiography, *Down These Mean Streets*, and ultimately his becoming a populist prophet dedicated to spreading the gospel of poetry. For Thomas, the innocence of a child, the belief in imagination, is humanity's natural state—as well as the state of being for the poet. The brutality of the mean streets of reality drowns that innocence. But one can be redeemed by returning to a state of grace—via poetry.

Walter Lowenfels (1897–1976) was another poet who shared Zeitlin's inclusive dynamic. *We're All Poets, Really*, proclaims the title of an anthology he edited. Lowenfels was a radical Left political poet, arrested for being a communist in 1953. His anthology called *From the Belly of the Shark* with the tagline *Poems by Chicanos, Eskimos, Hawaiians, Indians, Puerto Ricans with Related Poems by Others* foreshadowed multiculturalism by decades. By recognizing the variety of poetry traditions, Lowenfels was getting closer to Zeitlin's approach to poetry as the poetics of life—which I call "word art." My work with endangered languages has helped me realize that every culture has a word for art/ poetry of some kind—be it written or spoken or sung, whether it's aphorisms or stories or competitions. Papa Susso, the great Gambian griot, didn't consider his work to be poetry until we discussed how his words worked in the community. Now he says, "I'm a poet, a keeper of the oral tradition."

Zeitlin's definition of poetry in this book takes the art part for granted. See the poetry in the world, he says, and use language to the max. Like Walt Whitman himself, Zeitlin hears America singing. Unable to restrain himself, however, Steve Zeitlin the poet hears us—ALL of US! singing—in the rain! No surprise that he titled his book of poems exactly that, *I Hear America Singing in the Rain.*

It's that invincible optimism that gives this book its energy. I've spent years seeking a place for hip hop and spoken word inside the canon of English-language poetry. Zeitlin goes even further: he hears poetry in a homeless man's musings, in his wife's creating a melody, even in a poem! But he can't let the poem sit still. Here's what he has to say about Solomon Grundy, who, if you recall, was

> Born on Monday,
> Christened on Tuesday,
> Married on Wednesday,
> Took ill on Thursday,
> Grew worse on Friday,
> Died on Saturday,
> Buried on Sunday.
> That was the end
> Of Solomon Grundy.

For Zeitlin, "If we can create a society in which our apocryphal Solomon Grundy can play his heart out on Monday, raise hell on Tuesday, get a job on Wednesday, court all day Thursday, parent Friday, then retire, travel, and reminisce about it on Saturday—and if he finds traditional expressive material that is vital at every stage of his life—that really is not such a bad life for Solomon Grundy." Or for any of us.

Poetry has traditionally been thought of as a solitary art. There's Emily Dickinson in her upstairs bedroom in Amherst, secreted away, jotting lines on every available paper scrap, poems to be filed away, publishing only seven poems of the 1,789 she wrote. In a sense, poetry itself has been locked in that room with her, a true joy of life that has been kept hidden.

By showing us that poetry lives everywhere, by treating us readers like we're all poets, Steve seems to make the whole world into a poem, with all of us collaborating daily in the writing of it. Now, that's a poem!

Bob Holman
The Bowery, 2015

ACKNOWLEDGMENTS

Here's to all who helped me write this love letter to the world. This book features my name on the cover, but truly it was written collectively by family, friends, colleagues, and kindred spirits who contributed phrases, poems, and ideas. I would like to thank Esther Cohen for believing in this book when it was just a series of rambling thoughts and for showing it to my brilliant editor Frances Benson, who took up the cause. Caitlin Van Dusen also edited the book for me, helping to restructure it, adding her articulate light touch, and forcing me to clarify all my questionable metaphors. Amanda Heller copyedited the book, adding her wonderful turns-of-phrase throughout, as did Ange Romeo-Hall, the managing editor at Cornell University Press. Thanks to poet Jenny Factor for her twenty-three-page critique of the book, which helped immensely. My wife, folklorist Amanda Dargan, whom I accuse of being "uncreative" when she doesn't like something I've written, brought immense creativity and grounded common sense to this book, as she has with all that I have written.

Many of the essays in this book began as part of my regular column in *Voices: Journal of the New York Folklore Society*. I'm grateful to Ellen McHale, the Society's director, as well as to the two copyeditors for the *Journal*, Sherry Englund and Patty Mason.

This book has taken a lifetime to write, and my collaborators on previous projects have contributed to it: Amanda Dargan, Holly Cutting-Baker, Sandy Gross, Ilana Harlow, Mary Hufford, Marjorie Hunt, Marci Reaven, and Amy Warner. The staff at City Lore past and present has supported and inspired my work: Amanda Dargan, Hiroko Kazama, Elena Martínez, Sahar Muradi, Chris Mulé, Abby Ronner, Roberta Singer, and especially Catherine Fletcher, who directed the poetry programs at City Lore for many years. Thanks also to friends Flash Rosenberg, Alicia Vasquez, and Lisa Lipkin, and to my two brothers always, Murray and Bill.

My friend the poet and therapist Marc Kaminsky enabled me to explore my deepest self by pushing me to work at the outer limits of my intelligence—and contributed his prodigious intellect and empathy. Solomon Reuben, my lifelong high school friend, lived this book with me, making dozens of suggestions and engaging in endless conversations about the manuscript before he passed away. Among his final contributions is this poem, inspired by the book:

> Right here, right now,
> in everyday life,
> we love, we play,
> we create music, art and poetry.
>
> Enjoying and celebrating,
> we coax human nature out of suffering.
>
> We tune into the
> spontaneous creativity of Being.
>
> We are all lovers and poets—
> let's not skip a beat.

Introduction

Let the beauty we love be what we do.
—Rumi

A few years after I graduated from college, I ran into a former class-mate, Ross Abrams. He had started a medical practice by then, married, and had a child named Saul. I asked Ross if he told stories to his son at bedtime. "You know, Steve, it's a funny thing. I used to tell him fairy tales to put him to sleep. I told him 'Snow White' and 'Goldilocks and the Three Bears'—all the old fairy tales—until one night I just couldn't think of one. So out of desperation I said to him, 'Once upon a time, there was a little boy named Saul, and he woke up in the morning and had a bowl of Cheerios. Then he waited for the school bus, and then, for lunch, he came home for a bowl of Kraft macaroni and cheese.' My son loved it! After that, the only tale he ever wanted to hear was the story of his own day."

Always inspired to write poems based on everyday conversations and stories, I jotted down these lines:

> Once Upon a Time,
> My father, plumb out of fairy tales,
> Fashioned a tale about a boy named Saul
> Who wolfed down his Cheerios and waited for the school bus
> Came home to Kraft macaroni and cheese
>
> And it took me a moment to comprehend—
> That child was me
>
> But it became my favorite bedtime story
> The woof and warp of days
> Braided each night before my dad and I would part
> Wound by a childhood charmer
> Who spun life into art

The transformation of everyday life into art is at the root of all story-telling, memoir, autobiography, mythmaking, and legendry. We write "to order the mess."[1] Finding moments of artfulness and giving them the self-contained structure of a poem on a page or a picture on canvas or a tale that is told sets them apart from the chaos and the tedium of our daily lives and bespeaks their permanence.

We all have the capacity to express ourselves and respond aesthetically to our experiences. In the movie *Rocky*, the Sylvester Stallone character is asked why he became a boxer. "Because I couldn't sing and dance," he answers. Regardless of whether we are headed for the Broadway stage or the silver screen, we all have the capacity to express ourselves and respond aesthetically to our experiences.

Most of us tell jokes and stories, cook, dance, and celebrate. In these pages I explore the crannies of life where the aesthetics are nestled. "Only by imagination therefore can the world be known," writes Owen Barfield. "And what is needed is not only that larger and larger telescopes . . . should be constructed, but that the human mind should become increasingly aware of its own creative activity."[2]

The power of imagination lives, for instance, in the ability of children to transform ordinary objects for play. Particularly in years past, children leaping from the doorway as Superman or Batman had at their disposal an array of swords and shields that to the uninitiated more closely resembled dented garbage can lids and discarded umbrellas. "Let this broken antenna be a ray gun!" And through the magic of play, it was.[3] Urban children transform the cityscape. For the would-be circus performer or ballet dancer, the stoop provided the perfect stage. For a child with a ball, a fire hydrant was first base, second base was a lamp-post, and your little brother could be third base. As the poet Steven Smith writes, "We mistake the things we see for what they are."[4]

This book is part memoir, part essay, and partly a guide to maximizing your capacity for artistic expression. I begin by asking how we can tap into the poetics of things we often take for granted: the stories we tell, the people we love, the sports and games we play, even our sex lives. I explore how poems serve us in daily life, as well as the ways poems are used in crisis situations: to serve people with AIDS, or as a form of heal-ing and remembrance after September 11. I consider the tales and meta-phors of scientists as a kind of poetry that enables us to better understand the universe around us. I devote a section to art in the human life cycle and explain my own conception of "the human unit of time." I chronicle the contribution of daily artistic expression to our spiritual selves and echo William Blake's belief that imagination is sacred. We are at our best when we mirror the cre-ation of the universe in original, artful expression, for if we are not actively engaged in spinning new meanings for our lives, we are likely depressed or dying.

We are at our best when we mirror the creation of the universe in original, artful expression.

At one point many years ago, I made what my parents considered a "crazy" decision to study folklore, and I have dedicated my life to it. (As the folklorist Roger Welsch quipped, "You finally found a pond small enough.") This book offers this folklorist's take on the world. I explore the meaning to be found in the resonant experiences and evocative details of our own lives, in the shared humor of friends and lovers, the patter of cousins and uncles.

Folklore is often defined as traditions handed down by word of mouth across generations. But the definition of the term is perhaps best conveyed—and then intuited—by example. Like Edgar Allan Poe's purloined letter, writes Mary Hufford in *American Folklife: A Common-wealth of Cultures,*

> folklife is often hidden in full view, lodged in the various ways we have of discovering and expressing who we are and how we fit into the world. Folklife is reflected in the names we bear from birth, invoking affinities with saints, ancestors, or cultural heroes. Folklife is your grandfather and great-uncles telling stories of your father when he was a boy. It is the secret languages of children, the codenames of CB operators, and the working slang of watermen and doctors. It is the sung parodies of the "Battle Hymn of the Republic," and the parables told in church or home to delight and instruct. It is African-American rhythms embed-ded in gospel hymns, bluegrass music, and hip hop, and it is the Lakota flutist rendering anew his people's ancient courtship songs.[5]

In one of the most frequently quoted articles on the discipline of folklore, the folklorist and sociolinguist Dell Hymes writes: "The shaping of deeply felt values into meaningful . . . form, is present in all communities, and will find some means of expression among all. . . . Our work is rooted in recognition that beauty, form and meaningful expression may arise wherever people have a chance, even half a chance to share what they enjoy or must endure." He closes the thought by noting the "satisfaction in the voice of Mrs. Blanche Tohet of Warm Springs, Oregon, when, having finished fixing eels to dry one evening, she stood back looking at them and said, 'There, [ain't] that beautiful.'"[6]

In this book, I go beyond the traditions we share to the beauty and personal meanings we find in our individual lives. Sheila Ortiz, for example, the highly sought-after hairstylist in my hometown, tells me that when she's cutting a client's hair—even if she hasn't cut it in many years, even if many hairstylists have worked on it since—she can sense her own haircut in the hair. "Once, a customer I hadn't seen in a long time came into the shop. As I looked down at his head, I said to him, 'I once cut your hair, didn't I?'

"'But that was years ago,' he answered. 'How did you remember that?'

"'You always know your cut,' I said."

If Sheila's hair stylist's chair is her stage, so it goes, too, at the coffee shop in the Hastings, New York, train station where Avi Schwartz, the owner, greets me from behind the counter each day. On one occasion I asked him about the high prices for coffee. "That's because we give you the high-end experience." And indeed he does in a coffee shop that is cozy, warm, and inviting, with classical music or opera playing over the speakers. "Keep shining," he said to me one day as I ran to catch the train.

The next day I asked him, "Avi, are you shining today?"

"Actually, Steve," he said, "here I'm shining all the time—I have to be. Actually, I'm a very shy person. It's this coffee counter that makes me shine. It's my stage."

"So you're in show business?"

"Haven't you noticed?" he asked.

In my work, I've fallen in love with carnival pitches, children's rhymes, family stories, ancient cosmologies, and oral poetry traditions from around the world. The job of the folklorist is to ensure that great artistry doesn't slip through the cracks of other disciplines. Folklorists look for marginalized art forms and performers and ensure that they get the attention they deserve. We document songs, stories, and traditions that the world desperately needs to remember and be inspired by.

As a folklorist, I've become acutely aware of musicality in language. My profession aims to free the poetry in people—the things people say and the way they say them. My friend Marc Kaminsky, a poet and therapist, ran poetry and reminiscence groups for many years with older Jewish adults in Manhattan and the Bronx. He spoke about the sudden realization of the older women in his group: "We talk poetry!"[7]

Among the highest compliments I've received was from Marc, who once described me as "a poetic listener." He described the way a friend of his, the anthropologist Barbara Myerhoff, listened as "something akin to soul-flight: a period of grace, when she was granted the gift of leaving her own life to travel in another's."[8] Listening deeply is key to tuning in to the poetry of everyday life.

We all need to find creative solutions for how to be.[9] Even before I began to study folklore, I was a poet, which I define as someone who writes poems, not as someone who necessarily publishes poetry or is recognized by the academy. In this book my own approach is to combine a folkloric perspective, which documents the creative expressions of a culture, with a creative writing approach, which addresses our personal creativity. My career observing and collecting folklore melds with my creative writing; many overheard colloquial phrases become a potential poem or story. I believe this convergence of poetry and folklore gives birth to something new: a new way of seeing ourselves, and a new way of being in the world. I hope

My own approach is to combine a folkloric perspective, which documents the creative expressions of a culture, with a creative writing approach, which addresses our personal creativity.

to expand your consciousness of the beauty in your own world—and to inspire you to draw on words and other forms of creative expression to acknowledge and share this heightened awareness. To live a creative life is the best way to engage with the beauty of the everyday.

To live a creative life is the best way to engage with the beauty of the everyday.

In this book I use the word *poetry* as it is used colloquially: to suggest the poetics of life. I explore the many ways we "artify," "storify," and poeticize our daily lives.[10] I decided to focus on the poetry rather than the folklore of everyday life as a way of extending the book beyond the shared culture and traditional forms of folklore to include more personal forms of self-expression. Since I write about everything from Ping-Pong to cave paintings, I might have called this book *The Art of*—or *The Beauty of* or *The Patterning of—Everyday Life*. *Poetry* better expresses my own perspective, as it's through words and language that I try to understand the worlds I inhabit. For me, in the beginning, there truly was, and is still, the word—and human beings are, indeed, *Homo poeticus.*

We live in a world that advertises its products to us around the clock, often in ways we are not even aware of. Game apps for children made by the toy company Fisher-Price include ads targeted at infants. We are told what to buy, what to crave, and how to live; we are only kidding ourselves if we pretend the messages have no effect on us. It is therefore becoming more urgent to spend time expressing what is distinctive in our own lives. We need to cut through the cacophony of messages to hear our own voice. I've included a section that suggests ways to tap in to the artfulness and artistry of our own lives and that shows how doing this—in creative writing and other forms—enables us to find a voice to express who we are to ourselves and the world. I go on to make suggestions about how to find audiences for your work, to share your vision with the world. After all, no one's goal should be to sneak through the world unnoticed.

Language is grounded in poetry and metaphor. Our words come from simple sounds for natural elements or body parts (*foot, head, heart*). Through time and usage, these words are combined into metaphors that express concepts ("the head of the class," "the foot of the bed," "the heart of the matter"). *Window* originally meant "eye of the wind." In his essay "The Poet," written in 1844, Ralph Waldo Emerson wrote: "The etymologist finds the deadest word to have been once a brilliant picture. Language is fossil poetry. As the limestone of the continent consists of infinite masses of the shells of animalcules, so language is made up of images, or tropes, which now, in their secondary use, have long ceased to remind us of their poetic origin."[11] In a sense, every word is a poem.

And so it follows that every word in this book is plagiarized, swiped shamelessly from the poetry inherent in the English language. In truth, I owe a debt for borrowing fragments from everyone I meet. In poetry, as in folklore, I am a scavenger of the words and phrases expressed by people I've known and grown close to. So quotes from my readings and my friends pepper my own words and guide my thoughts.

As a graduate student in literature, when I learned to read *Beowulf* in the original Old English, I fell in love with the centuries-old tradition of poetic craft. I loved to engage deeply with the poets who wrote their masterpieces using forms like the sonnet, the ode, the villanelle, the haiku, and the ghazal.

Yet often when poets themselves define *poetry*, they go beyond these forms. A definition like "rhythmical composition, written or spoken, for exciting pleasure by beautiful, imaginative, or elevated thoughts" certainly transcends the set literary forms to include music and many kinds of speech. In his famous 1821 essay "A Defence of Poetry," Percy Bysshe Shelley writes about poetry in ways far removed from rhyme and meter. "It is the perfect and consummate surface and bloom of all things; it is as the odor and the color of the rose to the texture of the elements which compose it, as the form and splendor of unfaded beauty.... It is as it were the interpenetration of a diviner nature through our own."[12] My favorite definition of the term *poetry* is "the intensification of language."[13] This intensification begins with the poetry of everyday life.

In other parts of the world, particularly in the Middle East, poetry is far more integral to daily life than in the United States. Poetry is recited at births and weddings and is even used to settle disputes. Many immigrants from the Middle East carry poetry notebooks to jot down both their own poems and those by Rumi, Hafez, and the masters. A televised poetry contest, *Million's Poet,* was inspired by and has more viewers than *American Idol.*

My favorite example of this integration of poetry into daily life comes from the Lebanese American anthropologist Najwa Adra, who did her fieldwork in Yemen:

> Muslims try to perform a pilgrimage to Mecca at least once in their lifetimes. In the past, the journey was long and risky—pilgrims traveled by camel caravan, they were subject to heat exhaustion, robbery, and other dangers. Today, most travel by plane. In some parts of Yemen, when a member of the family leaves for the pilgrimage, the family left at home builds a swing, called a *madraha,* and hangs it from a sturdy tree. They then hang clothing belonging to the pilgrim over the same branch that holds the swing. What does this have to do with poetry? Two people at a time swing while singing songs for the pilgrim, and wishing him or her a safe return. One singer leads with a line, and the second repeats it. Women and men, young and old, chant these songs whenever they have time. The swing stays up until the pilgrim returns.[14]

Sometimes the songs, called the *darh,* simply assert that the singer misses the pilgrim; sometimes they list the gifts the singer expects from the pilgrim on his/her return. They are sung both to keep a traveler safe and to express the family's pain of separation." In one example:

Oh [protective] dove of Mt. Arafat   Hover over and circle down
To locate our pilgrim   Among the pilgrims from the North
You can't miss him   There he is, small and dark[15]

A few years ago, a reporter from the *Los Angeles Times* interviewed me about my work as a folklorist. When I starting talking about the poetry of everyday life, he tried to wrap his mind around my thoughts. "I guess what you're saying is that a folklorist is a scientist of human expression—and that our creative expression stands as evidence for the soul." He paused for a moment. "I think we've had a metaphysical breakthrough," he said, laughing.

We experience the arts in concentric circles. The outer circle is made up of the work of artists whom we don't know personally. Inside that circle are circles containing the art and stories of acquaintances, friends, and family, and the work of these inner circles is particularly charged because it is tied to memory, love, and passion, and it ripens with time. As my son, Ben, a film director (who in college decided to add a silent "h" to his name and spell it Benh), said in an interview with the *New York Times*, "Jokes around a dinner table—that is the art, as opposed to looking to the museum. My parents' appreciation for that—they definitely got that through to me."[16] Of course, Benh loves museums as much as we do.

The arts are not primarily a commodity. The arts are something we create, not just consume. Whereas our society generally contends that the outer circle of "great" masterpieces is the essence of art, folklorists consider the inner circle, the art of everyday life, to be the core. The rest of our lives revolves around it.

Masterworks of art can move us deeply through their intrinsic beauty. Most great novelists draw heavily on the grassroots cultures and the indigenous artistry of the places they write about. We know their writing has moved us when it gives us goose bumps or when we find ourselves referencing its images in our own lives. They can give us perspective, help us shape the way we view our lives—but our own life story takes precedence. Just as my friend's son Saul wanted to hear the story of his own day, it's our own lives that we ultimately need to hear told back to us in ways that provide us with increased understanding.

It's our own lives that we ultimately need to hear told back to us in ways that provide us with increased understanding.

"Our greatest desire," writes the psychologist Daniel Taylor, "greater even than the desire for happiness, is that our lives mean something. This desire for meaning is the originating impulse of story."[17] For me, sustenance comes not so much from the flour and water of the quotidian but from the yeast of humor and playfulness that infuses it; the artfulness makes the bread rise. In this book I take you into the universe of people and places and art forms that I love. Not only do I include a chapter on Ping-Pong, my favorite sport, but I also set up a game between the writer and the reader in which my experiences and yours Ping-Pong across a net and we come out, I hope, even—and exhilarated—by the end.

In each of these essays I have occasionally included short poems of my own to illustrate a particular point. I've done this when I believe the poems express an idea or a feeling that I couldn't explain in any other way, and I include them also to encourage you to find the forms—visual, written, musical—to express what is deepest and most distinctive about you and can be expressed only through your art. My poems are more numerous in the two chapters that treat the subjects of sex and death, since those are subjects that poetry can often address more potently than prose.

Among the subjects my wife, fellow folklorist Amanda Dargan, and I have studied are carnival pitchmen and others who use their voices to sell their products in the marketplace or their attractions on the midway. They were always the kings of hyperbole. As a sideshow barker might put it, in this book you will meet THE GREATEST CHARACTERS THE PLANET HAS EVER KNOWN, experience THE INNER LIFE OF PING-PONG, meet THE TRANSCENDENT AIDS POETS, discover THE MEANINGS OF SEX THAT YOU NEVER IMAGINED, see THE ASTONISHING CAVE PAINTINGS, and hear STORIES THAT CHURN IN THE CAULDRON OF SCIENCE. Bring out your inner folklorist and inner artist. I invite you to see through *my* worlds into those *you* inhabit and love. The cultural worlds that animate you lie just behind the worlds I write about, even if your own subjectivity and perspective on the world are nothing like my own. Take this journey with me, and then it's your turn to document, appreciate, and give voice to your life in your own art. "And above all," as Roald Dahl writes, "watch with glittering eyes the whole world around you because the greatest secrets are always hidden in the most unlikely places."[18] And there is always a chance to discover, like Saul, my friend's son, the story of your days.

Part I POETRY IN PEOPLE

1

Kindred Spirits

Sea of Souls

If a tree fell in the forest did it happen at all?
But the silence is deafening when the tallest tree falls
—Radoslav Lorković

Tony

"People think of me as homeless," said Tony Butler, who made his home in the tunnels of the New York City subway. "Hell, the whole world is my home. That's the way I look at it. And the beautiful thing about the whole world being my home is that I ain't gotta worry about no freakin' landlord evicting me anytime he gets ready. The only time I get evicted from this world is when I die. And that's a good feeling. Yeah, I dig what I'm doing—the only thing I complain about is the weather. A few times I had to refuse to freeze to death."

Someone once described Tony as an "African American subway Buddha." The description is apt: he'd take off his heavy shoes and make himself at home, sprawling on the subway benches with his butt firmly planted on two cushions that he carried with him at all times for comfort. He wore a gauzy, funky-looking veil, held on by a headband that covered more or less of his face, depending on his mood.

I first met Tony back in 1996 at the Broadway-Lafayette subway station in New York, where he sat with a newspaper spread out on his lap, playing cards dealt onto a wooden bench. "I'm breaking in a new deck," he told me. He was playing out bridge hands in the *Daily News*. Looking up at me, he said, "See all those people getting on the train this morning? The working poor. The *working* poor. That says it all, doesn't it? That's why I don't work."

Tony was not your ordinary homeless man—or, in fact, your ordinary man. He lived entirely off the grid. Once he told me, "I got arrested taking a pee from the platform onto the tracks. They confiscated my possessions and all my money. When they let me out they told me I could reclaim my stuff in Brooklyn. I show up there and they tell me I need an ID. How's a guy like me to get an ID? To get an ID, you need an ID. I'm outside the system. I don't pay taxes; I don't vote; I never had a social security card—I don't want any part of it."

Tony's "office," I discovered, was the last seat in the row of wooden benches on the east side of the platform. He'd commandeered an adjoining bench as his gaming table, where he dealt cards or moved chess pieces to pass the time—that is, when he wasn't busy with his real job of monitoring the trains on behalf of the greater New York City public. He made announcements whenever the trains were running late. "I consider myself a 'volunteer New York City Transit associate,'" he told me. "That word, *volunteer*, is important—that's where the humanitarianism comes into it. I help people who are lost on the platform. It really offends me, it really sickens me, to see customers down here not knowing where they're going. It sickens me to see people here at the Broadway-Lafayette stop who think they're at the East Broadway stop." His ongoing announcements set them straight.

Another time I ran into Tony, he was playing a game of solitaire. "The problem with this game," he told me, "is that there's an overabundance of losing combinations." In the weeks and years that followed, I realized that his observation applied not just to solitaire: this was his philosophy—and he said it poetically:

> Too many things go wrong, and not enough things go right.
> Wrong is what makes the world go round.
> Wrong is king.
> Wrong rules.
> Wrong dominates.
> The world is actually geared to go wrong.
> There's too many ways for things to go wrong,
> and it's impossible for everything to go right.[1]

Tony also had his own view of time: "Time is there and it's not there. If they stopped all the clocks and watches in the world, it wouldn't matter. It doesn't mean anything. Time exists for people like you, who live by the clock. I've got from now on."

After I had known him for a few months, Tony said to me, "Hey, Steve, I wouldn't mind if you laid some cans on me."

I brought him some cans of Campbell's soup a few days later. "Tony," I said, "living down here in the subways, how do you heat the soup up?"

"Steve, you know what I've discovered? The only difference between hot food and cold food is the taste." Tony steered clear of the Thanksgiving dinners given for the homeless about town. "Why don't you go to get your free meal?" I asked him.

"Too many undesirables," he said. "The one thing you don't want to mix is food and undesirables."

Tony and I struck up a friendship that lasted about five years, until 2004, when he died, at age fifty-three, from infections incurred in the tunnels. I took him on his last journey to St. Vincent's Hospital—when he finally admitted he was sick enough to go. As we rode there in an ambulance, I asked him, "Tony, what are you thinking about?"

"At times like this," he said, "you don't really think about anything."

He lost consciousness soon after and died about a week later. He was buried on Hart Island, the potter's field for New York City.

I remember a day when Tony reached into one of his many pockets and pulled out a scrap of newspaper. "Look at this," he said. "This is a little tiny obit. This woman, it says, was born in eighteen ninety-eight and died in two thousand and two. Can you believe that? She lived in three centuries. I want to do that." Tony made it for a little more than half of one century. He did not consider himself a homeless man; he was an "alternative lifestyler," as one his friends, Torin Reid, a subway motorman, suggested. Although we walked divergent paths, we both saw some of ourselves in each other. If I had seen my father killed in front of me, as Tony Butler did, would I have parted ways with society and found myself living in the subway? Perhaps our spirits are simply in closer proximity than our appearances suggest. Everyone, it seems to me, can expand their consciousness by finding friendship and common cause with those who are wholly different from themselves, people whom they would rarely meet in the ordinary run of life. It's up to each of us to find these kindred spirits.

For a project she called *The Architecture of Despair,* my friend the photographer Margaret Morton photographed the structures where many homeless people live in the tunnels and under the bridges of Manhattan.[2] Among the men and women she documented was a homeless Chinese man who lived underneath the Manhattan Bridge. I sought to capture a little of my relationship with Tony when I wrote these lines, inspired by Margaret's work:

Margaret

Photographing the structures of the homeless
in early morning light—

homes resembling a nest, a cave,
a house on wheels
homes built in the darkness of a tunnel
under the West Side Highway
in the ironic hollow of a Bloomingdale's bin

Mr. Lee's shanty covered with oranges
for the Chinese New Year

where Margaret arranged for the funeral
for she was the nearest of kin

When we document or celebrate another human being, we become part of that person's life. A few years before I first encountered Tony, when I was just beginning my career, I met the pioneering folklorist Alan Lomax at a party. He seemed interested in talking to me as a newcomer to the field. "I discovered Leadbelly and Muddy Waters," he said to me. "Who have you discovered?" The question left me nonplussed. I felt I hadn't yet discovered myself, let alone anyone else. And I didn't think that telling him about Tony Butler would get me far.

The Beatles were fond of saying that their manager, Brian Epstein, didn't discover them, as he often claimed; it was the Beatles who discovered Brian Epstein. I would love to have told Alan something to this effect: Perhaps you didn't "discover" Muddy Waters; perhaps Muddy Waters discovered you—and I imagine you both discovered something of your-selves in each other. Many of the singers and storytellers that folklorists claim to have "discovered" are themselves folklorists of sorts who have, in turn, collected stories and songs their whole lives and used them in their own art. In particular, there is a deep, often spiritual, if unusual, connection between folk musicians and the folklorists who document and promote their careers: for instance, between Alan Lomax and Lead-belly, between John Cohen of the New Lost City Ramblers and Roscoe Holcomb, and between folklorist Ralph Rinzler and Doc Watson.

In my work as a folklorist, I have long realized that we are not so much studying and documenting the folks we interview as we are part-nering with and learning from them in order to bring their stories and their artistry to a wider audience. They are not our "informants," a sorry term often used in the discipline, but our collaborators. Much of my work involves documenting cultural forms, but much of it, too, is about connecting with kindred spirits from other walks of life and col-laborating with them on a deep and personal level. The poetry of every-day life resides in stories, poems, foods, places, and songs. But it also resides in people—those endlessly complex beings whom we meet, poeticize, and storify in order to establish a kinship.

My uncle Jay, for instance, worked as a life insurance agent, but he was a poet at heart. For me, a quip he once made captures his true self. "You know, Steve, Joseph Campbell told us we should 'follow our bliss.' You know I can't follow my bliss. I have a job and two kids and a wife to support. But at least when he says 'follow your bliss,' I know what he means." This story stands for the philosophical side of my uncle Jay in my consciousness. It symbolizes him. I carry it with me as a touchstone.

Always a philosophical soul, Uncle Jay loved Robert Service poems, like "The Shooting of Dan McGrew," about a shoot-out in the Mala-mute Saloon in which Dangerous Dan McGrew—"in a buckskin shirt that was glazed with dirt"—and his rival shoot each other over the woman known as Lou. We read the poem together the day before he died. Uncle Jay also taught me how to fold a sports jacket so it fits neatly into a suitcase. But I always imagine him saying to me, "Clothes don't make the man. A poem makes the man."

Some people are "geniuses in the art of living." Seek them out.

The characters I've gotten to know in my work, many of whom have passed on, come back to me through stories. I discover again and again what the folklorist Sandy Rikoon narrowed into three words: "People are smart." Some people are "geniuses in the art of living."[3] Seek them out. Make them your teachers. Much of what I know about life I've learned from them.

As a folklorist, I hope in a modest way to document the lives of marginalized people who rarely see their stories writ large. My relationship with the extraordinary individuals I describe here is a testament to solidarity and connection across difference.[4] I am not denying the differences in our situations or walks of life, but they are kindred spirits nonetheless. Here I take notice of what I have learned from them.

Ethel

From Ethel Mohamed, the marvelous seamstress who began to embroider her memories after the death of her Lebanese husband, I learned lessons about how to grow old. When she was in her seventies, we brought her from her home in Belzoni, Mississippi, to the Smithsonian Folklife Festival for the Grand Generation Program. She told us:

Well, just the other day my daughter asked me, "Mama, do you feel old? When I see you sit on the side, I think maybe you feel old." Oh no, I don't feel old. I'm the age of whoever I talk to. Don't worry about that. If it's a little girl twelve years old, I'm her age, and I enjoy every moment. And if it's a young girl who's sixteen, I enjoy her, because I'm her age. I remember when I was sixteen. If she tells me about a boyfriend, I know about that, too. And if I'm with a twenty-four-year-old mother with young babies, I know exactly what she's talking about. And if I'm with seventy-seven-year-old folks, I know about that, too. That's one of the good things about getting old: you're the age of whoever you're with.[5]

I'm much older now than when we interviewed Ethel. But I think of her comments, too, when I am speaking to a much younger person—a student or a friend of one of my children. Yes, I've been the age that they are now. However, I realize that while the young person is cognizant of speaking to a much older person, I perceive the person as my own age. I need to constantly remind myself, "I am actually not their age." It's one of the strange things about getting older. My long-lost friend, the oncologist Ross Abrams, told me of an older woman in her late eighties who was treated by one of his colleagues. "You look at me and you see a shriveled old woman," she said, "but I'm that seventeen-year-old girl inside."

Moishe

Moishe Sacks, a retired baker and the unofficial rabbi of the Intervale Jewish Center, the last synagogue remaining in the South Bronx (since closed), taught me about retirement, aging, and death—as he put it, "how to live." Sacks, who was about seventy when I met him, had bushy eyebrows, a wide face, and immense wisdom in his words. Although his grown children urged him to leave the Bronx, with its high crime rate, he steadfastly refused. One time he even told me that he was worried that he hadn't been mugged lately: he thought it was a sign that the neighborhood was going downhill. Then one day, when he was about seventy, in the doorway of his storefront synagogue, he was robbed and pushed down a few steps. He went to the doctor and learned that he had a hairline fracture in his skull and that it would take ten years for it to heal fully. He told me that he was hoping to live until his head healed. He lived for ten more years, and died with his head fully recovered.

Until his death in 1995, Sacks remained a classic Talmudic reasoner. Every week he would try to put together the minimum of ten men, a minyan, needed for synagogue service, which was never an easy task in the South Bronx. If only nine men were present, Sacks would point out, "Let God come down and see that we only have nine. When he comes down, we'll count him in!" Once when there were only six men, Sacks noted that the IRS allows two deductions for each elderly individual.

If the U.S. government allows it, he reasoned, certainly God could do the same. On that occasion, he was apparently overruled.[6]

For the documentary *The Grand Generation*, a portrait of six dynamic elderly Americans, which I coproduced with Paul Wagner and Marjorie Hunt, Sacks shared these thoughts:

> Moses was the first one who formulated a form of retirement. He said the tribe of the Levis could work up to the age of fifty. At fifty, he told them, they should retire from hard work—but not from work. They became supervisors of others who came up. The only work that old age has is to keep on working and to be young.
>
> I have trouble too sometimes. You see that top button on my shirt, under the collar? Try to get that button through when you have arthritis in your fingers, and the button knows that you can't button it. So you don't look at the button. The way to button your top button is to ignore it. Say, "Button, go away. I'm not going to look at you." Look some other place and try it, and you'll see how fast you can button your button. I've tried it: it works.
>
> Death doesn't matter to me. I don't think I'll know death. I know only two things: the present, and how to live. And the present how to live does not include death. So why should I worry.[7]

"I don't think I'll know death. I know only two things: the present, and how to live."

Moishe Sacks also offered this reverie on the art of baking, which all of us can learn from. I added some line breaks:

> I love to braid a challah.
> I love to bake a cake.
> When I first learned, my hands flew into the process . . .
> I had a weekly schedule:
> Monday, I made a cake called *apple ness*,
> Tuesday strudel,
> Wednesday *bapkes*,
> Thursday this or that,
> But at the end of Sunday evening, I was happy,
> Because by Monday
> It went back to *apple ness*.

"I had accomplished what I had set out to do," he said. "Therefore, I was happy." Is there a better definition of happiness?

Kewulay

From Kewulay Kamara I learned about how an ancient mythology can shape a way of life far from its indigenous roots. Kewulay is my "friend and close associate," as we respectfully (and jokingly) refer to each other. For more than a decade we had the chance to work together on the documentary *In Search of Finah Misa Kule*. Directed by Kewulay, the documentary chronicles his quest to reconstitute an ancient epic handed down in his family. When he was a boy of fourteen in the village of Dankawali in Northeast Sierra Leone, Kewulay watched his father, a member of the Finah clan of oral poets and masters of ceremony, writing down the ancient stories in the Kuranko language in an Arabic script on an animal skin with a reed pen. His father was concerned that his children would no longer continue to pass down the stories in the oral tradition. Kewulay tells of his decision to leave the manuscript in the village as an heirloom after he immigrated to the United States. He then tells of the breakout of the Civil War in Sierra Leone and his journey back to his home only to discover that the manuscript was destroyed when the village was razed. "A thousand years of history lay in ashes," he says.

Kewulay returns with his son Kalie to Dankawali to re-collect and retell the ancient stories using cameras and computers rather than a reed pen. I was so pleased to travel with them to the village to meet this sweet clan of elders for whom "humility is nobility." Practicing, good-hearted Muslims who live in peace with the neighboring Christian populations, his brothers and cousins do not drink, but Kewulay and I did spend a magical evening telling each other stories of our very different lives in a bar set up in a veranda in downtown Kabala, the larger town where Kewulay went to school.

Kewulay's family mythology is of a people who live by the word. "A person who cannot bear to hear," he told me, "will have nothing of value said in their presence." "Words do not rust, words do not rot." His stories come from a time "when what was said was done, and what was done was said." As his cousin Momory Kamara put it,

> You are not a finah because you lie
> You are not a finah because you slash
> You are not a finah because you kill
> You are a finah because
> When the people want a word said
> But the word is hard to say
> *Finah, say it!*
> The people say,
> And the finah says it.

"Each word that a finah utters," Kewulay says as the film opens, "has his life in them. Each word that the Finah utters is beyond poetry, is beyond history. It's an instrument that can create the whole world." As the film closes, he says, "We live by the wisdom in these stories."

Kewulay brings the humility and the gift for words of the Finah clan of poets to bear on his life in Jackson Heights, Queens, both as a teacher and organizer of *baro* gatherings and Kwanzaa celebrations. He also teaches young people to write praise poems:

> If I tell you that my name is Kewulay, that might not mean a lot to you. But if I tell you that I am the son of Kamara and Mara, and I come from the village of Dankawali at the foothills of the great Loma mountains near the mouth of the River Niger, that starts to mean something. All of a sudden I am part of something much greater. A child to be praised may be just a little boy—but pointing out who his father is and who his grandfather is in a praise poem elevates that person. It's not saying that a person has a lot of money or that he is the president of the United States, but that he is a father or mother or a grandfather or a grandmother—and that's important enough.

Wow. So I am Steve Zeitlin, son of Shirley Stein, grandson of Bella Brodsky from the town of Shpola in the Ukraine near the banks of the famed Khovkivka River.

Though we all don't all have Kewulay's direct connection to a mythology of words to live by, we all do tell stories and can draw on those stories as a kind of mythology. Like a blessing delivered over a meal—"Keep us mindful and responsive to the needs of others," for instance—we cannot always live up to the words and ideals in our stories and poems and prayers. But they provide guideposts and enshrine our daily lives with meaning.

Fred

Former medicine show doc Fred Bloodgood taught me about the power of words to elevate the seedier sides of life. I first met Fred in 1979 when I was working for the Smithsonian Folklife Festival. I was planning a program with my wife, Amanda, on the old-time medicine shows that traveled to small towns throughout the country beginning in the years following the Civil War. We ran an ad in *Amusement Business* looking for performers who'd worked on the shows. Fred Bloodgood's son wrote to us and suggested we contact Fred, who worked from 1928 until 1939 as a medicine show doc throughout Georgia, Mississippi, Alabama, and Texas. He also worked as a carnival "geek show" pitchman in the North in the off-season. A geek show featured a seemingly deranged man who would bite off the head of a snake or a chicken as part of the show.

The way I got into show business? Well, my dad took me to the circus and the circus was just great but to me the sideshow—the sideshow was absolutely inspiring! And at that time I solemnly vowed that if I ever got out of school I would surely become a sideshow talker. I just thought that to be able to stand on that platform in front of a long, long line of pictorial paintings, meanwhile extolling the benefits to be derived by actually witnessing that congress of freaks and curiosities and monstrosities—surely that would be the best occupation a man could ever have.

Well the day I finished high school—that would have been in 1927—the very next day I hitchhiked to the nearest circus, and in no time I was over on the sideshow. Then occurred the most exciting, adventurous years that a youth could ever have. . . . It's a far cry from selling typewriters and adding machines, I'll tell you.[8]

Fred was, as one reporter put it, "a master jeweler in the timeless language of the pitch."[9] He was fond of stating the pitchman's credo: "Never, never use one word when four will suffice." Bloodgood presented "glittering galaxies of gorgeously gowned girls" and featured, among others, "Tillie Tashman, that teasing, tantalizing, tormenting, tempestuous, tall, tan torso-twister from Texas."

Bloodgood and other sideshow artists used similes to compare the outrageous antics of their attractions with the mundane, everyday experiences of their audience. He describes the wounds inflicted by "venomous reptiles" on his beleaguered "geek," a local drunk who was paid to bite off the head of a snake: "You will see the blood course from those wounds just as you'd pour water from a glass." Standing on a raised platform in front of the geek show tent, he'd announce:

> When I throw that live chicken you see me now holding
> Down deep into that steel-bound cage,
> You're going to see a most amazing change come over the old
>   woman.
> The eyes will dilate, the pupils glow just like two red-hot coals
>   of fire.
> You'll hear her emit just one long soul-searing scream,
> And then she'll leap clear across that steel bound arena
> Catch that bird between those massive jaws,
> Bite off the head with those long and tusky teeth.
> And then, ladies and gentlemen,
> You'll see her suck, drain and draw
> Every drop of blood from that bleeding, throbbing, quivering,
>   pulsating body
> With the very same relish as you or I
> Would suck the juice of an orange.
> It's one of the most disgusting,
> One of the most repulsive,
> Yet I'll say one of the most interesting sights
> you've seen in all your life.[10]

From Fred I learned that you can write or tell about the grungiest, most sordid aspects of life as long as your language is elevated and poetic. Good advice for any writer.

I think of Fred each time we run a public program at City Lore, the nonprofit cultural center I direct on New York's Lower East Side. When I stand at the door wondering if we'll be able to attract an audience—when the crowds are not necessarily flocking—I often think of Fred, who would stand in front of the gathered crowd on carnival midways, holding a chicken in the air and saying, "We are going to feed the geek this chicken you see me here now holding, whether one of you comes, all of you come, or none of you come."

Fred and I had a running joke that every few years I'd bring him out of retirement to perform his pitches "one more time, with feeling." Each time Fred performed for us, he would address the audience by saying, "Here we are presenting what conceivably may be the last, the final medicine show the world will ever know. The quaint rhetoric you hear will vanish, like the medicine show people themselves. As I used to say in the old shows: I want to thank you, one and all, for your kind, courteous, and undivided attention. Wishing you a safe return to your respective homes and destinations—and a very, very fond good night."

The phone in my office rang in 1997 and Fred's wife, Mary, told me that Fred had passed away. There would be no more medicine shows and no more Fred Bloodgoods. He had stepped out of retirement for the last time. I stood, closed the door of my office, and wept.

Annie

The Spaldeen is the New Yorkism for the ball that became ubiquitous on New York City streets and playgrounds, sold at the corner store and manufactured by the Spalding Company, from whence comes its street name. These balls bounced high and were soft enough that they did not generally break windows, except when batted with force. Passionate Spaldeen owners often made their fellow players guarantee "chips on the ball," meaning that everyone would chip in to buy a new one if the ball was lost, a child's first insurance policy. Generations of New Yorkers grew up passionate about their Spaldeens, but for the performance artist, writer, and storyteller Annie Lanzillotto, they became an instructive metaphor for life. From Annie

I leaned how an individual can draw on childhood experiences as powerful metaphors to address life's most difficult challenges.

"Spaldeens took on the smell of the street," she writes. "Spaldeens sweated and got dirty. Spaldeens taught me soul; to find adventure, to fly, to roll, to hide, to float, to be buoyant, to bounce back even after you rolled down the sewer." At night, "I'd wash my hands and face, and my Spaldeen. I scrubbed it in the sink with soapy water and a washcloth. It smelled clean, ready for the next day. I slept with it under my pillow."[11] She dreamed about where all the lost Spaldeens could be: "On rooftops in gutters, in sewer pipes, attics, basements, the East River, floating out into the ocean, washed up along the shore on beaches in far off countries, in the bellies of the whales."[12]

Annie was the first person in her family to go away to college and was admitted to Brown. One night before she left she had her first beautiful lesbian experience after playing ball on the beach in Coney Island. She then decided to get her portrait painted on the boardwalk as a going-away present for her mother. Her mom took one look at the painting and immediately noticed a small lump the artist had faithfully rendered on her neck, curved gently like a Spaldeen. It was as if the painter had X-ray eyes. Annie was diagnosed with cancer when she enrolled at Brown. She joined a support group in Providence for teenagers with terminal illnesses. She is the sole survivor of the group.

She has been in and out of hospitals ever since. She told me that she averages over sixty visits to Sloan Kettering each year. But she became a storyteller and performance artist, performing her first show, *Confessions of a Bronx Tomboy: My Throwing Arm, This Useless Expertise*, with a bucket full of fifty Spaldeens that she threw at an *X* on the theater wall over the heads of the audience.

In the summer of 2001, I brought Annie down to the Smithsonian Folklife Festival in Washington, D.C. It was featuring New York, and she came as the quintessential New York City storyteller. She held up a bent coat hanger and asked the visitors to guess what it was—calling it an artifact from the Smithsonian archives. Then she demonstrated how she bent it into shape and used it to rescue Spaldeens in the gutter.

She laughed when I told her that I was the smallest kid on my block in São Paulo where I grew up, but we didn't use a coat hanger—they lowered me into the gutter holding my feet to retrieve balls.

I visited Annie at Sloan Kettering a number of times, laughing as we walked through the halls with her hauling her IV around. We talked about her forthcoming memoir, which played on the Spaldeen as a metaphor.

"What do you think, you're made of rubber?" her mom called out as Annie skinned her knees playing on the street. "Yes, Mom, I am made of rubber,"[13] she answered, and her Bronx childhood supported and inspired her as she bounced back from Hodgkin's lymphoma at eighteen, thyroid cancer at thirty-seven, along with double pneumonia, a deflated immune system, and recurring tumors through the years.

In 2013, Annie finished her masterpiece, *L Is for Lion: An Italian Bronx Butch Freedom Memoir*. The book is essential reading as the most powerful depiction I have ever read of how a human being can draw on her folk culture, her humor, and her poetic insight to pull life-affirming meaning out of the gutter like a lost Spaldeen.

Captain Kellam

From Captain Kellam, a skipper-captain from the eastern shore of Maryland, I learned that, present company excluded, there is no such thing as an indispensable man. A gentle, imposing figure, he was in his eighties when Amanda and I met him, and he told us the story of seeing an old man on the lanes at a bowling alley. "Look at that old geezer bowling," he said. He went over and asked the man how old he was, and was told seventy. "I was ten years older than he was!" he said, laughing. "I don't feel old. I'm going to live to be a hundred."

In *The Grand Generation*, Captain Kellam talked about the importance of reminiscence in aging, echoing the influential psychiatrist Robert Butler, who noted that when the past seems longer and more vivid than the present, it is not a sign of senility but a healthy adaptation to the circumstances of age. "What do you reminisce about?" I asked Captain Kellam in the film. His disarming answer: "Girls."[14]

As a participant in the Smithsonian Folklife Festival, Captain Kellam performed recitations of classic poems. He particularly loved to recite a poem by Saxon White Kessinger:

Take a bucket and fill it with water,
Put your hand in it up to the wrist,
Pull it out and the hole that's remaining
Is a measure of how you'll be missed.

You can splash all you wish when you enter,
You may stir up the water galore,
But stop and you'll find that in no time
It looks quite the same as before.

The moral of this quaint example
Is do just the best that you can,
Be proud of yourself but remember,
There's no indispensable man.[15]

Skeme

From the young subway graffiti writer Skeme, I learned about what it means to be an artist. My friend the photographer Henry Chalfant produced the documentary *Style Wars*, directed by Tony Silver, which chronicles the intrepid teenagers who darted into the New York City rail yards to create the graffiti-painted trains of the 1970s and early 1980s. It depicts a classic interchange between Skeme and his mother, Barbara:

Barbara: Society should go down in the subway and lock them all up, because they don't have any business down there. It is dangerous down there. People that work down there for twenty-five years have accidents. But his contention is that he's immortal, I guess like most seventeen-year-olds are immortal.

Skeme: It's a matter of getting a tag on each line and each division. It's called "going all city." People see your tags in Queens, uptown, downtown, all over.

Barbara: I don't think he really knows how silly that sounds. He's going "all city." I mean, to what end? And when I asked him, he says to me, "Well, just so people see it and they know who I am." Nobody knows who he is.

Skeme: It's not a matter of so they know who I am. It's a matter of bombing. Knowing that I can do it. Every time I get on a train, almost every day I see my name. I say, "Yeah, I was there—bombed it." It's for me; it's not for no one else. I don't care about nobody else seeing it or the fact that they can read it or not. It's for me and other graffiti writers—that we can read it. All these other people who don't write: they're excluded. They don't matter to me. It's for us.

Barbara: You listen to them talk—it's absolutely ridiculous. Who died and left him king of any yard? He owns nothing in the subway. What you have is a whole miserable subculture.[16]

What you also have is a true artist, seventeen years old, who understood the significance of writing: for him, it was about having his name on a train. Both Skeme and Henry, who ventured into the yards with him, taught me about taking risks for art.

Mae

From Mae Noell I learned about publishing, finding your voice, and sticking to your guns. I first visited Mae in 1979, at her chimp farm in Tarpon Springs, Florida. I was conducting field research for the program on traveling medicine shows for the Smithsonian Folklife Festival; she and her husband, Bob, performed in shows in the 1930s and 1940s. She gave me a tour of her home for retired show business animals, which included a variety of dogs, monkeys, and horses given to her to care for by the Barnum & Bailey Circus. She even showed me an alligator with a wart on its tail, which no zoo would take.

She ushered me into her library, an RV parked in a corner of the farm and filled floor to ceiling with secondhand books on traveling shows and magic and the many other subjects both she and I found so fascinating. Mae regaled me with stories not only of medicine shows but also of the traveling gorilla show that she and Bob had toured with in the 1940s and 1950s. (Bob lost several fingers to the chimps.) They would pull into a town and put up signs asking for volunteers who were willing to wrestle a chimp in front of an audience for a cash prize.

Chimps, she told me, are eight times stronger than humans. For the show, the chimps would wrestle the town bully while the audience laughed and cheered as the bully was quickly outmaneuvered and out-fought. Her favorite story was about the well-known fighter Bruno Sammartino, who, long before he became famous as a wrestler, battled a chimp in his small hometown. According to Mae, the chimp tore his clothes right off him. "The crowd howled," she said, "as the chimp swung him around by his mainspring."

"I wish I could go back to those days," she told me. "But since you can't, you have go on like you are."

When she and Bob came to our wedding, she gave Amanda and me a traveling first aid kit in case we ever wanted to go out on the road. She told me she had written a book about the gorilla show and was trying to get it published. I later learned that Brooks McNamara, the historian of popular culture and author of the book *Step Right Up*, about traveling medicine shows, had helped her get it accepted by a major trade press. But the editors wanted some changes. They wanted it organized chrono-logically, while Mae wanted the book organized by chimp.[17] Mae refused to make the changes. In the end, she self-published the book, titled *The History of Noell's Ark Gorilla Show*, just the way she wanted it, with chapters on Kongo, Topsy, Snookie, and Butch.[18]

In my travels, I also picked up some wonderful expressions. From blues singer "Diamond Tooth" Mary Smith McClain, who performed in the traveling medicine shows and the med show performances we staged at the Smithsonian Folklife Festival:

"You can make it if you try—just keep on on." (Not "keep on keeping on," just "keep on on.")

From my good friend the Reverend Robert Butler, a gospel singer: "Black folks got all the sayings," he told me. "White folks got all the money."

And from an old mule trader named Ray Lum, who was invited years ago to speak at the annual meeting of the American Folklore Society: "You live and you learn, then you die and forget it all."

As I write this, just yesterday I had the honor of visiting the re-created eight-thousand-year-old Chumash Village on the bluffs of Malibu overlooking the Pacific Ocean. Mati Waiya, the tribal leader who led the reconstruction, spoke to a group of visitors from the American Folklore Society. He told us an origin story of the Chumash, who migrated to this spot from the barrier islands hundreds of years ago, crossing "a rainbow bridge" in their canoes. He told us about the need both to remember and to set aside the genocidal past of his people and work toward an ecologically sound future for all of us. Then he shared a traditional Chumash welcoming ceremony with us, blessing each of us with incense. I was so struck by his wisdom and the poetry in his speech that I raised my hand to ask, "Are there any books I can read, or documentary films where I can learn more?"

"There is nothing you can read, no documentaries to see," he answered. "You need to learn by giving yourself over to this ceremony, by being right here, right now, in this moment."

Many of these friends and collaborators have taught me not to take myself too seriously. Tucson-based folklorist James "Big Jim" Griffin told me about the research he was doing with a cattle rancher out west. "I was explaining my research to the man and I guess I used too many polysyllabic words."

"Hey," he told me, "I've heard ducks fart underwater too, and I have to tell you, I was not impressed." Jim thinks about those ducks whenever he is trying to ensure that what he is writing will mean something to the people and communities he is studying.

Rosina

From Rosina Tucker, a civil rights activist and the wife of a Pullman porter, I learned about history firsthand and about how believing that one has a purpose in life can enable oneself to achieve great things. Rosina was born in 1882, and her parents were born during slavery. They "never talked to us about their days as slaves. Very few former slaves talked about it. I overheard them talking to each other," she said. "But they didn't discuss it with the children." One day she overheard them talking about the meager rations they were given, even on holidays like Thanksgiving. Her father recalled that the turkey was forbidden for them, but they were given the strings with which the turkey was tied to suck on.[19]

She married a porter, a member of the first African American Union, the Brotherhood of Sleeping Car Porters. When he lost his job, she stormed into the boss's office and banged on the table until he agreed to put her husband back on the trains.

I met Rosina when she was 102. Paul Wagner, Marjorie Hunt, and I were producing our documentary about the memories of older Americans. In a resonant voice that conveyed the depth of her life experience, she spoke slowly into the camera.

> The poem that I want to read now is one that was written during the time that Black people didn't have the opportunities for education or other cultural pursuits. And you will see by it the bitterness that existed in the souls of men during that period. The poem is called At the Closed Gate of Justice by James D. Corrothers [1869–1917]. . . . I would prefer changing the word Negro to Black but it would spoil the smooth running of the poem.

> To be a Negro in a day like this
>   Demands rare patience—patience that can wait
> In utter darkness. 'Tis the path to miss,
>   And knock, unheeded, at an iron gate,
> To be a Negro in a day like this.

> To be a Negro in a day like this—
>   Alas! Lord God, what evil have we done?
> Still shines the gate, all gold and amethyst,
>   But I pass by, the glorious goal unwon,
> "Merely a Negro"—in a day like this!

> May I say this. I had worked with the brotherhood of sleeping car porters for thirteen years before we had a convention whereby I was elected the international Secretary Treasurer. I bring that out to show you that we have to put forth great effort for everything we do. Nothing is easy.

My friend the filmmaker Paul Wagner and the folklorist Jack Santino, who together produced a documentary about the sleeping car porters, introduced me to Rosina. Paul recalls the ham-and-cheese sandwiches she made whenever he visited her in Northeast Washington, D.C. She always made them with butter, he said. Rosina suggested that the key to a successful old age had nothing to do with not eating butter and everything to do with always having young friends. Once she said, "A young man asked me, 'What was the world like in your day?' You know, so often when a younger person will talk to an older person, especially a very old person, they seem to have in the back of their minds that those people are still living back in those days. I wanted to let this young person know that I wasn't living back then. 'My day?' I told him, 'My day: this *is* my day.'

"I feel that everybody has a purpose in life," she said, "whether they know that purpose or not, and I think there is a purpose for my life, and I will live until that purpose is fulfilled."[20]

"I feel that everybody has a purpose in life," she said, "whether they know that purpose or not, and I think there is a purpose for my life, and I will live until that purpose is fulfilled."

What connects me to these people is something beyond reason. Folklore as a source of great nurturance is palpable in their presence.[21] My friend the writer Christian McKuen wrote:

> It was early in November, I was riding home on the number six train from the Bronx. It was the regular scene on a mid-afternoon subway train, with riders slumped again the walls. Suddenly this one-legged fellow shows up in the carriage on crutches, carrying a paper cup. He goes up and down the aisle begging, and someone puts in a quarter and someone else turns the page of their newspaper. And then I hear this Hispanic woman sitting next to me shuffling in her little purse. She has two small children, maybe four and six. She gives a dime to one and a nickel to the other, and sends them up the aisle to this fellow.
>
> Swinging on his two crutches, he bends down very graciously so the children can put their money in. Then, instead of going on to the next person, he puts his hand over the top of the cup as if he's a conjurer, and shakes the cup up and down. And he takes out of the cup not the nickel and the dime the children had put in, but two quarters. He majestically pulls them out one by one, and he gives those quarters to the boy and girl. And the children look from their mother to the man, like "What is this?" And the mother says to the man, "No, no, no, I want them to give it to you." And the man pays no attention . . .

and swings on through into the next car, leaving the air shimmering with astonishment. And the children are staring down into their palms at these quarters as if a silver moon were shining out from each of them. The man then vanished into the next car. I guess that day he didn't want to be a panhandler. He wanted to be a magician.

I can think of no greater purpose in life than to share the wisdom and wit of these extraordinary people with the world. Many of these individuals have passed on. I carry them with me, these wise, luminous souls.

2

Intimacy in Language

Poetry in Family Expressions

We refined our communication into a work of art.
—GINGY CASWELL

I grew up as an American expat in São Paulo, Brazil. My parents, Shirley and Irv, belonged to that notable group called sojourners—those who immigrate but never fully assimilate. Since planes didn't fly at night in 1946, the journey from Philadelphia to Brazil took three days. Villa Villela, a friend of my uncle's, met my parents' DC-3 at the airport. His wife, Lillian Villela, my mother's first friend in Brazil, spent two weeks teaching her the language. Forty years later, Lillian joked that since then my mother had never learned another word of Portuguese.

My father persuaded my mother to leave their home in Philadelphia, promising that they would stay in Brazil for only two years. The two years became four, then eight, then sixteen . . . My mom passed away in 1999 in Brazil.

I was drawn to folklore because, even at an early age, I was aware of the beauty and power of folklore in my own life. As expats living in relative isolation, my two brothers and I grew up close. We developed our own accent and our own humor. To this day, my brother Murray and I still greet each other with "Yo, sire." Someone once asked my brother why we use that phrase. He answered, "Respect." Decades later my own children, Benh and Eliza, call each other "Swine" or "Swinedog": no respect! When Benh received an award at the Sundance Film Festival, he came to the stage and proudly announced, "I'd like to thank my sister, Swinedog."

My other brother, Bill, and I loved the movie *Jaws*, and we talked endlessly about Quint being eaten by the shark, nicknamed "the Big White." From this shared interest we came up with the phrase "speaking of the Big White," meaning something like "apropos of nothing," and which we use to introduce any extraneous or ridiculous topic.

In Brazil our family had an apartment on the first floor of a fifteen-story apartment building in a lovely beach town called Guarujá. One day Murray was passing out Chiclets, and rather than taking one, I took five. Mur said, "Why don't you just jump out the fifteenth-story window for a breeze on a hot day?" Ever since then, when I overdo anything, my brother calls it "jumping off the fifteenth-story window for a breeze on hot day." I knew, even back then, that this artful banter was at the heart of life.

I once told Eliza that she was born because my parents, on one of their early visits back to the United States, brought me a present: a yellow 78 rpm record with the tune "Red River Valley" on it. I thought it was the most beautiful song I'd ever heard. It inspired my love of folk music, and it had everything to do with my becoming a folklorist and meeting her mom, Amanda (a fellow folklorist), which led, eventually, to Eliza's (and her brother, Benh's) birth. She owes her very existence to "Red River Valley."

Besides the song, a few other incidents contributed to the serendipity of meeting Amanda. One day when I was studying Old English poetry in the library at the University of Pennsylvania, I took a break from my graduate studies and wandered aimlessly through the stacks. I chanced upon two or three books by a writer named Benjamin Botkin, who had worked for the WPA's Federal Writers' Project. One was called *New York City Folklore: Legends, Tall Tales, Anecdotes, Stories, Sagas, Heroes and Characters, Customs, Traditions, and Sayings*; another was *Sidewalks of America: Folklore, Legends, Sagas, Traditions, Customs, Songs, Stories, and Sayings of City Folk*. I opened one of Botkin's books to a random page and can still recall the children's rhyme I read there:

I should worry
I should care
I should marry a millionaire

He should die
I should cry
I should marry another guy

I immediately thought, This is the job for me, listening to people's stories and rhymes, searching for diamonds in the rough. Soon after this encounter I discovered that the University of Pennsylvania had a Department of Folklore and Folklife. I arranged for an interview with the department chair, Kenneth S. Goldstein, who explained to me that folklore is a religion, and folklorists are its missionaries. I promptly reported for duty.

Amanda took a different route to the field. Her wise and wonderful father, Lucas, a notoriously frugal child of the Great Depression, often brought home two-day-old bread that was on sale, and would rummage though bins of books that had had their covers torn off and were being sold for twenty-five cents. One evening he brought home John and Alan Lomax's *Folk Song U.S.A.* and gave it to Amanda, who had already developed an interest in folk music. At the bottom of the last page was a small notice: "For more information, contact the Archive of Folksong [now the Archive of Folk Culture] at the Library of Congress." Amanda wrote to the archive as a high school student. They wrote back suggesting that she get her undergraduate degree before she apply to one of the graduate programs.

In our respective folklore studies, both Amanda and I developed projects on family stories. After college, Amanda enrolled in the folklore program at the University of Newfoundland (after discovering it on the list of folklore programs in the response from the Library of Congress). She wrote her master's thesis on the folklore of her extended family in the South, around the same time that I was developing the Family Folklore Project to collect and publish family stories at the Smithsonian Folklife Festival. It was simply inevitable that we met—our first date was to attend the fiftieth anniversary of the Archive of Folk Song, in 1978—fell in love, married, and started a family of our own. On a trip back to D.C. many years later, Amanda discovered that the Library of Congress still had her letter on file.

Amanda grew up on a farm near Darlington, South Carolina. On one occasion her cousins went down to Black Creek to watch the boy cousins setting out in a small boat. Just as they were taking off, one of her cousins kissed his sister on the cheek and said, "Good-bye, Sis. Tell Ma the boat floats." After that, when family members called or wrote home, "Tell Ma the boat floats" meant "Everything is all right."

"Grey-haired and full of spirit," writes the African American folklorist Anand Prahlad, "my great-grandmother is a woman deeply attached to the land. A mother of two children, grandmother of nine, and great-grandmother of thirteen, she is a wellspring of stories and wise sayings. Granny was born in a log cabin on April 20, 1898, and has lived all her life in Hanover County, Virginia." Anand's mother, Jean, was born on January 15, 1934. He recorded their conversation on the origins and usage of the family expression "getting the butter from the duck."

> **Jean:** See the fat on the inside of the duck doesn't come away easy. You can't pull the fat from the duck like you can from a chicken or the other fowl. . . . It's between the skin and the meat, see? And sometimes you even rip the skin trying to get that fat out of there. But it's so rich and fat it's just like butter. You can use it in cakes and all those kind of things just like you would use butter.
>
> **Granny:** Yes, Lord, my momma used to use that one. 'Cause she used to go in the woods and cut wood. And sometimes when she'd get through cuttin' she'd be sweatin' and going on. And she'd have to set down and she'd say, "Ah, Lord, y'all go ahead, chillun, that thing done got all the butter from me.[1]

Family expressions, along with in-jokes and associations, are packed with alliteration, rhythm, and hyperbole. "Thank god for guts and gristle" is the rousing battle cry in one family whenever a dirty, difficult task needs be done. "Too tired to tuck" is another family's phrase, meaning that a task seems too exhausting.[2] Sometimes a child's mispronunciation creates a family word, like Eliza's term "cottontail hour" for cocktail hour. I've always liked Flash Rosenberg's recollection of the line spoken gruffly by her grandfather whenever her family gathered: "Consider yourself kissed."

As we become more intimate with one another, our conversation shifts from prose toward poetry. As my friend the therapist Solomon Reuben put it, "Heartful sharing becomes artful sharing." We condense our stories into brief phrases that sum up a story and that we know our friends and family will recognize. We begin to use catchwords and allusions, and much of our conversation is laden with these associations. At the same time, our talk becomes increasingly patterned and rhythmic. Linguists have shown that people who know each other well coordinate their talk. Social scientist Joseph Jaffe wrote that "the coordination of interpersonal timing involves the prediction of each partner's timing pattern from that of the other. This capacity for rhythmic coordination is essential to cognition and bonding."[3]

> **As we become more intimate with one another, our conversation shifts from prose toward poetry.**

Because of this, close families and friends often seem to be in sync. Without missing a beat, they can interject a teasing family expression that brings back a rush of memories. The better we know and love someone, the more layered and poetic our conversation becomes. As a friend of mine, Gingy Caswell, said about her relationship with her sister, "We refined our communication into a work of art."

Another friend, Ellen Dissanayake, author of *Art and Intimacy: How the Arts Began*, writes eloquently about the connection between love and art, envisioning both as emerging from the babble, coos, and patter—what she calls the "rhythms" and the "modes"—of a mother's play with her infant, a form of communication that goes back to the "pre-Paleolithic infancy of the human species." "Rhythms," she suggests, are patterns in time, while "modes" map the greater or lesser intensity of the experience as it unfolds. Mothers and their babies use their babble to establish a mutuality that, through an endless series of elaborations,

> **"Heartful sharing becomes artful sharing."**

evolves into art. She writes, "Each of us is born with a mind—sense and emotions—that moves us to seek and engage in intimacy with others before we do anything else."[4]

The human infant remains helpless and dependent on its parents for longer than other babies in the animal kingdom. This extended infancy, she suggests, has led to the development of rhythmic, emotive exchanges, and these exchanges, in turn, have evolved into the human receptivity to the powerful forces of love and art.

She describes studies that demonstrate how the babble and prattle of mothers and babies are "structured in time, like poetry or song: if transcribed, they reveal formal segments like stanzas, often based on one theme, with variations, that has to do with the looks or actions of the baby (frequently its digestion: burps, hiccups, and poops) or something about its lovability—for example, 'Mommy loves you. Yes. Yes. Did you know Mommy loves you? Yes, she does. She does. She loves you.'" Ultimately, "our conversations are built upon a nonverbal scaffolding of synchrony and turn-taking. Intimacy is replete with these nonverbal signs of attunement."[5] Mothers use words, but the patter is all about the rhythm and tone.

Watching Amanda babble and play with our two children when they were infants inspired me to write:

> The cat nestles on her breasts,
> the children's arms and legs
> branch haphazardly across her bough
>
> Until her laughter shakes the branches
> like the wind
> blowing limbs into their sleeves,
> and the cat out of the tree
>
> How many years must blow through empty covers
> till they calculate the value
> of that carefree intimacy,
> lost forever in the branches
> of the mother tree

In the babble of mothers and their babies, in the inscriptions of teens in their yearbooks, and in jump rope rhymes and expressions shared among family members lies a world of unself-conscious artistry and poetic expression that is always available to lift our spirits and inspire our creative expression.

Will the poetry of everyday life save the planet? Perhaps not, but for me it explains why the planet needs to be saved. "In my quirky way," the bandleader Bobby Sanabria said, "I imagine that the reasons aliens haven't destroyed us is that they looked down and said, 'They still jump rope, they still have their quaint expressions, they still make each other laugh. There's hope. Let them live.'"

Every semester for more than a decade, I taught a class in creative writing at Cooper Union, a New York City college. One of my students, Virginia Randall, was fascinated by the way personal associations and banter form bonds of intimacy. Virginia had recently lost her husband of twenty-five years, Michael. She wrote a beautiful piece about the private language they cherished. She called her piece "Losing My Italian." She begins by describing how her Italian mother moved into a retirement home after her father died. Her mother found it pleasant enough, but, as Virginia writes, "there was no one there with whom she could speak the dialect of the small Sicilian town from which her family came. 'I can't remember some of my words,' she said; 'I'm losing my Italian.'" Virginia goes on to explain how losing Michael was akin to losing a language:

In the babble of mothers and their babies, in the inscriptions of teens in their yearbooks, and in jump rope rhymes and expressions shared among family members lies a world of unselfconscious artistry and poetic expression that is always available to lift our spirits and inspire our creative expression.

> We were an unlikely couple. I grew up on the Lower East Side, in a neighborhood he would visit from his Ivy League college to score pot. He was an agnostic, I was a Catholic. He was an avid and skillful driver, I didn't even have a license. Still, despite all our differences, one day in August we got another phrase, courtesy of my Uncle Joe.
>
> Our wedding party was winding down. We had been toasted and everyone had been fed. Uncle Joe, with a refill of Asti, looked thoughtfully at Angie, his wife of fifty years, and told us, "You have to be willing to lose an argument." From then on, when an argument went around and around with no end in sight, one of us—usually Michael—would say, "I'll do an Uncle Joe," and that would end it. It was a big sacrifice for a man so competitive he'd argue every point in a trivia game.

Many of Michael's catchphrases were borrowed from rock-and-roll lyrics, punch lines of jokes, or dialogue from underground comics—I often teased him that he had a fourteen-year-old's sense of humor. Most of my catchphrases came out of the ether, things that I said without thinking that made him laugh. Others were linked to a certain time, place, or event. They made sense to no one but us, for comfort, for amusement, or sometimes, as any private language would, simply for the pleasure of recognition as the phrase slides into a well-worn groove, joining dozens—or hundreds—of other tellings and hearings, times and places. Every so often some comment of mine would make him laugh, and he'd say, "That's one of Virge's Greatest Hits." I felt so happy when he said that.

The "bump in the road" was a new one. It was mine. There was a speed bump on the road on the way to 95 South, when I would drive us to the hospital for yet another meeting with the transplant team. He had moved to Florida to improve his chances of getting a transplant, and I was commuting back and forth because the work was, for me, still in New York City. I was a very nervous driver, but I'd get in the car, and drive for hours, often in the rain, trying not to hyperventilate due to nervousness. That was my gift to him. He learned patience, finally, in the car while I drove. That was his gift to me. He'd speak in exaggeratedly soothing tones to tease me when we hit that speed bump on Summer Avenue with the sign that said "Traffic Calming." "Caaalming," he'd intone, while I maneuvered carefully over the bump. He'd gotten a ticket on that same road for hitting 60 in a 25-mile zone.

I'd had to say "It's just a bump in the road" more and more, encouraging him as he battled each setback, recovering each time but losing a little more ground each time, too. His fighting spirit was forged as a Long Island wrestling champion; he pinned his illness to the mat again and again, but each time he got up, he left a little more behind. We were buying time until he got the call for the transplant that meant health. I kept our "go bags" packed.

Even at the worst of times, the scariest of times, I could say something and Michael would laugh, and look at me with the same expression he had the day we got married, biting his lower lip in delight. Like when we'd spent all day in the hospital waiting for his appointment. It was a big one, a last-minute one, a life-or-death one, and we were nervous.

When I went to get us something to eat —I became a connoisseur of hospital cafeterias—I saw a worker so slow she seemed to be fetching

French fries one by one to fill the cardboard container. I told Michael about it and he laughed. He actually asked me to tell him again, while he was waiting to find out what was going to happen to him.

When you lose someone, you lose a language, too. I'm the only one who knows "Do you need a little 'there, there'?" has nothing to do with Gertrude Stein or Oakland.

That was Michael's light bulb moment, when he grasped that when I complained, I wasn't asking him to fix it, just to listen and sympathize. "Ah!" he said, his gunmetal-blue eyes widening, "you want a little 'there, there'!!" and he patted me on the shoulder. And so "Do you need a little 'there, there'?" meant "Do you need to vent while I listen for a while?" for both of us.

The first year after he'd gone, the memories literally paralyzed me. I got ambushed daily by situations that would elicit a familiar phrase either one of us would say. A chance phrase or song lyric locked me into the memory. I could function only by writing the flashback or the phrase on a note and putting it in the Mike Box, along with the cards and the photos, the comb with his hair, his cuff links. Only then could I resume whatever I was doing.

I'm still holding on to our language and memories with a record of our catchphrases. I add to them even now, six years later. I'm writing the dictionary of our relationship, but a language is a dialogue, requiring a speaker and a listener. You can't talk to a dictionary. I play both parts now. When I feel a nice breeze on a balmy day, I still hear his voice exulting, "The air feels like bathwater." But I turn and he's not there.

While making the arrangements for him, I found among his papers a scribbled note (now in the Mike Box): "the Polish Platter." The week before, I had told him about a diner in Greenpoint, and I had the "Polish Platter." "What's that?" he said. "It's pierogis and kielbasa," I told him, "but after you get it a German guy sitting next to you takes it away." He thought it was really funny.

But when I turned on his computer, I saw the reason why he wrote it down. He had an actual file he called "Virge's Greatest Hits." Long before the Mike Box, he had tallied the things I said, that he liked to hear or repeat, again and again: "I'll drink to that" and "Mauna Higha," the idioms of a relationship, the trip to Hawaii, or the dinner at Lutèce. "The Polish Platter" was his last entry.

I've been losing sleep over a turn of phrase he called "nups" because, he said, they were the opposite of puns. They came to me without thinking about them, and Michael was the only one who caught them and treasured them. He'd even email them to friends. I don't remember any of them. I've ransacked our papers and his notes, and checked the emails and I can't find any references. They're gone. Like my mother, I can't remember some of my words. I fear I'm losing my Italian, too, losing a language for a community smaller than a Sicilian village, a nation of two. Now one. But no matter what, I will keep looking, remembering, and adding to the list, appreciating each turn of phrase anew, and each moment and memory.

I can hardly do otherwise. I'm the last speaker of "us" now.[6]

3

Laughter for Dessert

Lightness of Being

Give humor its due.
—Albert Einstein

If my name be remembered at all, let it be remembered with
laughter.
—Sholem Aleichem

There's a big old goofy man dancing with a big old goofy girl
Ooo baby, it's a big old goofy world.
—John Prine

When our landlord, Henry Shrady, refurbished City Lore's former
offices on the Lower East Side, he divided one large office into two. In
the process, he made a serendipitous mistake. He neglected to put a
second light switch in the subdivided office. That meant that whenever
I needed to turn on my light, I had to visit my neighbor, Colleen's, office
to flick the switch.

Colleen Iverson works for the historic New York City Marble Cemetery. Her job was keeping records of the dead. What she did with the
dead, I couldn't be sure, but it kept her extremely busy late into the
night; I never saw her during the day. I often worked late as well, and as
a result, I frequently had to go into Colleen's office to turn off my office
lights.

Colleen has long hair, braided to her waist. She has a winning smile
and an infectious chuckle. She laughed heartily every time my arm
twisted into her office. One evening we joked about which of us would be
the last to leave; I began issuing daily points for whoever left earlier and
deducting points for whoever worked much too late. The assumption

was that neither of us should be putting in so much overtime. The points awarded for leaving early or deducted for staying late could range from five to five hundred thousand, based on whim. Some nights I would award myself ten thousand points for leaving early; sometimes she would lose two points for staying late. Colleen was forever bemused, claiming she couldn't grasp the rules, and couldn't tell if it was better to win or to lose points. She periodically demanded, "Where's the rule book? I want to see the rule book!" Sometimes she'd pretend to get it, exclaiming, "I think I'm getting there, I'm getting there—I just wish I knew where!"

One night when I left later than she did, I left her a Post-it note awarding her two hundred thousand points for going home early.

When she saw me again, she quipped, "Oh, really—where are they? Where are those will-o'-the-wisp points? Those shape-shifting points?" We thus created what I now believe may be the world's longest-running joke.

Laughter has played a huge role in my life. My brother Murray laughs harder than anyone else I know—and he caps it off by clapping in wild applause. "Let the din of merriment drown our flaws," I once wrote. When my daughter, Eliza, and her cousin Sarah Elizabeth tried, hilariously, to make gluten-free crêpes suzette and ended up with some disgusting crêpe scrapple to top off an otherwise delicious meal, the whole family burst out laughing. "We had laughter for dessert," Eliza quipped.

"Let the din of merriment drown our flaws."

I even imagined a mystery story in which the murderer kills by devising a perfect joke that convulses people with laughter till they die. And I can remember a girl whose infectious laugh inspired this poem:

Lily

Has my finger tweaked your rib bone
Is your clitoris in your funny bone
O how laughter turns you on

Laughter is the oil of life
You made it the lubricant of love
Glistening with it—and all alight

Climaxing
In paroxysms of laughter
Orgasms of delight

My friend and Ping-Pong partner Bob Mankoff, the cartoon editor of *The New Yorker*, is a student of humor; he also teaches a class in humor theory at the University of Michigan. On our way to play Ping-Pong, we often discuss our various perspectives on humor. Many theories, Bob says, "suggest that humor is about putting down others. In almost all humor, something or someone is diminished. Especially when you're laughing hard. The teller feels superior both to the butt of the joke and to the listeners in whom he created the involuntary response of laughter." But if humor is about putting others down, it's also conspiratorial: there's you and me, and then there are all those fools.

And then there is silliness. Once, our two kids were fighting in the backseat of the car, and Benh was sorely to blame. I told Eliza that she could take a free punch—and the "free punch" has since been enshrined in Zeitlin family folklore. The kids have now turned arm punching into an art form. We talk about the "music" a good punch makes when it smacks against an arm. We "tenderize" an arm by rubbing it before punching. Though the blows are sometimes heavy, they help to keep things light. The thumps have sound and rhythm, the poetry of the punch.

Whenever my wife and I do something really dumb or spacey, we call it "Steve and Amanda go around the world in a daze," and for a few years we had a notebook where we jotted down examples. Even though it has been lost for many years, we still take note of instances that should be "in the book." A recent classic came when a forty-some-year-old gentleman who was doing work in our basement told Amanda that he couldn't came back to finish the next day. I was working on my computer when he said, "I'm not coming on Sunday; I'll be back on Monday. Enjoy your weekend—it's going to be 65 tomorrow."

"Well," I said, looking up distractedly, "you don't look it."

Like many long-married couples, we've developed routines for our own personal comedy team of sorts. Every couple that has spent years

Every couple that has spent years together most likely has a comic and a straight man embedded in their humor and their folklore. together most likely has a comic and a straight man embedded in their humor and their folklore. In our comedy routine, I am a fountain of silliness to a bemused Amanda, who plays my straight man. In many photographs of our vacations, I am trying to pose as a Roman statue on a sheared-off colonnade, or make it appear that the sun is setting in my cocktail glass while Amanda takes the picture and laughs.

Professional comedy teams themselves are, of course, inspired by real life. Lucille Ball was already a successful comedian when she was offered a sitcom on CBS. She agreed to do it only if they brought on her husband, Cuban bandleader Desi Arnaz. At the time, her producers thought it was crazy to consider Desi for the show—"What television audience would believe that you were married to a Cuban bandleader?" they asked. "I *am* married to a Cuban bandleader," she told them. Commentators said the reason she wanted him on the show was to keep him closer to home, but she must have known from their married life that they could be funny together, with her playing the comic and Desi the straight man.[1]

The setup for which partner will be the straight man and which one the comic can change. George Burns and Gracie Allen, a team who

Figure 1. Telling Amanda a joke at our wedding. Photo by Mary Rogers.

from the 1930s through the 1960s took comedy from vaudeville to radio and then to television, switched their roles at one point. When they got started in vaudeville in New York, Gracie was the straight man and George had all the funny lines. At some point they noticed that audiences were laughing at Gracie's straight lines, not at George playing the fool. So they switched roles, with George playing the straight man and Gracie playing the ditsy lady with all the funny lines.

"For the benefit of those who have never seen me before," explains George in the documentary *Make 'Em Laugh*, "I'm what is known in show business as a straight man. After the comedian gets through with the joke, I look at the comedian and then I look at the audience like this," he says, rolling his eyes. "Then Gracie would tell a joke."

In one example, George walks into their living room and says, "Those are beautiful flowers."

"Aren't they lovely?" she answers. "If it weren't for you I wouldn't have them."

"Me? What did I have to do with it?"

"You said when I went to visit Clara Bagley to take her flowers. So when she wasn't looking, I did."

George pauses to bring on the laughter. "That is what is known as a pause," he says. "I'm famous for my pauses."[2]

In the same documentary, the actor Lewis Stadlen notes that "George Burns and Gracie Allen captured the idea that men are from Mars and women are from Venus: "the idea that two intellectual concepts will never meet, but they still love each other."[3] Perhaps the humor is what makes it possible for them to love each other, as it does with many couples.

Whether between comedians on the pop culture stage or partners in everyday life, what I call high banter is all about being in the moment. When you are totally at home with another person, you can free-associate, creating riffs that you could never have with anyone else. The great comedy teams react to and improvise with each other as well as respond to the audience.

Amanda and I are loyal fans of *Saturday Night Live*, which we struggle to stay up to watch every Saturday night. An entire book could and should be written on the folklore of *Saturday Night Live*, focusing on the improvisatory humor—the banter shared and created by the writers, as well as the banter improvised by the comics in rehearsals and then performed for the live show. In one of our favorite sketches, from 2007, comedians Amy Poehler and Maya Rudolph riff off each other as Betty Caruso and Jodi Dietz on their local TV show, *Bronx Beat*.

> **Betty:** It's bananas! The whole world is bananas. You know what I say? Live your life 'cause the world is gonna blow up!
>
> **Jodi:** She's right. Enjoy your family, enjoy your friends, have a glass of wine.
>
> **Betty:** Have two glasses of wine, have ten glasses of wine. What do I care? What am I? The police or something?[4]

If you're not in the moment, the world of high banter will slide right past you. It's a key ingredient of folk culture and family folklore. It's also the essence of the poetry duels that Amanda and I have studied in different parts of the world. On both street corners and stages, poets riff off one another in rhyme, participating in traditions ranging from *extempo* in Trinidad to *desafios* in Portugal, *contrasti* in Italy, freestyle rap in the United States, and *repentistas* in Brazil. The banter between couples and others is also reminiscent of what happens when jazz musicians riff off one another.

The balance for any creative person is to be in the moment, with no notion that the banter might make for a good story, and later to realize that—*aha!*—it *does* make a good story, then, when the time is right, shaping and telling the tale to friends or on paper.

For couples, moments of high banter are often enshrined in story—written about or retold. The balance for any creative person is to be in the moment, with no notion that the banter might make for a good story, and later to realize that—*aha!*—it *does* make a good story, then, when the time is right, shaping and telling the tale to friends or on paper.

The "Steve and Amanda go around the world in a daze" stories are told with great flair by Amanda. Not long ago Amanda attended her family's biannual "cousins' house party" at the beach in South Carolina, which brings together the women cousins of her generation for a three-day bash of drinking, joking, and storytelling.

Her cousin Martha's story took the comedy cake at the house party and has become enshrined in the Dargan cousins' folklore. Martha was in the supermarket when she heard a loudmouth cursing at his companion. Martha shook her head and said, "Mister, what is your problem?"

"My problem?" he shouted. "I don't have a problem."

"Mister," she said, "your problem's your mouth."

"Lady," he retorted, "your problem, your butt."

The line has become a stock response to anyone in the family who thinks they know what your problem is.

In his biography of Cole Porter, *The Life That Late He Led*, George Eells writes that the genesis of Porter's now classic song "It's De-Lovely" harks back to a remark made by Porter's friend Monty Woolley on board a ship just off the harbor in Rio de Janeiro. Watching the dawn break, Porter said to his wife, "It's delightful"; she replied, "It's delicious," and Woolley chipped in, "It's de-lovely."[5] Porter's agent later quipped that with friends like that, anyone could write a hit song.

So here's to high banter, the humorous jazz that occurs when we improvise in those you-had-to-be-there moments when the timing is perfect and conversations are elevated to the point where, as Porter put it, "it's delightful, it's delicious, it's de-lovely."

My delightful and delicious running joke with Colleen, in which I play the straight man and she the dazed comedian, has been carried along to an almost ridiculous extent. One afternoon, when I ran into her at Economy Candy, the great old-fashioned candy palace on New York's Lower East Side, a few blocks from our shared office, we both started laughing at seeing each other during the day. "You're almost too bright," I said. "It's like looking at the sun." I was stocking up on gummy candies and Jujubes, and she was looking for a type of Italian candy that could not be purchased anywhere else.

A few days later, offering her a handful of Jujubes, I told her that she didn't realize the fabulous prizes she could claim with her accumulated "points" from our joke.

She said, "Could it be a car? I could use a car."

"Yes," I said, "it could be a car."

"A real car or a gummy car?" she asked. "That could make a big difference."

When she asked about the car a few days later, I couldn't resist telling her that she had indeed won the car: a life-size, real, drivable car . . . but a gummy car. It was being manufactured especially for her in Detroit, I said, and was being driven to New York.

"When is the arrival date?" she asked.

I told her I would check. The next time we met, I passed on the bad news: somewhere in Pennsylvania, a steamroller had crossed over into the wrong lane and totally flattened the vehicle, leaving nothing but gooey colored liquid oozing along the highway.

Colleen and I have never had dinner or lunch or interacted in any other way—but in some sense we share the perfect relationship. I can open the door of her office anytime, and we both burst out laughing. Our relationship is pure laughter. We share a light.

Part II POETRY IN PLAY

4

The Poetry of Ping-Pong
The Art in Sport

"Focus for a split second before you smack the ball," said table-tennis coach Robert Roberts, born in the Bahamas.

"The ball is coming at me so fast," I said, "so where do I find that split second?"

"It's always waiting for you," he said.
—EXCHANGE AT THE WESTCHESTER TABLE TENNIS CENTER, 2013

According to Marty Reisman, the game of Ping-Pong died that day. Bombay, India, 1952. Marty Reisman, nicknamed "The Needle," is favored to win the World Table Tennis Championship. He brushes aside rumors that the Japanese have a secret weapon. A newfangled racquet? A killer shot? Then out walks Hiroji Satoh with a little racquet case under his arm. "I was the first American to see that racquet," Reisman later told me. "The sponge racquet. The Japanese did not expect him to win. They sent him as a substitute. He ran off with the world championship."

On that day, according to Marty, Ping-Pong became a game of obfuscation, concealment, and deception. "In the world championship today," he said, "the ball goes no more than three times across the net. In the old days, rallies would be thirty or forty strokes. There was a dialogue between two players that even a child could understand." With the advent of the sponge racquet, the beautiful sound of the ball hitting the racquet, then the table, went from *plock-plock plock-plock* to *squish-plock squish plock*.

"I cling to the racquet of my childhood," said Reisman, who grew up playing in the settlement houses on New York's Lower East Side. "It's a pimpled rubber racquet. It gives me perfect communication with the ball. It's a certain kind of feel that's transmitted from this racquet, and it lends itself to whatever neurophysiological makeup I have. I used to love using the sandpaper racquet as a kid. Hitting the ball would reverberate all the way up my arm in this sensual way. My reputation was a little better than my game—but the glory of it was to rise to the occasion."

As a folklorist, I should prefer the old racquet myself. As the old joke goes: How many folklorists does it take to change a light bulb? Two: one to change it and one to talk about how good the old one was.

But I love the foam racquet. That racquet transformed the game from a miniature version of tennis or badminton to a far more complex game of finesse, touch, and subtle spins. As player Phil Perelman put it, "To see what Marty can do with that primitive racquet is like watching Itzhak Perlman play a concert on a ukulele."

The great shots come from the foam. The foam gives players the flawless chop, or slice. Perfectly executed, it makes no sound. Then there's the chop slam. A slam is hard to hit back, but trying to hit back a chop slam is like trying to return a balloon that's flying wildly around with the air rushing out of it. When I was a teenager playing with my friends in Brazil, the *casquinha para dentro* was an apocryphal shot, endlessly discussed. *Casquinha* (peel) is when the ball hits the edge of the table. Instead of bouncing up, it peels off, and is impossible to return. But the *casquinha para dentro* occurs when a player spins the ball so hard that it does a double take, skidding off the edge of the table in one direction, yet spinning so hard it reverses direction in midair, making it more impossible than impossible to return. The shot was the stuff of legend. I never actually saw it happen.

The Westchester Table Tennis Center, in Pleasantville, New York, where I play, evolved from a basement community center with one table, in 1999, to a world-class athletic facility owned by *New York Times* crossword puzzle editor Will Shortz, who (as of this writing) has played Ping-Pong every day without fail for more than a thousand days, an occasion he celebrated with great fanfare at the club. Particularly in its early years, the players at the club shared an idiomatic lingo. When a ball just brushed the top of the net and went over, it "kissed the net."

A "Double Gordon" meant missing two serves in a row, named after Fred Gordon, who was famous for doing just that. I was known for the "Zeitlin Sidewinder." Before he offered up one of his spinny serves, the writer Stefan Kanfer would often say, "The only person who has ever known how to return this serve was an eighty-year-old woman in Peru, and she's dead." When Will and I were tied at deuce in the final game of a match, we called it a "moral tie," shook hands, and then went on to finish the game. When I showed coach Robert Roberts my paddle once, he told me I needed new rubber for it. He spoke to me as if I were a knight in armor wielding a Ping-Pong paddle: "You're going into battle with a dull blade."

The sound of the racquet, table, and ball lays down the rhythm of the game. I've always loved Ping-Pong because you can get into that rhythm, hit the ball back and forth across the net for hours, with any racquet, and simply talk. I remember having conversations with my friend Mike Kanarek to the sound of the Ping-Pong ball. We were both about fifteen years old. The ball would go *ping*, then "How did you" *pong* "reach over" *ping* "and manage to hold her hand?" *pong*. Just hitting the ball back and forth over a net allows for conversation.

But Ping-Pong players also talk to each other with their shots. On Tuesday nights, Stefan and I hit backspin to topspin. His backspin reads as topspin on my side of the table. So, defensively, a chop can be countered with a chop that negates the backspin. But I relish countering his chop with my loop. The loop starts at the knees and moves up to take the opponent's spin and double it; when he chops it back with the foam racquet, the spin quadruples. It's as if we're trading jokes with classic one-upmanship. Or engaging in a poetic dialogue written with a racquet and expressed in the movement of the ball. Marty would never approve.

Only another player could discern what is being expressed in the sidespin-topspin-underspin dialogue. Ping-Pong, like poetry, is a players' sport, not ideal for spectators.

Bob Mankoff, one of our fellow Ping-Pong aficionados and the cartoon editor of *The New Yorker*, talks about the palpable humor in the game: "The ball is so small and light that it's inherently humorous; it does funny things. So much aggression goes into that tiny ball that actually can't hurt you—it has the quality of a pillow fight."

When the ball hits the net and just rolls over the top, it inevitably causes smiles and laughter; when it hits the edge of the table and skids off, well, that's funny, too. But when it hits the net *and* then the edge, well, that's hilarious. When you're playing for fun in a competitive spirit, the game matters so much, yet it doesn't matter at all, which opens the way to enjoyment.

Mihaly Csikszentmihalyi once asked why Americans enjoy activities that offer little or no material reward. He concluded that play provides a feeling characterized by an unself-conscious sense of absorption. In the full experience of play, we act within a dynamic that he called "flow." "In the flow state, action follows upon action according to an internal logic that seems to need no conscious intervention by the actor. He experiences it as a unified flowing from one moment to the next."[1]

On a Saturday night in October 1998, at Empire Billiards in Hell's Kitchen on the West Side of Manhattan, I was lucky enough to be present for a match that's now almost as legendary as Marty Reisman's battle with Hiroji Satoh, almost a half century earlier. David Gonzalez, in the *New York Times*, described the scene: "Marty Reisman hunkered down and inspected the table tennis net. Wearing a purple shirt, red pants and a Panama hat, he looked like a retiree going to the deli for a nosh. But the $100 bill he held in his hand made it clear he wasn't about to retire anywhere. He folded the bill and held it against the net to check its height. It had to be exact."[2]

Marty was challenging Jimmy Butler, a world-class player in his twenties, for ten grand, just to prove that on a level playing field in which both players were using Marty's beloved, now outdated hardbat racquet, he could beat the young champion—and at the same time prove the superiority of the older racquet. It turned out that with so much money at stake, Jimmy Butler trained for this match with that racquet, and when the smoke lifted, Marty, the sixty-eight-year-old champ, went down.

Yet he remained undaunted. "Marty," I asked him a few weeks later, "were you upset about losing the ten thousand dollars?"

"Not at all," he told me. "I needed to put that money on the line to feel the intensity of the moment, to fully concentrate at the top of my game."

In his book *Sizzling Chops and Devilish Spins: Ping-Pong and the Art of Staying Alive*, Jerome Charyn describes how "concentration could often deliver a player into a kind of self-induced hypnosis that was somehow between dreaming and waking. Most of us at the table, in the middle of fierce competition, had experienced 'alpha' where we were outside our bodies in some mysterious immortal land of the unknown." Champion Dick Miles described the "alpha" experience following one of his marathon matches with Reisman:

> Once I was playing Marty and all at once this wasn't me any longer. I might as well have been sitting there watching myself do things I had never imagined myself doing. I understood—I just knew—that I wasn't going to miss anymore. This thing took over; and both of us fell into sort of a trance. When it was over and he had lost, Marty came out of it and said to me, "What happened? Where am I?" "Alpha" was a ping-pong player's paradise, where perfect harmony was achieved in the midst of battle, and mind and body moved in some mystical manner, and time itself seemed to bend to one's own will. This is what we longed for whenever we picked up a paddle.[3]

Both Marty and I would concede that you don't have to play Ping-Pong to experience the dynamics of flow. Volumes have been written on the poetry and flow of soccer, for instance. As *New York Times* sportswriter José Miguel Wisnik wrote, "Brazilian soccer transformed the 'British and Apollonian' game into 'Dionysian dance'; straight and angular European soccer became sinuous and curving as it took on the movements of samba dancers and the martial arts dancers and fighters of Brazilian capoeira. . . . To the Italian filmmaker Pier Paolo Pasolini, the Brazilian style was 'poetic soccer' based on dribbling and a nonlinear opening of unforeseen spaces, as opposed to the linearly responsible 'prose soccer' prevalent in Europe."[4]

The Italian journalist Beppe Severgnini wrote about Italian soccer during the 2014 World Cup: "[B]eauty is what we like to display on the field. . . . [F]or Germany, beauty is organization. For England, it is dedication and work rate. For Brazil, beauty is a dance. But for us . . . beauty is breathtaking speed."[5]

Writer and basketball aficionado Phil Hoose described "that aesthetic sort of sensual pleasure of having the ball rustle the net when it swishes through with backspin." Nothing but net, sometimes with the arc of a "rainbow jumper." On most New York City street courts, however, the nets have long been decimated by players trying to show they can dunk—so there's only the clang of a ball hitting a metal hoop. As a result, Phil said, in New York "you don't find many outside shooters . . . only great rebounders."[6]

According to former Knicks champion Walt "Clyde" Frazier, basketball today is all about the dunk. Players are happy to miss four out of five shots just to get one spectacular dunk that will get them on the television highlights reel. I once spoke to an elderly cab driver who had played basketball for Ohio State as a young man.

"Do you still play?" I asked him.

"Today," he said, "I couldn't dunk a doughnut into a cup of hot coffee."

Mastering the neurophysiological skills of a sport is not just about learning the game. It's about attuning yourself to the inner life of the sport. It's as if Ping-Pong balls and tennis racquets, bats and hockey pucks were tools with which we could create engaging experiences that were written into the sinews of our muscles and recalled whenever we play the games. Part of the construct of a sports experience necessarily concerns winning and losing. Whoever has better mastered the skills wins. But perhaps on a deeper level the sport has to do with training the body to move in certain ways that offer pleasure when executed correctly. Players become part of a community where everyone knows what it feels like when a shot is hit right. "When I swing the club just right," a friend told me, "and strike the golf ball just right, and it takes off in a perfect straight trajectory, there is such a feeling of satisfaction. Then the next ten

It's as if Ping-Pong balls and tennis racquets, bats and hockey pucks were tools with which we could create engaging experiences that were written into the sinews of our muscles and recalled whenever we play the games.

times when it doesn't do that I say to myself, 'Why can't I do it? Why can't I do it again?' "

"The language of baseball went beyond words," writes novelist Joseph Wallace. "In the end, all that mattered was skill and competition and the pure joy of being out there on the field, doing something you were good at. You couldn't truly understand it unless it was inside you."[7]

We are all capable of attuning ourselves to the hidden life of sports, a relationship that is about kinesthesia and embodiment (how the racquet feels, the absorption in the rhythm). When I'm playing Ping-Pong, I often feel that a particular spot on the other end of the table is in my hands. It's as if I could stretch my arm seven feet across the table to touch the place where I know the ball will hit. That may be a bit like the way Babe Ruth felt when (according to legend) he pointed to the center-field wall before he hit a home run.

> **We are all capable of attuning ourselves to the hidden life of sports, a relationship that is about kinesthesia and embodiment.**

During the 2012 Olympics I reveled in watching sports such as beach volleyball, where you could sense the depth of communication between the teammates. Players like Kerri Walsh Jennings and Misty May-Treanor were so in sync as they set up balls and dug shots out of the sand for each other, and were so joyously expressive after every volley. The game seemed elevated beyond sport to a grand human pageant in which viewers could witness the synchronicity between the players and the emotional roller coaster of each point.

Because they know this inner dialogue, the best former players often make the best announcers. Listen to "Clyde" Frazier calling a Knicks basketball game. He describes the players as "swishin' and dishin'," "shakin' and bakin'," "movin' and groovin'," "wheelin' and dealin'," "dancin' and prancin'," "improvising and mesmerizing," or "stumblin' and bumblin'," and, when they foul, "hackin' and whackin'." His commentary has even been mapped according to how many particular "Clydeisms" he uses in any given quarter. He uses slightly more when the Knicks are "winnin' and grinnin'." There is even a drinking game played during Knicks games in which spectators have to down a shot whenever he utters one of a set number of his classic phrases like "feline quickness" or "Swiss cheese defense." He rhapsodizes about "splendor on the glass" and preaches the poetry of basketball over the microphone. Every action on the court must be executed with "fire and desire." Clyde came to speak at City Lore on the poetry of basketball. An audience member asked him if he had ever actually written a poem. He answered emphatically, "No."

Yet to describe, some years ago, Latrell Sprewell's perfect pass to Marcus Camby, who, flying in midair above the basket, caught the ball for a slam dunk, Frazier had to turn to the sacred.

"Amazing grace," he said.

5

Days of Chess and Backgammon

Life's Game Board

Chess is a fairy tale of a thousand and one blunders.
—Savielly Tartakower

I dine, I play a game of backgammon, I converse, and am
merry with my friends.
—David Hume

Every afternoon during our extended family's annual one-week
stint at the beach in Garden City, South Carolina, I jog the two miles
from the beach house to the pier, where I listen to karaoke singers,
drink a beer, look over the shoreline, and dream. I imagine that if I kept
jogging south I would pass Georgetown and Charleston and head
around the Florida coast, jog along the Gulf of Mexico, run along the
shores of Central America and Venezuela and down through Brazil,
where I would sprint along the same Atlantic coastline, cross a bridge,
and end up in the little island resort of Guarujá, near São Paulo, where
I spent summers as a child, staring out at the same Atlantic Ocean. Tra-
versing five thousand miles and some fifty years . . .

Suddenly I am fourteen years old, jumping barefoot onto the hot hot
hot sand, approaching the bevy of beach umbrellas where a game of
backgammon is always in progress. Each weekend morning, Nina and
Tommy Tucker stroll down to our umbrellas, and my dad and Tommy
set the board across their laps and play game after game, using the dou-
bling dice to raise the stakes, while Nina, my mother, Shirley, and the
other women engage in some deep chat. They drink caipirinhas, Brazil's national cocktail, made with cachaça, derived from sugarcane,
mixed with sugar and lime, and purchased from beach carts. Tommy

and my dad mark the score with their fingers in the sand. My dad smokes cigars and always seems to have one in his mouth.

Once, when my dad doubled the stakes, I asked, "How do you know if you made the right decision?" He quipped, "Decisions, decisions, decisions. I just have to hope that by the time I die, fifty-one percent of my decisions will have been right and only forty-nine percent will have been wrong."

I was twelve years old in 1959, when Bobby Fischer won the United States Chess Championship 11–0, the only perfect score in the history of the tournament. I loved listening to the grown-ups under the beach umbrellas in Guarujá talking about Fischer (along with the Cuban Revolution). Though backgammon was their game of choice, I became fascinated by chess, and I thought about how a kid who was only a few years older than me could do so well.

Many years later, as a folklorist, I did field research on chess havens in New York's West Village. I interviewed the players in Washington Square Park and at the two warring chess clubs on Thompson Street, Chess Forum and the Village Chess Shop. I visited the Marshall Chess Club, where the pièce de résistance is the famous Capablanca table, with an inlaid-wood chessboard. José Raúl Capablanca, world chess champion from 1921 to 1927, is said to have won the World Chess Championship on that table, and, in 1965, when Bobby Fischer was banned from attending a tournament in Cuba, Fischer too played on that table, in New York, circumventing the ban by having his opponent's moves telexed in from the island.

I became intrigued by the philosophical side of chess, a "Capablanca table of the mind" where the players are locked in eternal combat. Over that mythic chessboard, players are, as Chess Forum player Gary Ryan described it, "locked into timeless space—there's only this kind of laser-like focus on the board. You make a move—I make a move, and I make a move that is totally riding the edge against your move. It's like a surfer catching a big, big wave."[1]

"You make a move—I make a move, and I make a move that is totally riding the edge against your move. It's like a surfer catching a big, big wave."

In this kingdom of the mind, chess mirrors the world. "Every chess piece has its own personality," chess expert Asa Hoffman told me. "Each is different and moves differently—it's quite different from checkers or Go. People of low self-worth think of themselves as pawns. We devious ones think of ourselves as knights, jumping around and foiling and tricking people. Rigid people are bishops who only move diagonally."

Ryan elaborates on the idea of the game as a metaphor:

In chess, the pawn is the only piece that can move only forward, never backward. Pawns remind me of the legend about the Gurkha soldiers from the days of the British Empire. They wore Gurkha shorts and were famous for their bravery. In a battle they were known to tie up one of their legs so they could not run from a last stand. They could move only forward. The pawn is like the poor soldier named as the point man in Vietnam or Iraq. Someone has to go first. I'm not sure chess is a game. Chess may be something else—like a dream. I think that dreams are probably our attempts to figure out problems. On the chess board that's exactly what's going on: it's us trying to figure out problems. I think maybe when I play chess I'm trying to figure out problems that have nothing to do with you.

Chess seems to lend itself to grandiose metaphors, perhaps because it marks one of civilization's most enduring, elaborated-upon creations, or perhaps because of the astonishing intensity of mental effort involved in playing serious chess—so intense that it becomes physical. The players at the Marshall Chess Club described the game to me in various ways: "Chess is a mathematical problem that hasn't been solved yet." "Chess is an absurdity." "Chess is a ball of yarn." "Chess is a language in which you have to develop your own vocabulary." Chess, said president of the club Doug Bellizzi, is "the search for the truth."

Metaphors also abound in in the down-and-dirty trash talk exchanged by the chess players in New York City parks. Raised in Brownsville,

Brooklyn, Maurice Ashley, the first African American grand master, remembers the Black Bear Chess School members who used to play in Prospect Park and taught him much of what he knows about the game. They were called the Black Bears because if you encountered a black bear in the forest, you couldn't just injure it; you had to kill it, because it would just keep coming. He recalls George, the best of the Black Bears, who at some point in the game would say, "Don't you like the way my rook is penetrating into the rear of your position through the hole created by your separated pawns?" Maurice added, "And you're so flustered that you blunder . . . and then he does his signature move where he gets up on the park bench so that everybody can see him, and he has his queen in his hand, and he jumps into the air like Michael Jordan and slam-dunks his queen on the square and says, 'Checkmate!' "[2]

My mother, Shirley, passed away in 1999. A year later, my dad met Audrey Walton, a British expat, and their relationship turned into a five-year loving courtship of tea and dinners in fancy restaurants, and ended when Audrey passed away. My dad, then eighty-five, retreated into his apartment in São Paulo and never came out. His salvation was the computer, which he embraced with gusto.

He read the *New York Times* online, printed out articles, and kept elaborate files of his favorite editorials. "Steve," he said, "I've always been an introvert, unlike your mother." (Shirley was the most social of people.) "This new life offers me the opportunity to express my introvertedness."

Through his friend Dick Alkema, my dad discovered the site itsyour turn.com, which enabled him to play backgammon with people all over the world. It became his favorite pastime, and he spent many hours playing on the computer each day. On one of my trips to Brazil, I asked if he wanted to play a game of chess with me online.

I had sent my dad the article I'd written about New York City's chess scene, which he seemed to enjoy, and he dutifully filed it away. He agreed to play a game of chess with me on the computer. Although he always used to beat me in person, he lost the first game we played online. "Steve," he said, "at the age of eighty-five, chess is just too difficult for me." So, eschewing the philosophical glories of chess, we made backgammon our game of choice, and an ongoing game of computer backgammon took place between us as regularly as the games between Tommy Tucker and my dad once had at the beach.

I was reminded of my grandmother Bella and her sister Rose, who engaged in an endless game of gin rummy, each cursing wildly when she didn't draw the right card. Or my sister-in-law Sarah Dargan and her daughter, my niece Sarah Elizabeth, engaged in the endless card game of spit. "The game started when I was about five," Sarah Elizabeth told me, "and Mom would let me win an occasional game just to keep me interested until I blossomed and could beat her—but only if I played on my knees, for some reason. The game is so competitive—and she cheats, and she drinks when she plays. The loser always contests the game and accuses the other of cheating." Watching them play, I realized the ways in which their game of spit, beyond the raging competition, expressed their intimacy.

As did, in its own way, the great rivalry between Boris Spassky and Bobby Fischer. When Bobby Fischer was living in Iceland, toward the end of his life, he was unable to return to the United States, where he faced charges for playing a 1992 rematch with Spassky, his archrival, in what was then Yugoslavia; the United States somehow could not forgive his violation of sanctions, despite all the benefits his world championship win had brought to the country in the midst of the Cold War. A clipping on the wall of the Village Chess Shop in New York tells of Spassky's offer to the U.S. government, asking to be punished along with Fischer. He suggested that the United States put them both in jail—in the same cell, in fact. Their only request: a chess set.

The online backgammon games between my dad and me were a gentle competition. We played a nine-game series over and over—and we each made a move only once a day. These games were hardly a search for truth, but they were philosophical in a different way. At a given moment during the maelstrom of each workday, I took a break and moved my piece. I don't think either of us cared who won. I was pleased that I could get in touch with my dad every single day and give him a small task to accomplish.

Like chess, backgammon has its own rules and complex strategies that can unfold in the almost unlimited combinations of the dice, the red and black pieces, and the spaces on the board. But for us the game was a form of communication on a different plane. Our moves online took less than a minute each day, and no hand reached out to reposition the round pieces or roll the dice. But though I was in New York and he was in São Paulo, with each turn my hand was on my father's shoulder, and his hand was on mine. The game was easy, and any long-standing conflicts and disagreements were set aside. Each day the game made me pause to remember my father and Tommy Tucker, the hot sand in Guarujá, and my boyhood.

For us the game was a form of communication on a different plane. . . . Though I was in New York and he was in São Paulo, with each turn my hand was on my father's shoulder, and his hand was on mine.

We were in the middle of a game that could have gone one way or the other when I noticed first a day, then a week, then two weeks passing without my dad having moved a piece. I received an email from my father's old friend Dick Alkema, who also had a running game of online backgammon going with him. I emailed, then called my father in Brazil to tell him how much the games meant to me and to Dick. He said he would try to keep them going for our sake. The contests started up again: one move a day.

But three months later he stopped moving in a round where he would have had just a few pieces left to take off the board to win the game. With his sight now impaired and his difficulty negotiating the computer, I knew that it was becoming just too hard for him. The game remained unfinished, and he passed away a few months later. Several weeks after his death, I received a note from itsyourturn.com telling me that I had won the game. My opponent, the note said, had "timed out."

6

Inventing a Language for Love

Sex as Poetry and Play

I come before you to stand behind you to tell you something
I know nothing about.
—TRADITIONAL CHILDREN'S SAYING

An old joke: Abe and Harry, two old codgers in a nursing home, have only each other as friends. Each dreads the other's death. As they're sitting side by side on two rockers, Abe says to Harry, "You know, we should make a pact. Whoever dies first should try to contact the other and let him know what life is like in the next world." Harry wholeheartedly agrees.

Abe dies first, and Harry is lonely. He sits by himself in his rocker week after week. Then one day he is called to the pay phone. He picks it up. It's Abe.

"Abie," he says, "I can't believe you did it. You reached out and called just like you said. Tell me, what's it like over there?"

"Harry, you're not going to believe it. It's incredible. We wake up in the morning and we eat and we eat and we eat. Then in the afternoon we have sex and we have sex and we have sex. Then at night we eat and we eat and we eat. Before we go to bed we have sex—"

"Abie, that's incredible."

"Harry, wait."

"What do you do after you eat?"

"We have sex."

"I can't wait to get there. That's unbelievable."

"Harry, you don't understand—I'm a bull in Wisconsin."[1]

Sex is an animal urge but also a human endeavor, so how do we—how can we—infuse it with meaning?

Our sexual experiences, it's fair to say, must rise above the rote performances of "a bull in Wisconsin" if they are to play a significant part in our lives. Sex is an animal urge but also a human endeavor, so how do we—how can we—infuse it with meaning?

"We are alone in this world," said Lissa, quoted in the writer and public radio producer Julia Hutton's marvelous book, *Good Sex: Real Stories from Real People*, "and we can't truly connect minds and hearts except through the tools we have—language, art, music, and sex."[2] No two people come to sex and sexuality the same way. After all, every mind is unique and every human body responds in a different way. For two people to get together sexually, they have to bridge not only two complex minds—which is difficult enough—but also two bodies with their varied responses and erogenous zones. That's a lot of variables—so many variables, in fact, it's a wonder that we manage to have sex at all. As Julia told me, "It's a process of discovery: the other person is a mystery. Are they not?"

Since everyone experiences sex differently, there is no way I can address sex that won't make both of us slightly uncomfortable. But to leave sex out of a book on how we aestheticize our lives would simply invite an elephant into the room.

This chapter does not explore the physical nuances of sexual response like the Kinsey Report or the *Masters of Sex* Showtime series; it does not tell you how to be more loving or improve your lovemaking, nor does it teach you new positions, like the Kama Sutra, or tell you how to arouse your partner, like *Cosmopolitan* magazine, or give you the ready-made fantasies of *Fifty Shades of Grey*. It looks at how we use language, story, poetry, and play to add an aesthetic dimension to sex; how we poeticize and humanize and create entire worlds of pleasure and angst based on the few ways that human beings can tuck ourselves into one another. Just as we create a world of subtle tastes and dishes from the simple act of ingesting edible things, so we create a world of visceral pleasures from the few limited physical ways we share sex.

Language and Poetry

We human beings have been having sex since long before we had language. In sex we hear primal moans, sounds that we don't hear anywhere else in our daily lives. Although I can't confirm this, it's fair to hypothesize that humans have been making these sounds at least since they became *Homo sapiens*. The rhythm and timing of the moans have their own aesthetic qualities. Because of this, rock-and-roll and blues singers play on those rhythms. Listen, for instance, to Ray Charles belt out the classic "What'd I Say." He chants "Ummmmh" with a bevy of backup women singers echoing back "Unnnnh." They trade back and forth: "Ummmmh," "Ummmmh," then "Unnnnh," "Unnnnh," faster and faster, leading to a climax of "Ahhhhhh."[3]

The beauty and grace of two people in love making love is a kind of poetry. The iconoclastic modernist Iranian poet Forugh Farrokhzad (1935–1967) wrote explosive, subversive poetry before she was killed in a car crash at the age of thirty-two. In "Inaugurating the Garden," she inverts the garden metaphor common to classical Persian poetry, re-examining desire as a source of pleasure and fulfillment:

> Everyone fears.
> Everyone fears, but you and I
> merged into one
> before the water, the mirror,
>   and the lamp,
> and were not afraid.
> I do not speak of the frail union
>   of two names,
> their embrace on an
>   old ledger's page—
> I speak of my hair,
> happy with your singed poppy kisses,
> our bodies' defiant intimacy,
> and our nudity's sheen
>   like fish scales in water.
> I speak of the silver life of a song
> a small fountain sings each dawn.[4]

Good sex, it's been said, is wordless, speechless, thoughtless. "The best sex," songwriter Cat Yellen told me, "is a dance. There is no talking. If he can't read my mind, the hell with it."

Whitman wrote, "I sing the body electric." The jolt of electricity that courses through us during an orgasm is seemingly tied to magnetic fields that hark back to the charges in tiny electrons inside an atom and the vast explosions that formed and continue to shape the universe. That rush of current is also the way we procreate the human race. That electric current shapes our powerful experience of sex, but we amp it up by adding language, poetry, story, and play. The aesthetic impulse plays a role in sexuality. We rely on the mind to quell the body restless.

We rely on the mind to quell the body restless.

Beyond our sighs and moans, we also need a language with which to talk about sex. You know exactly what gives you pleasure, and I know exactly what gives me pleasure, but how do we have that difficult conversation across our differences and societal expectations?

To engage in that conversation, we have a number of vocabularies available to us, none of them perfect. We have clinical terms: *penis, vagina, glans, vulva*. We have pornographic terms: *fuck, pussy, cunt,* and *cock*. We may have memories of childhood terms for sex organs, words like *tata, bicky, tweeny, widgie, pee-pee*. And we have a romantic vocabulary that doesn't mention sex organs but that is whispered in candlelight: endearments like *sweetheart* and *honey, I love you* or *I want you*. And we have the sound of the soft, sexy voices of our lovers whispering "mmmmm sweet nothings."

To help me find the language for this chapter, I spoke with Julia Hutton. I wanted to get a woman's take, but she went beyond that to give me a human perspective. "Some people are word people," she told me. "They want more language—that's how they enjoy the world. For some people, naughty words are a turn-on; for other people, they are a complete turnoff." But words, she says, "whether taboo or not, add more than a verbal dimension to sex, because the sound of your partner's voice can be very intimate. It's not just the content of the language; it's hearing each other. And the way sexual encounters affect the voice is unlike nearly all our other vocalizations. Part of the language of sex, too, is indirection. It's not just about being precise or saying, 'Should I put my hand a little higher?' We need to use language that conveys openness—playful language—to bridge the awkwardness."

I was reminded of my friend Lisa Lipkin's story. "I had only recently learned how to ask for what I wanted, both in and out of the bedroom," she told me. "Yet still, I used my sultriest voice to give instructions to my Irish American boyfriend. 'Move your fingers around and around in a circle,' I whispered."

"'Clockwise or counterclockwise?' he whispered back in the same sultry tone—before we both cracked up!"

Julia went on to say:

When AIDS became a reality, there was a strong cultural push to become more articulate about sex in order to establish safe sex. People needed to be more proficient in talking to each other, and there was a flowering of language, though it came out of responding to a plague. At that time, there was a lot of turning to sexual subcultures which had developed more specific vocabularies. Terms for sex acts, but also "butch," "bottom," "top," and "safeword" entered the mainstream. And they've stayed. Comedians on network TV now drop "safeword" into their stand-up routines. With expanded language, the ability to describe your experience opens. Along with the liberalizing of language came more discussion of a broader range of sex acts and the understanding that there was more to sex than intercourse. Today, technology is helping shape sexual culture, from dating sites and hook-ups to breakups via "ghosting." A wider range of sex behaviors may be getting noticed, yet language isn't necessarily advancing amidst short-format digital exchanges and pervasive sexual imagery, from Internet porn to nude selfies, sought or unsought.

In a sense, we invent love through language. We have to apply our own creativity and aesthetic sensibility to come together meaningfully, to develop a verbal or nonverbal language for sex, and to find common ground between us. Finding a common language is not always easy.

Do we reclaim vulgar language by putting love behind it and changing the meanings of words accordingly? Along these lines, I sought to romanticize the language of BDSM:

Will you share my sweet, sweet memories
of the pain?
(sadistic separation of souls)

Or will you regret
one treasured moment of our pirated pleasure—
so that we have to discipline our bad bad girl

bind you to the bedposts

lash you to a ship's mast
set the rigging aflame!

save you with a barrage of kisses
like a downpour of rain

Every couple is left to devise its own language, or a way to give the words their own meanings through the intonations and the way they are said. "They Call It Makin' Love," as the title of the Tammy Wynette song reminds us. Or as Bob Dylan wrote, "Love is just a four-letter word." The first thing I learned when I took a class on the history of the English language is that words like *fuck*, which originates from the Dutch *fokken*, meaning "to breed cattle," are passed down from our earliest Anglo-Saxon forebears. From their lascivious lips, to my libidinous heart, to your salacious soul.

Sex is also replete with similes and metaphors. The forbidden fruit is a theme in the biblical Garden of Eden. Fruits and flowers are easily distinguished from foliage; they are juicy and aromatic, and have irregular shapes, like our sex organs, lending themselves to metaphors. An ancient Assyrian text reads, "May my eyes behold the gathering of your fruit, may my ears hear the twittering of your birds."[5] Emily Dickinson writes, "Forbidden fruit a flavor has / That lawful orchards mocks— / How luscious lies within the pod / The pea that duty locks."[6] Lucinda

Williams sings, "I will open myself up to you like a rose." Cat Yellen learned from her parents that, when she was about five years old, her first big crush was on the Empire State Building. Classic phallic symbols include sticks, swords, clubs, towers, trees, missiles, rockets, and cigars. But as Freud supposedly said, "Sometimes a cigar is just a cigar."

The narratives and imagery that turn us on, and the language we use to describe our sex lives, harbor aesthetic qualities that are rarely explored or discussed. Sex workers often ask their clients what words they want to hear, and lovers need to agree on a shared language of the bedroom. One couple used the word "popped" to talk about orgasm. An element of verbal playfulness and fantasy contributes to what one of my friends aptly termed "fun in bed."

"Let me hear your body talk," as the song "Physical," by Olivia Newton-John, puts it. If the best sex is wordless, that doesn't prevent us from waxing poetic over its visceral grandeur. Witness these comments from Julia Hutton's interviews in *Good Sex*:

[Sex is] a body language for the hidden faces of the soul.

It's that sense of ultimate chaos. It's the journey to Ixtlán. Once you take the journey, can you go home again? Yes and no. Everything has changed because you've done what you've done. I live for times like that.

It was truly as if time stopped still. I remember thinking, "I'm in eternity. There is no past, there is no future."[7]

Story

In one episode of the *Moth Radio Hour*, Stephanie Summerville tells of her first kiss, at the age of thirteen:

The only things I had gleaned about sex were from the Harlequin Romance novels that my spinster cousin left at my grandma's house. And the things I got out of them were this: all intimate relationships begin with a kiss and, according to the writing, the women who got this kiss were somehow forever changed. [You knew that because] the writing got all flowery. . . . So here it is, after work, and I'm standing in the parking lot and I let Buster kiss me, and can I tell you it was the most amazing thing—it was delicious. When our lips met it was like somewhere in my mind a door swung open to a room full of incredible sensations, and that room, I realized, was called pleasure.[8]

I didn't lose my virginity until I was in college. One evening I was in the Van Pelt Library at the University of Pennsylvania, sitting across the table from a pretty blonde, a few years older than me. Later, as I walked the ten blocks back to my apartment, I became conscious of her walking behind me, carrying a suitcase. I thought nothing of it. I must have stopped in at one of the campus stores, because, as I recall, a few moments later she was ahead of me, ringing the bell of a row house. She turned away from the door and approached me. "I'm just not sure my friends are here," she said, growing quite distraught. "Could you wait with me for a moment?"

I stood there with her for a few minutes, and then she said, "Do you know any place where I could stay for the night?"

Stay for the night? Why, my place of course! When we arrived back at 4040 Spruce Street, my roommates were asleep. I actually shared a room, so that meant we were relegated to the sofa bed in the living room. I desperately needed a drink. At the time, I was drinking liqueurs: banana, peach, apricot—that kind of thing. I looked at the row of bottles along the bottom shelf of the bookcase. My heart sank: nothing left but the dregs. She didn't drink, she told me. So I took every one of those bottles and poured the remains into one glass, a banana-peach-apricot-strawberry cocktail.

I started making out with her on the sofa. "Why don't we take our clothes off?" she suggested. I went to the bathroom, and as I was walking out, I caught a glimpse of myself in the mirror. And so I waved my virgin self good-bye.

Firsts and lasts are constructs of memory, part of the ways we define and remember experiences. We divide our lives into chapters: "The First Time I Saw Your Face" or "The Last Time I Saw Paris." There is a first time for everything. But the first time is also the last time; that is, it's the last opportunity for the first time. There is a first time, and also a best time, and often our memory works to make us remember the best time as the first time. As one woman put it, "The saddest part of getting married was knowing that there would be no more first times." Yet lovers and other strangers who have done things thousands of times can still pretend they are doing them for the first time.

Once I waved good-bye to my virgin self in the mirror, I went to bed with this beautiful woman. In the afterglow of our memorable escapade, I learned just a little about her. Her name was Elizabeth. She was a member of a cult that sounded similar to EST, the Erhard Seminars Training. She had a child. She told me, laughing, that she was on a mission to de-virginize young men who looked liked me. She walked out of the apartment and I never saw her again. I took a shower and went to class with a sense of raging, euphoric exhaustion. I smiled through the whole lecture. Life craves these vivid memories—and we rely on them for stories.

In *Southern Ladies and Gentlemen*, the humorist Florence King writes hilariously about "the self-rejuvenating virgin." Many of her fellow southern women adapted to the mores of their culture by enjoying as much sex as possible while still remaining "virgins." As long as it wasn't premeditated, it didn't happen. As long as it wasn't in a bed, it didn't happen. On a vacation, they could enjoy a frenzied sexual fling, believing it hadn't really occurred because (1) they'd never see him again; (2) they didn't remember his name; (3) he'd never told them his name; (4) they didn't tell him their name; (5) it happened in New York.[9]

In our sex lives, we reinvent virginities in other ways, and many other memorable moments might be classified as rites of initiation: our first kiss, our first orgasm, the first time we have sex with a new person, the first time we try some new sexual variation or have an encounter with a member of our own sex. Framing our experiences in terms of first times and last times is among the ways we "storify" our lives. Fantasies are often framed as first times, which is ironic, since most people's first times are awkward and unsatisfying—though of course in one's fantasies they aren't.

T. S. Eliot wrote, "We shall not cease from exploration, / and the end of all our exploring / will be to arrive where we started / and know the place for the first time."[10] Our first-time fantasies point to our deeper selves as adventurers always longing to encounter experiences for the first time.

My friend the writer Alicia Vasquez told me about her initiation into sex with women as a series of firsts:

I remember the first time I was attracted to a woman. I was walking along Lexington Avenue in New York City toward work, and as I crossed the street she stepped right in front of me. I was awestruck by her beauty. I felt a sudden need to follow her. It confused me and I didn't understand what had just happened.

That first time was followed by the first sexual experience with a woman. The first time I was with a woman I was struck by how sweet her scent was; she was soft and yielding. Her moans drove me crazy and when she whispered my name I was hooked. Once morning came and the alcohol wore off, it once again felt awkward, and I was afraid. I thought something must be wrong with me. It took many years before I was willing to accept the fact that it is a part of me, who I am, how I'm built, my DNA.

Then she talks about giving her partner her first orgasm: "My first girl-friend, and the woman with whom I could practice, freaked out when I first made her come. Score! End-zone dance! I suddenly jumped out of bed and spiked my pillow. Probably not the best way to go."

Not all the stories of sex and sexuality are positive, charming, or fun. Sex can spill into violence and abuse and leave behind searing memories or untold, sometimes festering, stories. Alicia also wrote this powerful poem about her childhood's untold story:

As a young girl
I was sodomized
by a man.
He hurt me.

Me.

When it was over
I packed up my pants
tucked in my blouse.

I did not tell anyone.
Not anyone.
Not even myself

Fantasy

Folklorists have often described the core structure of fairy tales as "interdiction/violation."[11] We could stop reading as soon as we get to the point in a story that says, "You will not travel into the forest," "You will not kiss the prince," "You will not open the box," for we know that the princess *will* travel into the forest, kiss the prince, open the forbidden box. It's inevitable. In our sexual fantasies, if not in our real lives, we are always opening Pandora's box. That's the way the story is meant to unfold.

Our sexual fantasies often reverse conventional norms of good and bad (as they are often portrayed in fairy tales and other traditional stories): in our fantasies, what's good is bad, and what's bad is good. Angels presumably don't have sex. And the women on the television series *Orange Is the New Black* engage in delicious "hate sex." The reversal evokes saturnalia, the masks and role reversals that take place during carnival celebrations. I tried to express this in a poem I called "Dark Light":

> wash away your inhibitions
> divulge the naked urge
>
> haunt the dark places
> where spirits troll
>
> for inebriated laughter
> in the lipstick's red glow
>
> no one casts a shadow
>
> the light shines from below

"An orgasm has no memory," the writer Lisa Lipkin told me.

> The memory is of the buildup to the orgasm, and that's a story. The story of getting fucked on the floor is one I've come back to again and again in my memory, as a single woman, lonely sometimes. You don't remember the time he didn't kiss you; you remember the time he kissed you. You remember the time he brushed up against you, not the time he didn't. You remember it in your memory, in your memory tissue. Sex is really about stories. The stories of how you were seduced, how you'd like to be seduced. Your sexual fantasies are the stories you tell to yourself.

Or as another woman put it, "You really have to hold on to your fantasies. I have just two basic fantasies, and they've gotten me all the way through my married life."

Sexual fantasies work for an individual not so much when they tell new or original stories as when they match a kind of proto-story that is already programmed into our bodies and our minds. How do those proto-stories arrive there? From things we read and watch mixed with how our bodies respond to mental images, perhaps. And perhaps we inherit particular erogenous zones or predilections from our parents in ways that it pains us even to think about.

I asked Julia Hutton how particular sexual fantasies become implanted in our brains. "The development of the erotic imagination seems to be haphazard," she said.

> One of the things that really impressed me when I was interviewing people for *Good Sex* was the profound impact of the first erotic media—usually print—that people had been exposed to. The male ritual of being handed *Playboy* or *Penthouse* by an older brother—or stealing it. A black man told me he had concluded—indelibly—that white women were the naughty ones, because they were the women in the first porn films he saw. One woman talked about discovering the book *Peyton Place* while babysitting, and always seeking out a particularly steamy page. I was impressed with how early turn-ons and ideas got set—and became fantasy material or stimuli that people returned to again and again. Sometimes entirely private: they may never even share that with another person.

Sexual fantasies themselves are a form of folklore. They are a body of culturally bound and transmitted stories whose plotlines are passed along through magazines and movies and word of mouth. Our sexual lore is handed down much as children's games are: intragenerationally rather than intergenerationally. The knowledge and lore of sex are often shared between young people coming of age at the same time, rather than passed on from parent to child. But unlike playground games, sex is not a phase of play we pass through. It stays with us, and evolves into an ongoing dialogue with ourselves and others throughout our lives.

"It was a hot night in Los Angeles" was how a friend always began the bedtime stories he told his wife. He referred to them as "forbidden lullabies." Often, shared fantasies help couples continue to enjoy their sex lives, even over the course of a long relationship.

Sordid or not, telephone and Internet sex, as well as sexting, are forms of storytelling, as are the stories told or enacted by lovers in the night. Even though they are using the stock phrases of "talking dirty," their success depends on using them playfully and in sync with each other. We can be creative with the clichés.

The language is often completely formulaic, beginning with "What are you wearing?" Phrases and fantasies are a bit like the motifs in fairy tales, which can be moved around and combined with greater or lesser degrees of imagination. In fact, the conversations are so formulaic that sex workers in other countries can sit in their rooms with a keyboard and text (or "sext") phrases like "Do you want to fuck?" in a language they don't even speak or write. But of course there is a difference between sex with a partner and sex for money. The financial exchange affects the lovemaking and inserts an element of exploitation into the encounter; doing this kind of work can take a significant toll on women's and men's psychic well-being.

Couples' sexual fantasies often seem simpleminded, particularly when taken out of context. When sex is not on our minds, the lure of these fantasies escapes us. Like pornography, they may have story lines that are as predictable as those of a campfire skit or an Easter pageant. Yet they harbor a power in the moment because they produce a visceral response in our physical selves. A poem or a story can give us goose bumps, but a fantasy is wired deeper into the body's circuitry: it can make us come. I tried to capture some of the experience on a cosmic plane:

> the current of the cosmos
> zigzags through you
>
> not quite enough to kill you
> just to put you under
>
> a grand orgasmic sigh—
> then a night of peaceful slumber
>
> as lightning zaps a distant moon
> creation spurts
> life starts

stars burst
galaxies die
the cosmos churns and heaves
a grand orgasmic sigh

Since acting out all of our momentary urges and desires is not a viable option for most of us, we need creative metaphors and fantasies as a way of establishing close relationships with individuals with whom we share a bond and an attraction but with whom sex is not an option. Since we can't live out our fantasies, we often use poetic metaphors to add a sexual charge to nonsexual relationships. I recall going out with a friend for coffee and a cookie at four in the afternoon. "You know, sharing a cookie is a bond," she said as she broke the cookie in half in a way that didn't seem totally innocent. Dancing is also a safe way of expressing one's sexuality. What do women want? I've heard the question answered "They want to dance." Yet dancing, too, is often an obvious metaphor for sex, which becomes perfectly clear as dancers shake and grind their hips on the dance floor.

I jotted down these lines to express the way an attraction can be played out symbolically in the course of a conversation or over a meal:

Perfect Love

When all the ions are charged
and I'm in the zone with you
in the ozone just above your eyes
your spirit comes wafting into view

As we speak
our spirits promenade
down Second Avenue
dance on restaurant tables
crisscross the rivers and the bridges
zip across the skyline
like some crazed angels from above
our spirits gallivanting
making perfect love

Whooshing back as we pay the bill
to whisper and coo—
that's why I traveled all these miles
to spend an hour with you

Perhaps we need fantasies because most of us make imperfect love.

To a greater or lesser extent, people try to live out their fantasies in real life. Often the effort fails, or appears ridiculous or pathetic to outsiders. The partners in our fantasies are always beautiful, and it is always the first time; the real-life versions have a hard time competing. Describing a mechanic and a receptionist acting out their fetishes at an S&M club, author Mark Baker writes: "The standard plot is totally undermined by the fact that real people are playing the parts. Their humanity interferes with the story line." Nonetheless, we can't help but be taken with people who seek to play out their fantasies within safe boundaries. Perhaps from them, as Baker suggests, "the rest of us can extrapolate the true depth and power of our own sexuality, gauge the noble and venal limits of our mysterious human condition."[12]

We outgrow some of these fantasies in the course of the life cycle, or at least become less driven to act them out. Songwriter Cat Yellen, who danced in strip clubs, expressed the visceral pleasures of sexual fantasy from her unique perspective as a performer of make-believe. I put my interview with her in poetic form:

> I was a stripper.
> I lived in a make-pretend world of sexual images. I lived in costumes.
> I was happiest when I was in a dark room full of men, scantily dressed.
> Not that I wanted to fuck anyone, but it was a dream.
> They say that every man wants to fuck a hooker and every woman
>   wants to be one.
> And I was very caught up in those games.
>
> I got up onstage three weeks ago at this place where I'd danced in
>   Chelsea.
> I just wanted to capture the old feeling one last time—and it had
>   changed.
>
> Leaving all that behind is a grieving process, but you can't help but
>   mature.
> It no longer works for you.
> You're given the time that you're given and then it's gone. . . .
>
> If I long for anything, it's the ignorance I used to have.
> Every bit of wisdom that I get narrows my path.
> It's cool; I've got to walk the good path, whatever that may be.

But sometimes I long for just the fucking banal ignorance that I had
    of a little-girl junkie stripper motherfucker whore,
And that wildness, and that leniency I had on myself before.

Play

In the early 1950s, the anthropologist Gregory Bateson observed that monkeys nipping at one another in the cages at the San Francisco Zoo were clearly not fighting. They were playing. This meant that the monkeys must somehow have communicated this distinction to one another. Bateson termed this "meta-communication."[13] In the S&M subculture of New York City, consenting adults, negotiating the thin line between pleasure and pain, often use the safeword "red light" to signal to their partner "This is not play," and "green light" to mean "This is play."

While these adult play activities share much in common with children's games like Red Light, Green Light and Simon Says, when my wife, Amanda, and I studied the broader concept of play for our book and exhibition *City Play*, we came across few studies of adult play and no studies of play that considered sex.

Years later, when Amanda and I were teaching a class on the folklore of New York City at the City University of New York, we asked students to write an ethnography of a New York City community that harbored a rich expressive culture. We were surprised that three of the students independently selected topics about the city's subcultures of sexual play: an African American S&M club, a Latino swingers' group, and the city's vampire scene. All of the papers were excellent, but we were even more impressed when one of the students brought in an "artifact" to illustrate her presentation: a nipple clamp.

"In this society," says Morgan, a thirty-eight-year-old interviewed by Julia Hutton in *Good Sex*,

> adults are not supposed to play. We're supposed to work, to be consumers. One of the things that lies at the core of who I am is that I want to go play. Adopting a persona provides me with the ability to sidestep daily roles. . . . I can fall into these characters and play at them in an adult way—a sexual way. I can learn what grovel means and get off on it. What does virginity mean, and how many times can we re-create it? I can be the blushing bride, the proud groom—or the

jockey, for that matter. There are aspects of all those characters in us. . . . I can make up my own characters, play those roles, do the things that most people only do in a sedate way on Halloween.[14]

Never leaving a stone unturned in my work as a folklorist, I began to consider the question: Is sex play? Fellow folklorist Kay Turner suggested interviewing a friend of hers, Claire Cavanah, who owns several women-oriented sex-toy shops in Lower Manhattan and Brooklyn that were then called Toys in Babeland (since shortened to Babeland).

During our interview, Claire mentioned an NPR program featuring Stuart Brown, director of the National Institute for Play. "He never mentioned sex," she told me. "I was waiting for it and waiting for it, but it never happened."

Claire, who is also a mother, spoke about the freedom of play she experienced during her childhood in Wyoming:

In the park near my house there was a creek, and we would build things and hide from each other. Time would disappear. You lost your sense of everything that weighs you down. That's very much like sex, if you think about it. When you're very close to orgasm—when you're in that kind of zone with someone or even just yourself—things fall away, all of it. As a child, too, there are those moments when everything feels right, the air is right, the music is right, you're with the right people— you feel safe, but you're also risking something . . . and it's worth it.

Claire was quick to point out that sex is not just about play, however. "It's also serious business. It's also abuse, recovering from abuse; it's coming out of the closet; it's being rejected by your family; it's contracting AIDS. There's a lot of darkness, too."

I was struck by Claire's passion for the mission of Babeland, which aims to serve both the dark and light sides of our sexual lives. She explains:

What we try to do is heal the wounds and support people in sexual liberation, which is following the basics of life—your hunger, your thirst, your desire. That's the play element of sex. Here at Babeland, we feel that we're standing on the shoulders of all those who fought for reproductive rights for women. Our mission is taking the shame out of having sex, honoring it as a life force, and treating it as a place where grown-ups play. Sex is where adults let go and are joyful and follow their curiosity, their pleasure, their bliss, in consenting situations with other adults. That's really basic to what we do here—and the toys carry the metaphor.

In Claire's view, the sex toys the store sells are useful when they fit into and enhance the stories and fantasies that her clients tell themselves and/or one another. "Oftentimes, people who shop here fall in love with a toy—sort of like a nice pair of shoes. They say things like 'That vibrator is me—it expresses me!'"

Humor and laughter also play a part in good sex. Julia Hutton quotes Ricky, a woman from San Francisco:

I want to be in his car, laughing—preferably him laughing at something I'm saying. . . . I want him to tease me in a personal way that implies he knows me. I want him to mimic me, say my words back to me. . . . That whole notion of being conspiratorial is what's sexual to me: "It's me and you against all these morons." That's fun; that's intimate. If you can't answer me, if you can't talk to me, if you can't laugh at my goddamn jokes, don't touch me. . . . I want to touch somebody when he says something wonderful. If he gives me a sense that he's trying to figure out something to say that will either catch my interest or make me laugh, it drives me mad with desire. And gratitude.[15]

> "I want him to tease me in a personal way that implies he knows me. I want him to mimic me, say my words back to me."

"I just loved that comment of Ricky's," Julia told me. "Shared humor is a way of creating intimacy and conveying acceptance and tolerance, and you need tolerance when you're dealing with a real human being. You want to be nonjudgmental, and to have an openness—the thrill of not knowing what's going to happen, even with a longtime partner. And if you work out the cues with one another, well, then you have your own private language, just the two of you together. You're keeping the secrets of the relationship, and it's both protective and potentially very sexy."

The colorful language of love and sex revs up our heartbeats. Our communication is most powerful when we're physically excited, when our bodies are responding to another's. We live in order to live vividly,[16] and sex and the language we use to express it is at the heart of this pursuit. We are never so alive, and we testify to the power of these stories in the beating of our hearts.

Part III POETRY IN SERVICE

7

Poetry on the Porch
A Time Set Aside

A WORD is dead
When it is said,
Some say.
I say it just
Begins to live
That day.
—EMILY DICKINSON

My family and I love August in New York. Parking is easy, and we even get a seat on the subway. But during the first week, like other New Yorkers, we flee the sirens and horns, abandoning the clatter of City Lore's offices on the Lower East Side for a week at the beach in Garden City, South Carolina. My wife's parents rent the same house every year, and all of her sisters and our nieces and nephews pile in, spending afternoons and evenings on the screened porch overlooking the sand dunes, the beach, and the sea.

Among our traditions is an evening spent reading poems on the porch, which Amanda's dad, Lucas, eagerly anticipates, bringing along his *101 Favorite Poems*, published in 1929. But we all bring a few poems to the porch—even the children. At age ten our nephew Aidan Powers came equipped with a full set of Shel Silverstein's ingenious poetry.

Masterpieces and ditties are treated with equal weight: poems by Shelley, Keats, Wordsworth, and Byron are interspersed with children's poetry and nonsense verses. The poems that waft into the sea air carry with them not only the finely wrought words of their creators but also the family stories, personalities, and ethos of the family gathering. Once, a family story reminded Lucas of a limerick, and he began to

The poems that waft into the sea air carry with them not only the finely wrought words of their creators but also the family stories, personalities, and ethos of the family gathering.

recite: "A wonderful bird is the pelican. / His bill holds more than his belly can"— but then he forgot the next line, which we were able to find through Google. With relief, Lucas finished the poem for us: "Ah, that's it! 'He can take in his beak / food enough for a week, / but I'm damned if I see how the helican.'"

Each year, Amanda's sister Sarah reads "The Minuet" by Mary Mapes Dodge, in honor of their mother, Frances. "Grandma told me all about it, / Told me so I couldn't doubt it, / How she danced—my grandma danced!— / Long ago." Sarah reads that poem every year because it reminds us all of a story that Frances loved to tell about how she once jumped up onto a table at her college's Junior-Senior Ball and danced to "Minnie the Moocher." When she was still alive, the recitation gave Frances a chance to tell that story, and, now that she's gone, it recalls the memory of her telling it.

Lucas, a forester and an environmentalist, never misses a chance to share Shelley's "The Cloud," which he reads in full and I quote in part: "I am the daughter of Earth and Water, / And the nursling of the Sky; / I pass through the pores of the ocean and shores; / I change, but I cannot die." Each year he remarks, "I just think it's amazing that a poet could capture the hydrologic cycle so well."

My nephew Patton, who has lived and worked in Beijing and speaks Chinese, often recites a poem by Li Po, "Quiet Night Thoughts," among the most quoted poems of the Tang dynasty, which he himself translated:

Before my bed
there is bright moonlight
so that it seems
like frost on the ground:

Lifting my head
I watch the bright moon,
Lowering my head
I dream that I'm home.

"I thought it would be appropriate for poetry night at the beach," Patton later explained, "because the moon was shining on the water; because of the extreme contrast between a frosty tundra and Garden City in August; and because being at the beach in the summer with my grandparents is one of my models for 'home.'"

In *The Second Life of Art*, the Italian poet Eugenio Montale suggests that the journey of art is an "obscure pilgrimage through the consciousness and memory of men." He explains that music, painting, and poetry exercise their powers outside of the moment of creation, when they free themselves from "that particular situation of life which made them possible." It is in those moments—when the poem is appreciated in situations and for reasons the poet could not even have imagined—that the "circle of understanding" closes and "art become[s] one with life."[1]

> **It is in those moments—when the poem is appreciated in situations and for reasons the poet could not even have imagined—that the "circle of understanding" closes and "art become[s] one with life."**

The poems our family reads were composed at different points in human history, but as part of their "obscure pilgrimage," they come to rest for a few moments each summer at a beach house in Garden City.

At the beach, the poems have become part of the way our family members share what they love with one another, and, in the process, share something of themselves and where they are in their lives each summer. In the end, poems are simply expressions of how people, employing an act of imagination, relate to one another and the world.

The evenings of poetry on the porch at the beach were so enjoyed by the family that they spawned poetry nights in the Dargan living room back in Darlington, South Carolina, on a weekly basis. Enter David Brown, a neighbor, a poet himself, and his closest friend, Stanley, who sings and plays guitar. They keep the tradition of poetry nights going long after summer's end, when Amanda and I are back in New York. Lucas often recites "Elegy Written in a Country Churchyard" by Thomas Gray ("The curfew tolls the knell of parting day . . ."). Then he tells of his visit to the site that inspired the poem, St Giles's parish church not far from London. "The place didn't look anything like how it did in my head. But the good thing is that whenever I read the poem, I still picture it just the way I do in my mind."

David and Stanley added a new tradition of calling themselves officers in the South Charleston Road Literary Society, drawing on their mutual nicknames, Rooster and Smoke, and writing comic poems to each other. The two memorized "The Shooting of Dan McGrew," which they recite in tandem. Then Stanley came up with a parody that closes, "I'm not as wise as those other guys and my mind don't work like it used to, but that, boys and girls, was the night that started the legend of Smoke & Rooster!"

They end each night on the high road—and the low road—singing the Scottish song "Lock Lomond" for Amanda's dad, whom they call Mr. Lucas.

But on this night, on the porch in Garden City, the evening wouldn't be complete without my daughter, Eliza, reciting John Masefield's "Sea Fever" from memory: "I must go down the to the seas again / To the lonely sea and the sky." Eliza has the gift of memorizing poetry easily; she talks about learning some poems by accident—she just hears them once and they stick. Amanda's grandmother, whom she called Mugga, told her to memorize as many poems as she could when she was young because she would need them when she grew older: "You'll know people who are sick, and you can recite the poems to them when there is nothing else to say. And when you get to be an older woman, going over those poems in your head will keep your mind sharp."

On the porch, Eliza finishes hers: "And all I ask is a merry yarn from a laughing fellow-rover, / And quiet sleep and a sweet dream when the long trick's over."

"Oh my god: look at that beautiful sky!" Amanda says. We look up to see the moon casting its reflection on the water as the sound of the waves grows louder, and the rustle of the wind makes it hard to hear what's said. Then Amanda's sister comes out to tell us that supper is on the table, and the poems, like children, are put to bed.

8

All My Trials

The Healing Powers of Poems and Tales

All my trials, Lord, soon be over.
—TRADITIONAL SPIRITUAL

From our family's poetry night, I understood how poetry can be used to share feelings and thoughts with loved ones, but I became interested in the role that poetry could play in getting people through hard times. I asked my friend Jane Preston, managing director at Poets House, and she suggested that I talk with her colleague Alice "Ollie" Kaasik, who has been the Poets House bookkeeper for twenty-five years. Ollie was a mirthful person who loved Broadway musicals, spent much of her free time on Shelter Island, and occasionally read poetry aloud to children at Poets House with accompaniment from a full cast of hand puppets. During the holiday season, Ollie and her husband could be spotted moonlighting as Mrs. and Mr. Claus at parties in the area.

A long way from the beach house in South Carolina and some twenty years ago, Alice "Ollie" Kaasik was overcome with anxiety, a vague, powerful angst she couldn't place. "One day," she said, "I was walking through my office at work and I saw a poem Scotch-taped to a computer." It was called "The Guest House," by Rumi:

This being human is a guest house.
Every morning a new arrival.

A joy, a depression, a meanness,
some momentary awareness comes
As an unexpected visitor.

Welcome and entertain them all!
Even if they're a crowd of sorrows,

who violently sweep your house
empty of its furniture,
still treat each guest honorably.
He may be clearing you out
for some new delight.

The dark thought, the shame, the malice,
meet them at the door laughing,
and invite them in.

Be grateful for whoever comes,
because each has been sent
as a guide from beyond.[1]

"Different people are sitting at the table," Ollie says, "but the poem just tells you, 'don't be alarmed.' So when I had the panic attacks I understood that it's not me—I just have a really bad visitor. I need to sweep out our house, to let him in, and let him go."

Her brother loved the poem, too. "It's become a metaphor for us. 'I got a really bad visitor,' he'll say. We must have used this poem two thousand times. You see, it's not our anxiety that is visiting us; it's just some gribbley guy—that's our family term for a weird, crazy person. You see, anxiety doesn't really have a source. But if you think of it as a visitor," she said, "it becomes something you can focus on. You can let him sit there and then you can let him go. Right now I have new demons, an illness called cancer that is far more real than anxiety. So I have to find a new poem." Ollie passed away in February 2016, and I never learned whether she found that new poem.

On the porch in South Carolina, with all of us kicking off our shoes on vacation, the poems express our personalities far from the madding crowd. From the window of my office on the corner of First Street and First Avenue on the Lower East Side, I watched human beings use poetry in a different way. Between May 1990 and April 1991, a sculpture by the performance artist Karen Finley stood in the corner park on First Street that was populated by drug dealers and the homeless. Called *The Black Sheep*, the concrete monolith was inscribed with a poem cast in bronze. Here is an excerpt:

We are the black sheep of the family . . .
There's always one in every family

Even when we're surrounded by bodies
we're always alone—
You're born alone
and you die alone . . .
Black Sheep folk look different from their family—
The way they look at the world
We're a quirk of nature—
We're a quirk of fate—
Usually our family, our city, our country
never understands us—
We knew this from when we were very young
that we were not meant to be understood.
That's right. That's our job . . .
Usually we're outcasts, outsiders
in our own family.
Don't worry—get used to it.
. . . Sometimes, Black Sheep are chosen to be sick
so families can finally come together
and say I love you.
Sometimes, some Black Sheep are chosen to die
so loved ones, families, countries
and cultures
can finally say
Your life was worth living!
Your life meant something to me!
I loved you all along![2]

Day after day I watched homeless men and homeless women reading the poem. Many reached up to touch it. Once I watched a homeless man kneeling before it, praying.

"There never was a story without a poem," writes Harold Scheub in *The Poem in the Story: Music, Poetry, and Narrative.* "It is in the nature of storytelling that the narrative is constructed around a poetic interior."[3] Stories, he suggests are formed around a lyric center in which the storyteller's present and the mythic past become metaphors for each other. Both stories and poems share some of the qualities of prayer. Rabbi Edward Schecter offers his proof by example with a story he told on Yom Kippur in 2011:

On Friday morning, I got a call from a member of my congregation telling me that one of our members, Alan, was in the hospital, and that the situation was grave. This was Columbia Presbyterian, and I've been there so often that I've become friendly with the Jamaican guard who sits at the front desk in front of the elevators. This time, when I got to the hospital I was surprised to see he wasn't there. Another Jamaican man was at the desk. He was waving everyone else toward the elevators, but for some reason he asked me to show identification. I was a bit flustered, carrying a cup of coffee and just through fighting the traffic on the West Side Highway. So I reached into my wallet and pulled out my Board of Rabbis card.

"Rabbi," he said, "we can let you in even though it's not visiting hours. You have special permission."

"That's good," I said.

"That's because you have special powers." Then suddenly a question occurred to him: "If you pray to your God to heal this man upstairs, can your God do it?"

My first response was to say, "Yes, God can do it," even though I didn't believe God would do it even if He could. Then I could just get into the elevator and get my day moving. I even had a chance because other visitors were lining up behind me and I was keeping people waiting. But I didn't say that, and the guard kind of waved the other people on their way, as I had hoped he would have waved me on. He looked at me again: "Well, Rabbi?"

And without knowing exactly what I was going to say, I responded, "No. I don't believe God will cure him if I pray asking God to do it. But I do believe that prayer opens us up to the healing powers that God has already placed in the universe."

"I like that, Rabbi," he said.

"And now," I added, feeling a bit encouraged, "let me ask you a question. What kind of God would He be who would heal only those who prayed to Him?"

The guard nodded his approval and I got into the elevator, a bit relieved and overwhelmed by this man's probing questions. But then as the elevator went up, it dawned on me: Maybe this is a test. Perhaps I should say the traditional prayer for healing, the Mi'She'berach: "May He who has blessed our forefathers bless this man with health." So I said it then for Alan.

I walked into Alan's room and sat down. Within a few seconds, Alan's doctor walked in. "Mr. Janger, your tests came back just fine. You can go home tomorrow."

We visited for a few minutes, but Alan was already making those mental transitions from hospital to home.

I ran for the elevator, now in pursuit of that guard to tell him about it. When the elevator reached the lobby, he was no longer there. Instead, at the desk sat my good friend the other Jamaican guard. He said, "How is Mr. Janger?"

And I said: "Fine. He's going home. Where is the other guard?"

He said, "What other guard?"

I said, "The other Jamaican man who was here earlier."

"Earlier? Rabbi," he said, "I've been here all morning. I haven't left this spot."

When I got to the parking lot, I thought Isaac Bashevis Singer, who wrote stories like this one, was going to deliver my car.

Later, I ended up telling the story to a fifth-grade class—even though I thought the kids wouldn't get it.

Five years later, I got a call from the parents of one my students telling me that their daughter was in the hospital and was going to be facing potentially life-threatening brain surgery the next day. They wanted me to come say the healing prayer for her. So I rushed to the hospital.

"Would you like me to say the Mi'She'berach?" I asked her.

She said, "No, that's all right. I don't need a prayer. I just want you to tell me the story about the hospital guard that you told us in fifth grade."

That girl is now married with three children.

Perhaps stories and poems, like prayers, have the power to heal—or perhaps they open us to the healing power of the universe, as the rabbi said. Or perhaps they provide comfort and insight into our situations when our prayers don't work.

Perhaps stories and poems, like prayers, have the power to heal.

9

The AIDS Poets

Living with Dying

Living with death as my everyday little friend.
—IOLENE CATALANO

When I called Lila Zeiger in the early 1990s to ask if I could visit the AIDS Day Treatment Program, on West Twentieth Street in New York City, where she ran an informal writing workshop, she found it difficult to give me a date and time. At the center, people with AIDS came from 8:30 a.m. to 4:00 p.m. to listen to music, eat lunch, and receive professional support. "You see," Lila told me, "the patients get their social security and disability checks on the first of the month, and many squander them on drugs, so they are completely out of it for the first week. That's why I need to let you know the best time to come. This is the new AIDS population," she told me.

At the same time she empathized with them: "What can you expect? They're already taking all sorts of drugs for AIDS—why not also take the ones that make them feel better?" At the center, the wall leading to the cafeteria is lined with poems, many from poets who have passed away. The poems, she suggested, show the shift in New York City's AIDS population, from the gay men and drag queens who died in such great numbers in the 1980s to the many African Americans and Latinos who succumbed to the disease in the 1990s.

"When people hear where I work," Lila told me,

they often make the assumption that I am a combination of Mother Teresa and Lady Bountiful. While I do not deny the difficulty and the pain, I hasten to explain how lucky I am to have found this place—and this work, which enriches me more than anything I have ever done. How do all of us at the program live with the loss of so many people whom we have known and cared for and loved? For me, by now, it must be close to a thousand too-early deaths. We know that life is finite, but this modern plague, of which we still understand so little, has been marked by a poignant variety of endings: the handsome face covered with Kaposi's sarcoma lesions, the robust frame reduced by wasting, the brilliant brain dimmed by dementia.

Lila, an accomplished, widely published poet herself, taught creative writing informally at the center for eighteen years, from the early 1990s until 2000, some of direst years of the epidemic. Her goal was to help her clients express their pain and leave a legacy. The program is "a place where people are stopped in their tracks, where we appreciate the irony that for many the diagnosis signaled a poignant desire to break out of self-destructive patterns and live fully," Lila told me. "Seeing those we love dying among us every day, the very idea of mourning becomes so intense—and so intolerable—that we almost need to reject it. Our emphasis is indeed on living, on using all of our abilities and resources to experience as much fulfillment and joy as we can. Therefore, I am part archivist, part tummler," she says, referring to the social director–comedians who used to entertain at the Jewish hotels in the Catskills in the middle of the last century. "An important facet of our program is to relieve the stress we face each day—to do the unexpected, the unconventional, and to have fun."

As the creative and social director, Lila worked with the AIDS-afflicted to organize a prom and a yearbook. "It all began," she said, "when Laura [a patient] said plaintively one spring morning in 1998, 'I never had a prom!'" Lila continued:

Our Laura, who struggled every day with her obesity, with her addiction to drugs, which could make her nod off into her cereal many mornings. Laura, who cried with the frustration of not being able to mother her beloved daughter or prevent her own mother from taking over her life when she herself could not function. Why never having had a prom, of all the many severe deprivations in her life, should suddenly emerge so painfully was not for us to ask. We knew only that the month of May had come once more, and with it a romantic possibility entirely within our reach. . . .

The prom was a huge success. It went off as planned on May 28. Everyone had received an invitation and a program. We dined, we danced, we flirted, we voted for a king and queen. The invitations wisely advised, "Creative Prom Attire Requested." As the photo montages in the yearbook show, this could be anything from a tux to (of course!) drag to a striped T-shirt. The staff had collected as many formal costumes as we could to provide for those who might need them. I wore a little constantly-falling-off-the-shoulder number from the free bin at a Vermont thrift store. But Curtis, who was chosen king of the prom, and who had once worked on a cruise ship, looked elegant in his own tuxedo, his blond tresses flowing as he paraded and even danced, although he had just been hospitalized and was still so seriously ill that he could barely walk. (That is the kind of incredible courage that we are accustomed to seeing all the time.) Robby, the queen, who frolicked on Curt's arm, really is a queen, which made everything more wonderful. A professional female impersonator and talented performer, Robby was gorgeous in a faux diamond tiara and pearls, and had secretly lobbied the other clients to gain well-deserved votes for Curtis as the king.[1]

The yearbook Lila helped them put together includes photos from the prom as well as the patients' hobbies, nicknames, favorite things, ambitions, and a list of "Most likely to"'s, including "outlive my ex"; "find an apartment in Queens"; "be a bad influence"; "build my own home from found objects . . . and a little glue"; "make music—and make love"; "win a gold medal at the First Argentinian Tango Olympics"; "be just an old, penniless queen"; "be the one to land a big old jumbo jet—without experience or a license!"; "be finally recognized as a Glamazon and a great artist"; "embarrass myself in public"; "be on *Oprah*"; "build my own racing bike"; "party all the time"; and, of course, "SURVIVE!" Yearbook entries were often read at memorials for the center's denizens.

Lila long ago gave up on the idea of teaching a formal writing workshop at the center. When I visited, she was just a roving writer recording her students' words when they felt they had something to say. She related to each person individually, relying on her intuition to figure out when the moment was right to urge them to create a poem or a story. For someone living with AIDS, time is of the essence. Her one rule was that all the poems must be typed up right away and "published" on the walls of the center.

In these poems and stories, grandmothers, homeless people, drag queens, drug addicts, exconvicts, and former attorneys come face to face with mortality; the writing is filled with pain and pathos. Whenever Lila approached one writer, Carlos Bermudez, he used to tap her hand as if to tell her gently, *Go away*. Eventually, he trusted her with his words. In his poems he struggled against the demon of drugs, fighting the battle all of us wage each time we summon the will to resist putting something into our mouths or bodies for a quick fix of momentary pleasure. "Your soul," he writes, "has a good guy and a bad guy. / When the bad guy does something, the good guy feels it. . . . / The good guy tries to tell the bad guy, 'You're not supposed to do that!' / And the bad guy says, 'You can't tell me what to do.' " As I read Carlos's poems, Lila told me that although he died three years ago, he is still at the center: in his will he had requested that his ashes remain there. She pointed to a simple metal box, which now serves as a bookend.

Like Carlos, Iolene Catalano was among the center's poets whose darker side could not be told what to do. When I met Iolene, an attractive musician and former bisexual prostitute, she talked to me about Lila: "She was always there for me. I think that really helped a lot. I need a sort of creative catalyst a lot of times. The poems are there, but they're not broken down into poems. Really, it's me trying to find the space where the poems are written from and to be in it, 'cause I don't have that much serenity in my life." She showed me some of the lines she wrote to express this feeling: "Trembling hands, tormented brain / Broken shards in the devil's rain."

She then gave me a copy of a poem she had written about needles in her life:

> Needles
> all of my life . . .
> to get immunized for school,

with a hoop and a thimble
for flower embroidery
on the top hems of sheets,
knitting potholders,
hooking rugs . . .
needles

And then the changes.
What a mysterious
metamorphosis!
"Works! Works! Works!"
I can still hear Flaco
hawking the gimmicks
on his corner . . .
in the shooting galleries,
the gaunt faces waiting
to feed the hungry veins,
staring at the bloody
cups of water holding
needles.

Iolene died just a year after I met her. During our interview, she offered an insightful reflection on living with death and on dying young:

Since I learned I have AIDS, I've tried to find closure on emotional issues that I probably would not have thought about until I was very old. But because I'm not going to be very old—or at least it looks that way, you know—I've thought about my life, and I myself am surprised about the things that surface as turning points or moments of special significance to me. If someone would have asked me while I was healthy what was one of the most significant moments of my life, it wouldn't have been any of these things. But since living with death as my everyday little friend, the things that I see as important now are affected by my awareness of a dark side of life.

I think that my writing before I was ill—without my being conscious of it—attempted to be happy or have something positive to say. And then, after grappling with the illness and learning to accept its effect on my everyday life, it's sort of like all this little happy horseshit that people do dropped away. Not because I wanted it to but because the reality of living in the presence of death as your everyday little friend changes you spiritually, so you don't have this need to make reality into some little sticky, unrealistic, happy fuckin' pipe dream.

For instance, I had to come face to face with my own mortality in order for the years of my active heroin addiction to take on a meaning. Because that behavior, even though it looks meaningless and negative and stupid to other people—you have to realize it's the best attempt that the person can make to stay alive. And if the best attempt you can make to stay alive is to punish and mutilate yourself and celebrate death through a blood ritual every day, the things that are causing you to see your life that way are really important.

My life is really chaotic and it's unrehearsed: they're no guidelines about, like, how to drop dead when you're young. I have learned from each one of the other people here by watching the way they are dealing with their own mortality. I learn that the things that I'm feeling are not strange or inappropriate. I don't know what "normal" is for this situation. And I don't think anybody else does either.[2]

Iolene's best friend, Cat Yellen, also a recovered addict, spoke at her memorial service, at St. Mark's Church-in-the-Bowery. She'd met Iolene at wild parties near the "Ho's Stroll" on Twelfth Street in Manhattan.

"We ran together for a long time," she said at the service.

And we did a lot of destruction. You know what, though? In the lowest, darkest, deepest, murkiest delevation of addiction, we loved each other; we loved each other's souls. You know, I keep flashing on all the hysterical stuff we did. We never slept. Never. And she would spaz out. You know, we'd spend all day getting a hit together, and since we never slept we'd fall asleep in midair, holding the cooker—and she'd spaz! And everything would go flying. It's the dirtiest, darkest stuff—but you know, I can laugh about it today. I still lust after the damage we shared so lovingly.

"I still lust after the damage we shared so lovingly."

Cat met Iolene again when they were both in recovery. "It's really beautiful to have relationships in recovery, but it's ultra-beautiful to have been at that level of insanity with somebody. I still have her in my heart with the two of us arm in arm, strolling on Twelfth Street, singing 'Chain of Fools.'"[3]

Lila retired in 2000, partly because she could no longer officially work at the center without social work credentials. She passed away in 2013, at the age of eighty-four. Though it had been thirteen years since she'd worked there, her family chose to hold her memorial service at the AIDS Day Treatment Program.

I attended the memorial and read aloud from Lila's description of the yearbook project:

> Each time we look at the yearbook and see our almost-unrecognizable faces and preposterous getups, each time we read the special things we had to say about ourselves, we know how well we have commemorated our existence. We remembered our past, and gamely made up for what each of us had lost. We tried to define who and how we were at present. We looked to the future with hope and with humor. What better way to praise our distinct being and our common humanity? What better way to give the finger to time? To death?[4]

10

Oh Did You See the Ashes Come Thickly Falling Down?

September 11 Street Poems

There are some things about which nothing can be said and before which we dare not keep silent.

—T. S. ELIOT

In the days and weeks that followed the attack on the World Trade Center, the streets of New York lay eerily quiet and deserted. The avalanche of ashes from the towers created a black and paralyzing snowfall. Hours and days fell out of kilter.

The first memorials were written in the dust and debris—on a car hood, a single word: "Pray."[1] On the window of a McDonald's a block away from the World Trade Center: "We are not afraid." In the early hours and days, family members and friends, in their grief, came as close as they could to Ground Zero, the place where their loved ones had died, where their souls might have lingered. Written by a child in the dust of a shopwindow close to the scene: "Daddy, I came here to find you." Another: "God Be With You Dana—Love, Mom."[2]

The poets did not wait for the dust to settle. As streams of water poured over the smoke at Ground Zero, the city, awash in emotion, hosed itself down with words. Distraught and bereaved New Yorkers scrawled missives in the ash. On the afternoon of the first day, Jordan Schuster, a student from NYU, laid out a sheet of butcher paper in Union Square; he was the first of many to inspire his fellow New Yorkers to set down their thoughts. He told me:

My friends and I went to get the paper, pens, and tape, and met at Union Square at three o'clock on September 11. We taped down the first two pieces of butcher paper and started writing. People walked up and we'd offer a pen and say, "Do you have something that you want to share?" "Do you feel like getting anything out?" And some people would say, "Yeah." And they'd take the pen and write. . . . And it just started growing. It grew really quickly. Like, within half an hour there were probably fifty people there. Within an hour there were about two hundred and fifty people. Within two hours about five hundred.[3]

Words proliferated into a barrage of written feeling that vented rage and offered solace.

The poets did not wait for the dust to settle.

From the first day's writing in Union Square: "Strength through diversity in the most diverse place the world has every known. Tim, born September 11, 1971."[4]

Written in chalk on Union Square, September 13: "Hate breeds hate / Love breeds love."[5]

Posted on an index card in a Times Square storefront, September 14: "Bastards!"[6]

Posted on Canal Street, September 17: "I felt as if the Twin Towers were injured, and they fought hard to stay up as long as they could. They couldn't hold out anymore, but we can. USA!"[7]

By the time the staff at City Lore was able to get back to our Lower East Side office, we found email messages waiting, asking us to document the spontaneous memorials and poems and to collect stories. Our staff photographer, Martha Cooper, had been out in the streets since the day after the tragedy. Before we had time to think too much about it, we'd decided to respond to the requests and eventually mount an exhibit that would chronicle and share this unfolding tribute to the city's indomitable spirit. As participants in grief and as New Yorkers ourselves—as well as folklorists, photographers, and historians—we saw our work as a tribute to this great city in desperate times. Though tragedy might have resulted in a sense of alienation and anonymity in a city of this size, the opposite occurred: people created places where humanity could restake its claim.[8]

Brightly colored, candlelit improvised shrines and memorials cropped up in every corner of the city. In a cathartic burst, emotions etched themselves onto the cityscape: on chain-link fences, on banners pinned on fences, in sidewalk chalk, on tiles. Inscriptions cited heroes from Gandhi to Jerry Garcia. Even random scraps of office paper that blew into the air after the explosions and fell to the streets like black confetti were interpreted as poems. On her Brooklyn patio, folklorist Marion Jacobson found a balance sheet from an unidentified company showing a profit of several million dollars—an ironic poem of sorts.

> **In a cathartic burst, emotions etched themselves onto the cityscape.**

On September 15, a ten-year-old boy stood outside the firehouse of Fire Squad Company 1, in Park Slope, Brooklyn, passing out a poem.

> In the graveyard,
> The gravestones are silent,
> The people are even more silent
> This tragedy will leave all of us
> With unhealable wounds
> That only an angel can heal.
> That, my friend, is the angel of hope,
> An angel of light,
> An angel named phoenix
> That angel will find you;
> Together, we will rise up
> Out of the dust
> Out of the ashes
> And out of the dark.

Particularly in the weeks immediately following the disaster, most of the posted poems, like this one, were anonymous. In the months that followed, new poems continued to appear, but they were often stamped with copyright notices and website links.

Fliers featuring missing people were taped to walls throughout the city. As days went by, hopes dimmed, but the posters proliferated.

Kinko's offered free copy services, and soon mailboxes, bus shelters, telephone booths, firehouses, pizzerias, and subway station walls became bulletin boards. Snapshots and wedding photos pleaded with passersby. They included detailed descriptions of clothing and jewelry worn by the missing person on September 11, as well as date of birth, height, weight, tattoos, and other distinguishing personal details. Sometimes there was a heartbreakingly cryptic line, pleading for a special dispensation: "Had no hate in his heart for anyone," "Expecting first child this week," or "Please help me find my daddy."[9] As one person put it, "If I just put up enough of these fliers, maybe there will be a miracle." But only a few days after the attack, *New York Times* reporter Amy Waldman wrote, "Manufactured in hope, the fliers have now transmuted into memorial."[10]

On a flier at Grand Central Terminal seeking Clyde Frazier Jr., a visitor expressed on a Post-it note a sentiment felt by all of us who were haunted by the faces of our fellow New Yorkers:

> Every morning
> I see you
> smiling.
> I miss you.
> We never met.

On the streets, ordinary people set up memorials, sustained them, made them meaningful. Thousands took part. They neither asked permission from city officials nor waited for religious or civil authorities to tell them how to respond. New Yorkers showed an amazing ability to use public spaces to gather and express themselves, and, in many cases, to give others an opportunity to do the same. The plethora of shrines and memorials was notable for its dispersion across all five boroughs and beyond, distinct from the similar but more centralized shrines following the 1995 Oklahoma City bombing, which grew up along the chain-link fence surrounding the Alfred P. Murrah Federal Building.[11] Sacred spaces cropped up on street corners, in housing projects, beside handball courts. So often characterized as unfriendly and cold, New Yorkers created places where poetry was a common language.

All space is contested space. As sociologist John Urry writes, "The spatial dynamics of conflict can be explained by the fact that no two objects can occupy the same point in space."[12] Inspired by Michel Foucault, who insisted that "space is fundamental in any exercise of power,"[13] David Chidester and Edward T. Linenthal, authors of *American Sacred Space*, write: "Sacred space is often, if not inevitably, entangled in politics. . . . Sacred places are always highly charged sites for contested negotiations."[14] No need to tell any New Yorker who has ever tried to rent an apartment, to commandeer a parking spot, or to paint a mural on the side of a building about contested space. But after September 11, all over the city an unspoken partnership sprang up between landlords, the city, policemen, and the grieving public. Behind every shrine was a group of property owners and city authorities condoning it, choosing not to contest the space, not to impose their vested authority. With the notable exceptions of Union Square and Washington Square Park, where, in the name of restoring a sense of normalcy, the city sent sanitation workers numerous times in the first few weeks to clear away the shrines, city agencies and landlords allowed New Yorkers to express their sorrow in public spaces. They allowed the city to become a memorial garden on public property. The magnitude of these public expressions of grief seemed to mirror the enormity of the loss.

In Inwood in Upper Manhattan, by the neighborhood handball court on 207th Street and Seaman Avenue, family and friends of Brian Monaghan waited for four days and nights for him to come home. Eventually, his friends Ray Martinez and Mick Fitzgerald lit a candle, neighbors began to contribute objects and poems, and the street corner became a place for people to gather. A discarded bookcase was found to hold their offerings. A shrine evolved over four months, eventually embracing a good portion of the block. Police and the sanitation department issued no summonses.

The city made arrangements for the families of those who had died to visit Ground Zero. City Lore, too, made a pilgrimage to the ghost town of Lower Manhattan, while it was still smoking.[15] Standing in front of the shrine at Battery Park, which was lined with countless teddy bears—selected, perhaps, for their association with comfort and children, and perhaps with Smokey the Bear, who prevents fires—we shook our heads in wonder. But on the wet and cold October day of our visit, what had initially seemed almost silly and overly sweet gradually took on significance as we started to read the inscriptions. Across the city as well as at Ground Zero, we realized, the shrines were becoming portals where the living and the dead could communicate directly.

> **The shrines were becoming portals where the living and the dead could communicate directly.**

"To Lee," one inscription read. "We came here today to tell you how much we love you & miss you. We are trying to remember all of the good times. We're just saying hello because there will never be good-byes." At the Inwood memorial for Brian Patrick Monaghan, a girl casually addressed him on a Post-it: "What's up Babe. It's me, ROSIE—I'm here in the corner looking at all your pictures and candles."

Many of the notes were written as poems from the living to the dead, such as this one at the Battery Park shrine, from a wife to her husband:

> Where did you go?
> You gave me a beautiful little angel,
> But didn't stay to see her grow.

The shrines were also places where the dead could, in turn, speak to the living.

> Do not stand at my grave and weep
> I am not there, I do not sleep.
>
> I am a thousand winds that blow
> I am the diamond glint on snow.
>
> I am the sunlight on ripened grain
> I am the gentle autumn rain.
>
> When you wake in the morning hush
> I am the swift, uplifting rush

of quiet birds in circling flight.
I am the soft starlight at night

Do not stand at my grave and weep.
I am not there. I do not sleep.[16]

One of the most striking missives was from the dead to the living, written by Alicia Vasquez and posted at the Grand Central memorial.

don't look for me anymore
it's late and you're tired
your feet ache standing atop the ruins of our twins
day after day searching for a trace of me
your eyes burning red
your hands cut bleeding sifting through rock
and your back crooked from endless hours of labor

It's my turn
I'm worried about you
watching as you sift through the ruins of what was
day after day in the soot and rain

I ached in knowing you suffer my death
rest in knowing that my blood lies in the cracks and crevices
of these great lands I loved so much.

In addition, street shrines served as portals for the living to talk directly to the terrorists, whose remains also lay in the Ground Zero rubble.

Well you hit the World Trade Center, but you missed America
You hit the Pentagon,
Again you missed America
You used helpless American bodies to take out other American bodies,
but like a poor marksman, you still missed America

Why? Because of some things you guys will never understand
America isn't about a building or two, not about financial cen-
    ters not
about military centers

America isn't about a place, American isn't about a bunch of
    bodies
America is about an IDEA.

> An idea that you can go someplace where you can earn as much as you can figure out how to live for the most part, like you envisioned living, and pursue Happiness

> (no guarantees that you'll reach it, but you can sure try . . .)![17]

The philosopher and historian Mircea Eliade suggests that sacred space is set apart from ordinary, homogenous space. In his work he writes about the "axis mundi," a sacred space that permits passage between worlds.[18] In a sense, the improvised shrines became axes mundi where the living and dead conjoined and could communicate in the language of poems and letters. At the same time, the many images and miniatures of the towers that proliferated after the event also suggested axes mundi symbolically penetrating the universe, allowing a passageway between worlds. For months the World Trade Center site was a smoking pit that contained the remains of the dead; perhaps the miniature towers suggested to viewers a world below the point where they once had touched the ground.

I was reminded of Haitian Vodou, whose adherents believe there is a crossroads where a great tree penetrates the earth, creating a passageway from the world of the living to the land of *les invisibles*, the spirits. At every Vodou ceremony, this tree is symbolized by a *port manteau*, a pole in the center of the prayer space that enables this passage. In New York, public art in response to the event seemed to attest to the toppled towers' evolving symbolism as a kind of *port manteau*. The Municipal Art Society mounted (and continues to mount each year on September 11) an installation called *Tribute in Light* near Ground Zero: two high-powered beams are projected skyward to represent the towers. Also each September 11, artist Ze'ev Willy Neumann draws the two towers in white marker on the pavement of his Brooklyn block, from which they were once visible.

Although the city under Mayor Rudolph Giuliani cleaned up Union Square repeatedly and tried to disperse the ongoing vigil that was always part peace rally and part political protest, officials did save the gathered objects, creating a large archive of memorabilia that was eventually stored in the women's locker room of the Hamilton Fish Park swimming pool, on the Lower East Side. (Later the items were given to different historical societies and museums.) City Lore had a chance to go through the materials for our exhibit *Missing: Streetscape of a*

City in Mourning, which took place at the New-York Historical Society in 2002. We were touched by these anonymous verses on a weather-worn sheet of paper:

To the Towers Themselves

They were never the favorites,
Not the Carmen Miranda Chrysler
Nor Rockefellers' magic boxes
Nor The Empire, which I think would have killed us all if she fell.

They were the two young dumb guys,
Beer-drinking
Downtown MBAs
Swaggering across the skyline,

Now that they are gone,
They are like young men
Lost at war,
Not having had their life yet,
Not having grown wise and softened with air and time.

They are lost like
Cannon fodder
Like farm boys throughout time
Stunned into death,
Not knowing what hit them
And beloved
By the weeping mothers left behind.

In our culture, we think of art as culling elements from what passes for real life, rearranging them, and offering them as a commentary—metaphorical or lyrical—on our lives. In response to September 11, poems were written with the urgency of art but put back into the flow of life to take their place anonymously alongside ritual objects that were part of the mourning process. Words were forged into poetry not for art's sake but to pierce the barrier that separates the living from the dead. In this worldly city, along our secular sidewalks, stoops, and parks in all five boroughs, New Yorkers spoke to one another in a language of symbols and ritual acts, refusing to give death the last word.

Words were forged into poetry not for art's sake but to pierce the barrier that separates the living from the dead.

As New Yorkers inscribed poetry on the cityscape, the United States was preparing for war, first in Afghanistan and then in Iraq. These very same artistic expressions of grief were continually referenced, drawn upon, and co-opted by politicians and journalists to support these wars. Many New Yorkers, including those of us at City Lore who were documenting the memorials, felt increasingly uncomfortable with this use of public grief for political ends.

Yet the sentiments on the ground were deeply felt. On the day of the disaster, a copy of Shelley's poem "Ozymandias" crisscrossed the Internet. Along with the poem came the suggestion that if the World Trade Center were ever to be rebuilt, it should bear a plaque with the inscription "My name is Ozymandias, King of Kings; / Look on my Works, ye Mighty, and despair!"

At City Lore in the days immediately after September 11, the poet Bob Holman and I conceived of a collaborative poem—in fact, two poems—in honor of the Twin Towers. Each would have 110 lines, mirroring the number of stories in the two buildings. Assembled and edited by Bob, the first "Tower" consisted of lines contributed by the public, the second of lines by invited poets, many of them major figures in American poetry. The "Twin Poem Towers" were displayed in dramatic graphic fashion at City Lore's 2002 New-York Historical Society exhibit.

The well-known poets whose work appeared in "Tower Two" sought to move outside the well-worn ideas of the street poems. A number of them were concerned with words themselves:

Quraysh Ali Lansana: I hold these syllables like hands on a clock feeling the sound of time through its fingers.
Patricia Smith: With one sullen syllable, I peel back a segment of sky.
Saba Kidane: Afraid of syllables used to attach wings to breaths.
Maggie Balistreri: Words on page, mete out this woe; words on page undo sorrow.

The poets searched for images both accessible and obscure:

Eliot Weinberger: The emptiness at the center has made the city sacred.
Galway Kinnell: That is our own black milk crossing the sky.

Adrienne Rich: "Love should be put into action," screamed the dirty hermit of another poem.

The poetry of the streets had a different kind of work to do. It addressed the ruptures in time-tested ways and sought to make the horrific bearable. The dead are still with us. The Towers can be re-created in our hearts. We are all one family in the wake of tragedy. "Kill the bastards." The people's poetry of September 11 engaged the city in a rhetoric that affirmed and reaffirmed these simple ideas. The dead address the living; the living address the fallen Towers. As in much folk poetry, emphasizing the sentiments through repetition seemed more important than expressing original ideas in an original way.

A few years after September 11, a student in my creative writing class, Esther K. Smith, inspired by the poem "I Am Waiting" by Lawrence Ferlinghetti, wrote about undoing the damage of the events of September 11:

> I am waiting
> for the World Trade Center
> to unimplode and rise again
> for the broken glass to heal
> for the flames to stop
> for the planes to fly
> backward to Boston
> first the second
> and then the first
> for the security guards there
> to have checked that day
> to have cared
> to have been paid better
> to have had health insurance
> to have actually been educated
> in the Boston public schools
>
> I am waiting for those jumping
> falling people to fly back up
> in through the windows
> and back to their cubicles.

The bereaved spoke to one another in a language that cut across gradations of religion and belief, drawing upon basic human impulses. Mourners communicated in a shared language of symbols, regardless of whether their religion was Catholicism or fly-fishing, whether they believed in the power of flowers and candles as a way to speed the arrival of a soul in heaven or whether they offered objects simply in a spirit of commemoration. As folklorist Ilana Harlow writes, "At shrines, red, white and blue candles flickered alongside Christian votive candles, Jewish memorial 'Yahrzeit' candles and offertory candles petitioning a range of intercessors from St. Anthony to the Virgin of Guadalupe to the 'Siete Potencias de Africa' of the Afro-Cuban religion of Santeria. The candles dripped into and onto each other, as our differences seemed to melt away."[19]

The POEMobile Dreams of Peace

Writing with Light

Llegó la poesía a buscarme (Poetry came in search of me).
—Pablo Neruda; inscription painted on
the front of the POEMobile

The Brooklyn-Queens Expressway is bumper-to-bumper—an accident somewhere up ahead. Up in the cab of the POEMobile, I can see a clear and beautiful view of nighttime Manhattan on my left. I'm returning home from the POEMobile's celebration for the Muslim holiday of Eid al-Adha (which commemorates Abraham's sacrifice) at Diversity Plaza in Jackson Heights, Queens.

The POEMobile is a magnificent art truck with brightly painted iron wings arching above its roof and poems in two dozen languages emblazoned on its sides—beneath which hides a dilapidated 1988 Chevy step van that could conk out at any moment.

Jointly sponsored by Bowery Arts + Science and City Lore, the truck projects poems onto walls and buildings in tandem with live readings and musical performances in neighborhoods throughout New York. As poets perform in their native languages on the street or plaza, a beam of light soars past them and the words float in light above their heads, often several stories high. The projections open with an animated feathered wing brushing words onto the building, an idea inspired by a Martin Espada line: "God must be an owl, electricity coursing through the hollow bones, a white wing brushing the building."[1]

The door of the POEMobile is inscribed with lines of poetry in some of the world's endangered languages. When the POEMobile drove to Bridgeport, Connecticut, for an arts festival, one woman was moved to tears when she saw a line in Tlingit, her native Alaskan language, inscribed on the truck. She exuded unabashed joy as she called her mother in Alaska to let her know. A few minutes later, an inebriated visitor saw me in the driver's seat and asked if he could purchase a hot dog.

In each community we appoint a poetry ambassador to co-curate the program with us. We look for interesting architectural features on a church or movie house façade or just a blank wall for our projections. From then on, it's a ragtag operation. The POEMobile drives up, we pull out the ladder, hoist the high-powered projector onto the roof, then string party lights around the truck and through the performance area, creating the feel of a European piazza. We set up a stage with sound, assemble a few benches, and then turn it over to the poets and musicians who perform with their words soaring high above their heads. Specially designed software enables the projected poems in their original language to dissolve into English, and vice versa. The community experiences the impact of the poetry in their spoken tongue, while the English-speaking visitors and neighbors are able to grasp the life experiences of the foreign-language poets they live among. The beams appear and disappear, underscoring their ephemerality to a surprised and often enchanted crowd. When it's over, the POEMobile pulls away, leaving the street and building as if nothing had ever happened.

As traffic inches forward, one car length at a time, I muse on this guerrilla poetry, set up in diverse urban neighborhoods, creating momentary beauty and wonder in words and music and light, and traveling under the radar of both news outlets and, for the most part, the authorities.

In the driver's seat I think back to the Pakistani *mushaira*, a gathering of poets, we held at Shaheen's Sweets in Jackson Heights. Working with poetry advocate Ashraf Mian, we asked eight poets to compose ghazals for the occasion. When the poets read in their native languages, the community audience burst forth with "Wa Wa, Wa, Wa!"—a call-and-response that prompts the poet to read the line again. A local college professor composed literal translations of the Hindi and Punjabi poems into English, and when those translations were read, the audience remained silent. Then Bob Holman, our collaborator on the POEMobile, read his freewheeling translations of the poems, and the audience went wild with their "Wa Wa"'s. The poets were especially pleased, so happy to have their poetry appreciated by an English-speaking audience. Here is one:

Song
after Dr. Shafiq

I've left
Got a mortgage
Sold the house didn't repay the mortgage
So marry me
In my last life you said no
This time around—I am rich and on the lam
So let's do it do it do it
Let's invent love
And spin in the opposite
Direction from the world.[2]

Still stuck on the BQE, I reflect on some of the POEMobile's great moments. "Sing in Me, O Muse!" highlighted Greek American poetry at the Federation of Hellenic Societies in Astoria with poets, musicians, and dancers honoring their Greek heritage. We projected poems onto the nearby Amtrak overpass and offered a commemoration of the one-hundredth anniversary of the birth of Nobel laureate Odysseus Elytis.

Until the advent of printing, poems were made to be spoken. Since then, most literary poems were intended to be read silently, to one-self. There is something wonderful about having them spoken and read simultaneously, as well as about seeing the poems brushed by an animated wing onto a building and then disappear. Holman described the event this way: "The vision of the show from a vantage point behind the crowd was heartbreakingly beautiful, truly Cinema Paradiso come to town. And the central moment of audience communing silently with the projected bilingual text of Sappho while traditional musicians played provided a moment of sheer delight. For this was Pure Poetry of the Moment, gentle, clear, demanding, individualized. We were simply living it. It was New and Old and the fact that it was Greek, Classical & Modern, created a marvelous blend of orality, tradition, and high-tech."[3]

With Brooklyn in the rearview mirror of the POEMobile, I remember another event, our Haitian Poetry and Music program at Five Myles Gallery in Crown Heights, in collaboration with Haiti Cultural Exchange. A highlight was the Haitian poet Denize Lauture, who was accompanied by master Vodou drummer Frisner Augustin, just a few months before Frisner died of a stroke in Haiti:

> Our poet is
> A vodou priest
> Who makes words
> Sound like conch shells
> Who makes words
> Sound like bamboo trumpets
> And who turns words
> Into beautiful Rada drumbeat
>
> Our poet is a wizard
> Who juggles
> Wondrous literary sounds
> Inside a magic jar
> A wizard who knows how to twirl
> The most beautiful words
> Who knows how to jam
> The small drum of heavenly sounds
> And who knows how to sing the blues
> On the tip of his mother tongue
> Until all priestesses, all angels
> And all souls become possessed
>
> Our men and women poets
> Are shining masters of midnight
> Who draw magic symbols
> at the crossroads
> Of knowledge
> With the sacred dust
> Of all gone master poets[4]

I recall other recent programs—a Russian-Ukrainian Yevgeny Yevtushenko tribute on the Bowery; and both a Korean and a Chinese New Year celebration in and around Flushing Town Hall, in Queens. We covered many of the world's hotspots in their respective New York City

Figure 2. Live from the POEMobile at Eldridge Street Synagogue, 2012. Photo by Abby Ronner.

neighborhoods. My favorite line came from the poems we projected at our Persian/ Iranian Norooz (New Year) celebration in **"Remember flight, the bird is mortal."** DUMBO. From the poet Forugh Farrokhzad: "Kus ölür sen uçusu hatırla" (Remember flight, the bird is mortal).[5]

This line was found scribbled on scraps of paper that were found in the trenches during the Iran-Iraq War.

I began to wonder if poetry could indeed save the world. If global tensions did boil over and conflict erupted, certainly all support for the arts would be summarily axed, and I would be out of work. I imagined that I would take flight in a new POEMobile—some wildly decorated, poem-bedecked Chinook helicopter left over from the Vietnam War careening into the world's war zones to bring a message of peace. I imagine projecting lines from the Yevtushenko poem "Babi Yar" in tension-ridden towns in Russia and Ukraine:

> I am
> each old man
> here shot dead

I am
every child
here shot dead.[6]

I began to think of anthropologist Steve Caton's book *Peaks of Yemen I Summon: Poetry as Cultural Practice in a North Yemeni Tribe*. He describes how tribal leaders use the *zamil* tradition of poetic couplets to resolve obstinate disagreements. He relates a dispute that broke out between the Banī Shadād and 'A'Rūsh tribes over a pasture straddling a tribal borderline. One side argued, "[It was] my grandfather's property after my ancestor's and my property after my father's; / [and so it goes] down the past generations all the way to Shem, the son of Noah." The other side responded with a verse arguing that the presence of their sheep grazing on the land was proof that it belonged to them. The Yemeni poets explained to Caton that honor is a window into the tribe's innermost character. "[H]onor, like glass, is fragile and easily broken; and once honor is shattered, it cannot be mended." So, in this situation, to avoid conflict, a mediator interjected, "War is not a wedding; / beware: honor is like glass."[7]

If only resolving the world's problems were so easy.

Not long ago I had a conversation with my friend and colleague the performance artist Ruth Sergel. In 2011 Ruth ran a vast array of events to commemorate the one hundredth anniversary of the Triangle Shirtwaist fire of 1911, in which 146 garment workers, mostly young immigrant women, perished in a blaze caused by unsafe working conditions in a factory on New York's Lower East Side. The tragic event helped spark the American labor movement. Ruth's myriad programs included youth poetry, a play by Elizabeth Swados, street processions, several exhibitions, and discussions with women from Bangladesh who faced similar unsafe conditions in their factories. I loved the programs, and frequently joked that she should wear her tiara at all times in honor of what she had accomplished.

When I asked Ruth how she felt about her festival in retrospect, she said, "I thought it was an absolute failure—I thought the events would change the world and they didn't." I was taken aback; her entire initiative had been an unqualified success.

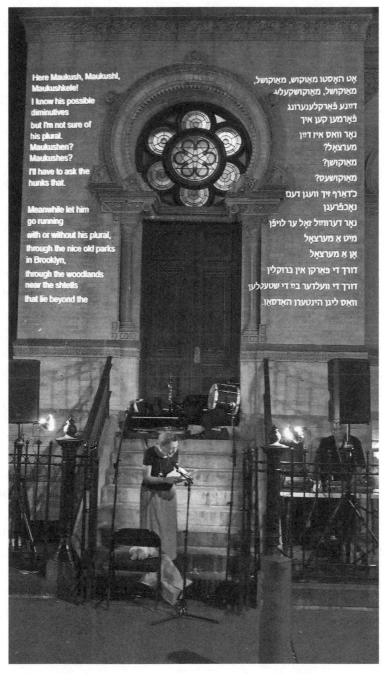

Figure 3. The POEMobile projecting onto the façade of Eldridge Street Synagogue, 2012. Photo by Abby Ronner.

"Ruth," I told her, "if you're going to change the world through the arts, it's going to be a slow process. It's like righting a great ship of state that turns oh so slowly." And in fact, there are a lot of countervailing winds to overcome. Besides, as I've often said, judge me not by what I did but by what I tried to do. We're always up against our own limitations and the limits of human endeavor.

Perhaps poetry expresses the ethos of the poet or the performer. It expresses people's inner life, illuminates their humanity, but certainly does not justify their actions. Hitler, Mao, and Bin Laden all wrote poetry, and great American poets such as Ezra Pound and e. e. cummings had fascist tendencies.

With the POEMobile still at a standstill, my mind turns on a recent article I'd read in *The New Yorker* called "Battle Lines: Want to Understand the Jihadis? Read Their Poetry." Robyn Creswell and Bernard Haykel write "It is impossible to understand jihadism—its objectives, its appeal for new recruits, and its durability—without examining its culture. . . . [U]nlike the videos of beheadings and burnings, which are made primarily for foreign consumption, poetry provides a window onto how the movement talks to itself. It is in verse that militants most clearly articulate the fantasy life of jihad."[8]

How can we wrap our minds around the fact that the brutal jihadis love poetry and that their poetry undergirds their brutality? They imagine themselves recapturing past glories atop a steed, swinging sabers as warrior poets. The jihadist Awshan wrote: "I announced there would be no more rest / until . . . / I strapped on my machine gun with a mujahid's resolve."[9]

Reading one another's poems can tell us where someone else is coming from, even someone with a radically different worldview—and can be used as a tool for building empathy if we first put down our guns.

Perhaps it is not the writing but the sharing of poems across cultures that can create intercultural understanding. Reading one another's poems can tell us where someone else is coming from, even someone with a radically different worldview—and can be used as a tool for building empathy if we first put down our guns. We don't need to "study war no more"—just the poetics of peace.

The BQE starts to move, putting an end to my reverie. The tractor-trailer wreckage has been removed. I am reminded of the day the performance artist Annie Lanzillotto stopped traffic on Third Street in New York. Walking around her old neighborhood haunts with the POEMobile following the procession, she stopped to sit on mailboxes and tell stories, and to project her prose poem "Catching a Fly Ball in Oncoming Traffic" onto the wall high above us:

> I grew up playing in traffic. Under the arcs of balls, balls hit high—
>   'til they became small and black in the sky.
> The ball's going back and all the while you have your inner ear on
>   the car at the intersection.
> You don't miss the ball.
> You don't get hit by the car.
> With a car coming at you, you face the open sky.
> You never miss a pop fly because a ball is coming at you.
> You listen. You turn your ear to the horizon. The ball is in the air.
> Your feet are moving beneath you.
> Your ear tracks the speed the car is coming at you.
> Your eye you keep on the ball.
> You know a car is coming without needing to look.
> You don't want to stop the car, just like you don't want the car to
>   stop the play.
> With your throwing arm you flag the car around you.
> You figure which side of the street the ball is favoring in
>   the wind.
> You wave the car to the other side of you.
> You may temporarily halt the car 'til the ball is square in your hands.
> The car inches forward 'til the ball is in your hands, then the car
>   proceeds.
> The car is your audience rushing to find you.
> The car came all this way, down this particular street, around
>   several corners, jumped the exit ramp, to back up around the
>   corner to see you make this play.
> The car in the middle of the play is part of the play.
> It's all in the timing.[10]

The gathered audience read the poem out loud along with Annie. Then she walked out onto the street, waved her arms, and signaled for the cars to stop. Amazingly, they did. Even the yellow cabs didn't blow their horns. She held up a Spaldeen, the classic New York City rubber ball, smacked it with a broomstick, and watched it arch over and above the POEMobile. If Annie's poem could stop New York City traffic, well, then perhaps poetry can change the world.

12

Free Market Flavor

Poetry of the Palate

Human beings feed on metaphors. . . . [W]e hunger for, cannibalize, spice it up, sugar coat, hash things out, sink our teeth into, and find something difficult to swallow or hard to digest, so we cough it up and then have a bone to pick with someone, which is their just desserts.
—Michael Owen Jones, "Food Choice, Symbolism and Identity"

"I am the accumulated memory and waistline of the dead restaurants of New York," writes the poet Bob Hershon, "and the dishes that will never be set before us again, the snow-pea leaves in garlic at the Ocean Palace, the blini and caviar at the Russian Tea Room, the osso buco at the New Port Alba, the kasha varnishkes at the Second Avenue Deli, the veal ragout at Cent' Anni."[1] I'm with Hershon—for where else but in memory can I ever again find the spicy taste of the prah prig sod at the Lower East Side's long-gone Siam Square, an indescribable mix of lemongrass and spiced peppers? These tastes imbue our social gatherings and, later, serve as catalyst for some of our fondest remembrances.

In the Zeitlin fold, some of our deepest shared family memories waft back to a tangle of lemongrass, peppers, and fish sauce, or goat curry, combined in dishes cooked from half-remembered, reimagined, and reconstituted recipes from Thailand, other parts of Asia, or the Caribbean via the Philippines, by immigrant cooks and entrepreneurs trying to match their home country's cuisine to American ingredients for New York City's global palate. At Thai House in Ardsley, New York, for example, our family savors one, sometimes two orders of "Tiger Cry" and pad thai noodles, eaten with chopsticks, which allow only small, savory bites that alternate with soothing sips of wine. As I watch our four faces discussing our lives across the small table, surrounded by carved wooden figures of Thai gods and goddesses, the sensory overload elevates the occasion.

Whenever our family ate at Ubol's Kitchen, a Thai restaurant on Steinway Street in Astoria, Queens, the owner, perhaps prodding us to try something new, joked that she could put in our order as soon as we walked through the door. We celebrated every birthday and special occasion with Ubol's spicy barbecue beef, flaming chicken, and, of course, pad thai; we finally did try something new and added "Pork in the Garden." Ubol's was what my daughter, Eliza, calls a "re-creatable good experience," like riding the Cyclone at Coney Island. Re-creatable, that is, until the sad day when we sat down to eat and felt a little disconcerted not to see the familiar staff. We tasted the pork only to realize that the chef had left the garden. A mouthful of memorable tastes would never again grace the tips of our tongues.

In the mid-1960s, changes in immigration law, and subsequently the Vietnam War and the breakup of the Soviet Union, ushered in a new wave of immigrants and expanded the American palate. Culinary entrepreneurs confronted the marketability of their cultural heritage. They brought with them their native languages, memories, customs, and cuisines. English speakers might not understand their language; their songs and poems had little value to anyone but themselves—but their foods and the vocabulary of tastes they could express through their cooking might be easily appreciated across cultures. They could use their "native tongues" quite literally to taste, adjust, and adapt their cuisines to the American palate.

A painter's palette and a cook's palate are more than homophones. The taste of a favorite food, deliciously prepared, can make you close your eyes and *mmmmm*-out for a moment, in much the same way that a beautiful painting can create a blissful moment of silent appreciation. My friend Linda Atkinson, an actress, did a brief stint in divinity school. She was asked to write a twenty-page paper that she simply could not wrap her head around. She grew increasingly frustrated, and on the day it was due she told her teacher, "I must say you would learn a lot more about how I thought about things if I handed you my favorite recipe than if I wrote this twenty-page report."

The poetry of the palate is part of our palette of personal and cultural expressions. Is tasting your favorite dish akin to hearing your favorite poem? No, of course not. One mixes ingredients, the other words. But both have aesthetic qualities that lead me to see them as part of the poetry of everyday life.

The poetry of the palate is part of our palette of personal and cultural expressions.

A language of tastes from immigrants' home countries is a marketable currency—and it adds not only flavors but also delicious words to our English vocabulary. Words like *masala dosa, callaloo, lo mein, baklava, momo, chimichanga, injera, sashimi,* and *halo-halo* now salt-and-pepper the English language. Our daughter once quipped that she would have become a vegetarian long ago if it were not for moo shoo pork, a Chinese dish and a name she savored.

Just the names of these dishes can evoke their flavors and a longing to taste them. But food and foodways give us more than just words; the dishes served are themselves a language that we savor as we eat. Ingredients combine like the images in a poem to deliver a delectable experience. The different cuisines harbor a corpus of artful expression embedded in their unique tastes.

The different cuisines harbor a corpus of artful expression embedded in their unique tastes.

Two books by Mark Kurlansky—*Cod: A Biography of the Fish That Changed the World* and *Salt: A World History*—make the case that the entire history of the world can be told through a single food.[2] Foodways can provide a lens through which to explore geography and cultural history. On a recent visit to a Filipino bakery in Queens, New York, folklorist Bill Westerman ordered a traditional dessert, halo-halo, from the Tagalog word *halò*, meaning "mix." "You can see the history of the Philippines in this dish," he said. "The purple yam, plantains, garbanzos, mangos, and macapuno [sweetened coconut meat] are the indigenous Asian ingredients; the ice cream and crème caramel come from Europeans, beginning with Magellan, who arrived in the Philippines in 1521."

Our family first heard of the Filipino restaurant Cendrillon, in New York City, from the scholar Jack Tchen, who had brought a mutual friend of ours there. "I am going to order a dessert," Jack told her. "It's called the mango tart. It's big enough for four people—but do not ask me to share. If you want some, you'll have to order your own." When we first dined there, we made the same mistake: we ordered one for the table to split four ways, then promptly ordered three more.

A few years later, I sat in a booth at Cendrillon with Romy Dorotan, the Filipino owner and head chef, whose unusual story speaks to the immigrant experience. He immigrated to Philadelphia in the 1970s to study economics at Temple University. He and his wife, Amy, were activists, organizing against the Marcos dictatorship. He started out as a dishwasher, became a cook, then moved to New York. He opened Cendrillon in SoHo in 1995. A strong advocate of using fresh, local ingredients, he built the menu around his unique cooking style. But as food critics visited, "they started calling us a Filipino restaurant," he said, "so we added more Filipino dishes."

I asked about the origin of our family's favorite appetizer, the goat curry wrapped in a scallion pancake with mango chutney. "Where in the Philippines does that come from?"

Romy laughed. "The origin of the goat curry is that we lived in Flatbush, Brooklyn, and it's a West Indian community. So that's my own take on their goat roti. I used a scallion pancake instead of the roti for the bread. It's what I call 'fusion confusion.'" Of course, West Indian food itself is a combination of African, East Indian, and native influences.

"Filipino restaurants have lagged behind the other Asian restaurants," Romy said. "Filipinos have been here since the nineteenth century, but there are not many Filipino restaurants. For one, the Filipino restaurants mostly cater to other Filipinos; secondly, a lot of Filipinos are not entrepreneurs, and they can get other jobs because they speak English. They can go into nursing and other services."

Cambodian, Thai, and Vietnamese restaurants in the States, he said, "use a tremendous amount of sweetness, which always attracts people—it's the most accessible taste, sweetness—far more sweetness than they would use in their home countries. Filipino food is different from that of the other Asian cuisines. We love anything sour—tamarind, vinegar, citrus. Sweetness is not a big thing, but it's starting to encroach."

When SoHo began attracting mostly tourists—who, unlike the priced-out artists, were looking for more standard fare—he decided to move the restaurant to Flatbush and changed its name to the Purple Yam.

Like Cendrillon, the city's eateries are in perpetual motion. In the vast culinary marketplace of New York, the spring roll faces off against the empanada; the Brazilian caipirinha takes on the margarita; the piragua shaved-ice cart takes to the streets against the Mister Softee truck. Restaurants continually have to adapt to changing tastes and to the competition—as Yonah Schimmel's knishery did by inventing the cheddar and jalapeño knish. Chinese restaurants serve fried chicken in African American neighborhoods. Korean restaurants in New York City sometimes serve a hot dog smothered with bulgogi.

In New York, world history, immigrant history, and shifting demographics create an ever-changing range of eateries offering a panoply of tastes, often concocting new flavors by mixing ingredients. The dishes capture the movement and blending of cultural traditions across space and time. Our personal memories engendered by the tastes and the dining experience derive in part from the histories of each dish and the movement of peoples they represent. As my family tucks the goat curry into the scallion pancake and brings it to our lips, currents of world and immigrant history seem to swirl around a single point on the tip of our tongues, the taste ineffable.

13

The Poetry in Science

Metaphors to Explain Mysteries

How do you wear the universe?
Does it drape across your shoulders loose or snug?
Are you lost in it?
Does it need some alterations?
Is it a rag or shmatte thrown across your shoulder?
Or is your life resplendent
in that intergalactic diamond cloak?

I jotted down these lines, inspired by the new popular cosmologists: scientists who use homespun metaphors to make the mysteries of the universe as comfortable to lay audiences as a well-worn coat. For example, in this new form of literature, a beam of light—almost impossible to catch, because time slows down as you approach it—becomes, for scientist Michio Kaku, a ghost ship about which old sailors once spun tall tales.[1]

I marvel at the enormity of what was accomplished by men such as Thales, Democritus, Euclid, Archimedes, Galileo, Newton, and Einstein, as well as the many scientists who collectively devised quantum theory. They make me proud to inhabit this planet, about which science has learned so much, given only subtle clues—and working with our mere kilogram of brain. Yet the metaphors and analogies of scientists are an art in their own right. And although we must never mistake the map for the territory, we can also appreciate their poetic prose, which enables us to understand scientific theories that would otherwise be beyond our grasp.

Once, human beings looked up into the sky and imagined stories about the gods written in the constellations; science and storytelling were one and the same. Today, a folklorist investigating science sets forth on a journey into a very different world. In modern times, storytelling and science appear to be different realms entirely. Nonetheless, scientists still turn to storytelling in order to explain the mysteries of the universe.

Beyond their discoveries, scientists share an evolving body of stories—a kind of folklore of science—that conveys their ideas in lay terms. The cosmologist John Wheeler, for instance, who coined the terms "black hole" and "wormhole," uses an old-fashioned image from his adolescence to explain how a black hole can be visible in the darkness of space. At a prom, when the lights are low, you can see the girls in white dresses whirling around; the young men in black tuxedos are barely visible. Yet the white whirls give convincing evidence that there must be something holding them in orbit. The girls are like bright stars, the boys like black holes. The black hole, Wheeler said, "teaches us that space can be crumpled like a piece of paper into an infinitesimal dot, that time can be extinguished like a blown-out flame, and that the laws of physics that we regard as 'sacred,' as immutable, are anything but."[2]

Often we can understand the science only through the metaphors. Einstein's general theory of relativity tells us, for instance, that gravity is not the weight of one big object pulling on another because of its size; it's not the sun pulling on the earth, or the earth pulling on the moon. The explanation of the behavior of the planets has to do with the way those heavenly bodies bend space-time. How can we wrap our minds around that? A number of scientists and science writers, including Brian Greene, John Briggs, and F. David Peat, suggest the image of a sheet of rubber stretched thin.[3] Place a heavy ball on the sheet, and the sheet warps as the ball weighs it down. Then roll a lighter ball onto the warped sheet and it will circle, in smaller and smaller orbits, around the depression made in the rubber sheet. As one journalist put it, imagine the way a bowling ball circles on a trampoline. This is more like the way heavy objects affect one another. Suddenly, I begin to grasp some essential elements of Einstein's theory.

My interest in cosmology began with books about popular science. I read Michio Kaku's *Hyperspace: A Scientific Odyssey through Parallel Universes, Time Warps, and the Tenth Dimension*, Gary Zukav's *The Dancing Wu Li Masters*, and Brian Greene's *The Elegant Universe: Superstrings, Hidden Dimensions, and the Quest for the Ultimate Theory*.[4] I sought out scientists and interviewed them about the relationship between science and stories.

My favorite scientist-as-storyteller parable, referred to by many contemporary scientists, is the nineteenth-century novel *Flatland: A Romance of Many Dimensions*, by Edwin Abbott, headmaster of the City of London School. The novel presents an allegory for string theory, which posits that within some of the smallest known units in the cosmos, called quanta, there exist still smaller units, made up of tiny vibrating strings. The notion of tiny vibrating strings is not that hard to understand. We know that there are things so small we can't see them—atoms, electrons—and so why not vibrating strings? But here's where it starts to get a little dicey. The strings are vibrating not just in our three-dimensional world but in ten dimensions.

In *Flatland*, Abbott uses a powerful parable that conveys the notion of a multidimensional universe.[5] The characters are squares, lines, and triangles. They live in a world with no height; they're flat as a page; they cannot picture what things look like in our three-dimensional universe. One day, a character named Lord Sphere, from a different universe called Spaceland, rolls across their world. The novel's hero, Mr. Square, can't see the sphere because he lives in two dimensions. But as Lord Sphere moves through his world as if he were a flat piece of paper, Mr. Square sees a circle that grows bigger and then smaller. Lord Sphere tries to describe what he looks like to Mr. Square. He asks him to picture a direction that is "upward and not northward." Mr. Square remains unconvinced. Frustrated, Lord Sphere resorts to action to prove his case. He peels Mr. Square off the page, and Mr. Square then floats like a sheet of paper on the wind. Returning to his flat world, Mr. Square is thoroughly convinced. He tries to convert his fellow Flatlanders, but they label him a heretic and throw him in jail.

Brian Greene spoke with me about *Flatland*. "By exploring readjustments of worldview that are required in moving from a two- to a three-dimensional universe," he said, "we can get a sense for what it would be like for us to go from our three-dimensional world into four or five dimensions. Because it turns out that string theory demands that our world actually has more dimensions than we are aware of from common experience."

Nobel Prize winner Leon Lederman and writer Dick Teresi titled their 1993 popular science book *The God Particle: If the Universe Is the Answer, What Is the Question?*[6] The "God Particle" was their term for the infinitesimally tiny Higgs boson particle, which, in 1964, the British scientist Peter Higgs and others theorized must exist in order to explain inconsistencies in the way electrons and other particles behave. Lederman claims to have mentioned the "God Particle" once in a speech, and Teresi, his coauthor, decided to use it as the working title for their book, assuring Lederman that "no publisher ever used the working title on the final book. The rest is history," they write. "The title ended up offending two groups: 1) those who believe in God and 2) those who don't." With great humor, they quote from "The Very New Testament":

> And the whole universe was of many languages, and of many speeches.
> ... And they said to one another, Go to, let us build a Giant Collider, whose collisions may reach back to the beginning of time. And they had superconducting magnets for bending, and protons had they for smashing.
> And the Lord came down to see the accelerator, which the children of men builded. And the Lord said, Behold the people are unconfounding my confounding. And the Lord sighed and said, Go to, let us go down, and there give them the God Particle so that they may see how beautiful is the universe I have made.[7]

Their book traces the history of the search for the smallest and most fundamental building blocks in the universe. To help readers understand quantum physics, they conceive of a conversation with the Greek scientist Democritus, who imagines a knife repeatedly cutting a loaf of bread in half, till a "mental knife" is needed to halve the pieces; eventually what's left is the atom.

Today, particle physicists use the Large Hadron Collider in Geneva as the "knife" to physically collide and split particles that scientists have used their "mental knives" to theorize about. As the collider breaks apart the world's tiniest particles, it reveals the infinitesimal pieces from which all of creation is structured.

Lederman and Teresi offer an extended metaphor to explain the search for the Higgs boson particle.[8] They imagine scientists sent on a goodwill mission from a planet called Twilo. When the scientists arrive, they are brought to a World Cup soccer game as a cultural experience. They are far smarter than we are, but they have a significant shortcoming: they have trouble distinguishing black from white—although they can watch the game, they can't see the ball.

They try to understand the plays. They discern that there are two different uniforms, two groups in conflict, and that each player moves in a certain way within a certain part of the field. They actually identify the players' positions. They even realize that symmetry is at work, because for each position there is a counterposition. They create tables and charts—but with only a few minutes left in the game, and still unable to see the ball, they still don't have the foggiest notion of what's really going on. Suddenly, the smallest Twiloan, a young whippersnapper, pipes up with a theory. Just before a large cheer erupts, he tells them, there appears to be a round bulge at the back of the orange net. "There must be a ball!" he cries. That said, all of the other rules and positions suddenly make perfect sense. Similarly, the Higgs boson particle could be predicted before it was actually discovered, to great acclaim, in 2012, thanks to the Large Hadron Collider. The documentary *Particle Fever* captures the modesty of Peter Higgs, who predicted the particle, as the audience of scientists at the collider burst into wild acclaim right after its discovery.[9]

Lederman and Teresi go on to explain some of the other mind-bending paradoxes of particle physics. To illustrate how the electron can be a mathematical point with mass, charge, and spin but no radius, they cite Lewis Carroll's Cheshire Cat: "Slowly the Cheshire Cat disappears until all that's left is its smile. No cat, just smile. Imagine the radius of a spinning glob of charge slowly shrinking until it disappears, leaving intact its spin, charge, mass, and smile."[10]

Lewis Carroll's Wonderland imagery is a favorite of quantum physicists, who seem to imagine that Carroll intuited the paradoxes of quantum mechanics and knew that the world was put together in the same wild, crazy quantum way. John Briggs and David Peat wrote a book called *Looking Glass Universe*, which concludes: "Science itself is a looking-glass. When we look into this glass we see wondrous things which may have a truth like that of Alice's strange worlds: a mixture of fantasy and metaphor, reality and something else, something not quite effable. But the point has come in our discussion to abandon this image and return nakedly to the theories themselves—to recognize that the looking-glass has been another name for the ceaseless activity of science which in the end is nothing more than our own habitual and fanciful curiosity."[11]

The scientists I spoke with gave different reasons for using stories, and I was surprised to learn that they serve as more than just a way to convey their ideas to lay audiences. As Brian Greene told me, "I don't feel I understand anything if I understand only the mathematics." In a public radio interview, the astrophysicist Margaret Geller described how the creation of stories guides her research. In her daily work, she posits a smooth-running story and then tests it against reality. She suggests that "science is 'creativity in a straitjacket' because you can make up lots of stories, and the ones that don't match nature are worthless. The only ones that are good are the ones that are consistent."

Though scientific theories have challenged or discredited many of humanity's most deeply held myths and beliefs about how the world works, the continuing efforts of scientists to create metaphors and parables to understand and explain the universe attests to the enduring and universal human need for stories. The universe goes on seemingly forever, and particles are endlessly small. As creatures trying to grasp the universe, we still find that we need a beginning, a middle, and an end.

Some scientists postulate that the universe itself is an unfolding story. In *Journey of the Universe*, Brian Thomas Swimme and Mary Evelyn Tucker write: "With our empirical observations expanded by modern science, we are now realizing that our universe is a single immense energy event that began as a tiny speck that has unfolded over time to become galaxies and stars, palms and pelicans, the music of Bach, and each of us alive today. The great discovery of contemporary science is that the universe is not simply a place, but a story—a story in which we are immersed, to which we belong, and out of which we arose."[12]

Some scientists postulate that the universe itself is an unfolding story.

"The universe is made of stories, not atoms," writes the poet Muriel Rukeyser. To which the Buddhist writer David Loy responds: "Not atoms? Of course it is made of atoms. That's one of our important stories."[13]

Several scientists have suggested that we are actually the consciousness of the universe, a koan of popular science that I sought to express in a poem called "Animated Stardust":

> Sentient being,
> are we on a quest to understand the universe
> or some aspect of creation's quest
> to understand itself?
>
> Frail and human creatures of the cosmos
> Can we sense the presence
> of our own creator
>
> in this animated stardust?
> This dust that renders visible
> a stream of light—
>
> particles dancing in a beam of light

The scientist Leon Lederman jokes that this notion that we are the consciousness of the cosmos places us right back at the center of the universe—which is just where we were before Copernicus discovered that the sun does not actually revolve around us here on earth.[14]

The search for beauty and meaning in the cosmos goes beyond the stories scientists tell to explain their work. Knowing of my passion for popular science, my wife gave me a copy of *It Must Be Beautiful: Great Equations of Modern Science*, edited by Graham Farmelo, for Father's Day a few years ago. The book presents essays by scientists from several fields, and suggests some points where aesthetics and science intersect. Mathematics, Brian Greene told me, is a language, just as English is a language. Literary metaphors are like equations, albeit a little less precise than a mathematician's might be. Farmelo compares Einstein's $e = mc^2$ to a powerful poem that, like a perfect sonnet, would be spoiled if even a word or comma were changed.

The premise of Farmelo's book is that the universe can be expressed in equations that are beautiful in their simplicity, suggesting that God is either a mathematician or a poet—or both. Scientists look for simple, elegant formulas that can explain the complexities of the universe. Paul Dirac, the Nobel Prize–winning Cambridge physicist and creator of the Dirac equation, suggested that God used beautiful mathematics in creating the world.[15] Thomas Huxley once said, "The great tragedy of science—the slaying of a beautiful hypothesis by an ugly fact."[16]

As I read Farmelo's book, Keats's famous line from "Ode on a Grecian Urn" popped into my head: "Beauty is truth, truth beauty,—that is all / Ye know on earth, and all ye need to know." Keats's *beauty = truth*; *truth = beauty* and Einstein's $e = mc^2$ both have explanatory powers in the real world, albeit from slightly different vantage points. Einstein's equation explains the relationship of energy, matter, and the speed of light; Keats's elucidates the power, allure, and seeming permanence of art. Keats's formula is written in the English language, Einstein's in the language of mathematics. Although they don't often use the word *truth*, scientists seem to be looking for the same elegant simplicity as the poets.

Although they don't often use the word *truth*, scientists seem to be looking for the same elegant simplicity as the poets.

Michio Kaku told me about a formula that string theorists are developing. The formula will have the beauty of $e = mc^2$ and will accomplish what Einstein himself tried to accomplish during the last thirty years of his life but never achieved: bringing together the insights of quantum mechanics and general relativity, the theories of the smallest and the largest bodies in the universe, known as "unified field theory." Before string theory, Kaku explained, scientists had devised equations that were a foot long, contained dozens of variables, and were anything but graceful. It was like "trying to put together the most beautiful animal in the world by pasting together giraffes, whales, and mules with Scotch tape," said Kaku. In an effort to explain the equation, he came up with his own twist on the *Flatland* story. Once, he told me, a gorgeous gemstone fell into Flatland and broke into two parts. One piece was general relativity and the other was quantum mechanics. The Flatlanders simply couldn't find a way to tape them together to create a unified theory. Then a sage suggested that they shift one piece not "left or right" but "up" into another dimension—and the two parts fit together perfectly.

The figures and stories that the ancients found in the stars may have been a product of their imaginations, but there are still plenty of stories out there in the universe. And so the folklorist, like the scientist, can feel quite comfortable under a canopy of stars in our humble corner of the Milky Way galaxy, within the Virgo supercluster of galaxies, nestled within the known universe.

Part IV POETRY IN THE LIFE CYCLE

14

Navigating Transitions

Poetry in Rites of Passage

Doctor, Doctor, will I die?
Yes, my child, and so will I
One, two, three, four, five
I'm alive!

—TRADITIONAL CHILDREN'S RHYME

"Solomon Grundy: born on Monday, christened on Tuesday . . . died on Saturday, buried on Sunday." So the childhood nursery rhyme goes, ending with the simple postscript: "That was the end of Solomon Grundy."[1] In our songs, children's rhymes, and proverbs, we comment on the life cycle. "If a man is twenty and not a revolutionary, he has no heart," goes one saying. "If he is forty and is a revolutionary, he has no mind." When you are young, goes a frequently remembered adage from the Bible, you fasten your own belt and go wherever you wish. When you grow old you stretch out your hands and someone else will fasten a belt around you and take you where you do not wish to go.[2] A comedian described the three stages of life as youth, middle age, and "Gee, you look good."

On the streets of Chinatown in New York, Ng Shung Chi sings, a cappella, the Muyu laments he learned as a boy in Toi Shan, in southern China:

A person's life seems like a weeping willow.
Middle age is the arrival of fall,
Withering and waning away as the fall goes on.
Who will pity this fading figure?
Green willows come back with the spring,
But old age will never go back to youth.[3]

Shakespeare's seven ages of man from *As You Like It*, too, are often quoted, ending with "Last scene of all / That ends this strange, eventful history / Is second childishness and mere oblivion / Sans teeth, sans eyes, sans taste, sans everything."[4]

The life cycle continuously changes our relationship to time. Many say, and I agree, that time moves faster as you grow older, because each new year is a smaller percentage of your life span. When you're one, the next year will be half of your life. When you're fifty, each year is just one fiftieth of your life. On New Year's Eve, 2016, Lucas Dargan, my wife's dad, observed, "It's almost 2016, and I was born in 1917. Almost one hundred years! That's a long time! Well, it doesn't seem as long looking back as it did looking forward."

Throughout the life cycle, the complex cycling and recycling of customs and rites of passage is reminiscent of the classic children's toy the Slinky, not only because we can imagine the metal coil playfully walking up and down the "stairs of life," but also because it spirals as it curls end over end. Along with the rites of passage that mark linear time, seasonal customs and holidays shape a sense of cyclical, recurrent time. As the holidays arrive year after year, like the spiraling Slinky birthdays also come and go, as we gradually move forward and grow older.

Rites of passage are the mileposts that guide travelers through the life cycle. Ethnographer Arnold van Gennep, writing in 1909, compared tribal rituals in different parts of the world and noted the similarities "among ceremonies of birth, childhood, social puberty, betrothal, marriage, pregnancy, fatherhood, initiation into religious societies and funerals."[5] All these rites of passage, he observed, consist of three distinct phases: separation, transition, and incorporation.

Half a century later, the anthropologist Victor Turner examined the transitional or "liminal" stage in the well-developed initiation rituals of the Ndembu of Zambia. He analyzed the momentous reordering of the neophyte's world that occurs while he is in limbo between his childhood and adult selves. "Rites of passage," Turner observes, "are found in all societies but tend to reach their maximal expression in the small-scale, relatively stable and cyclical societies, where change is bound up with biological and meteorological rhythms and reoccurrences rather than with technological innovations."[6]

In the twenty-first-century United States, our rites are not nearly so complex or of such magnitude as the Ndembus'. Rarely do we find elaborate three-part rituals, and the symbol-laden liminal phase in all our life-cycle rituals is probably the least developed. In fact, although we frequently use the term *rites of passage*, what we have today more closely resemble customs rather than rites of passage.

Erik Erikson was the first social scientist to divide the full life cycle into stages. In his 1950 book *Childhood and Society*, Erikson discusses four childhood and four adult stages, each characterized by a particular dilemma or issue.[7] Each of Erikson's stages yields a recognized corpus of customs and lore: adolescence is marked by the lore of the teenager, young adulthood by courtship customs and stories, adulthood by the folklore of parenting, and maturity by the traditions of old age.

The accompanying chart illustrates how, in the course of our life spans, we pick up and discard certain kinds of folklore and traditional behavior, leaving behind a body of material that remains associated with a particular age.[8]

Van Gennep's phases of "separation, transition, and incorporation" may have lost some of their power, but in contemporary American life the ritual urge still continues to engender folk customs and simplified rituals that mark the growing number of transitions in our increasingly complex society. For instance, many of us wed more than once, marry across religions, and have blended families. Contemporary American rites of passage tend to stress incorporation over separation or transition; many are celebrations welcoming an individual into a new status or role. Coworkers in an office may host retirement gatherings or play occupational "initiation" pranks on new employees. Families may celebrate birthdays with a party or by dining at a favorite restaurant, anniversaries by opening a bottle of champagne, or a child's first step by a

Informal rites define our movement through twenty-first-century American life.

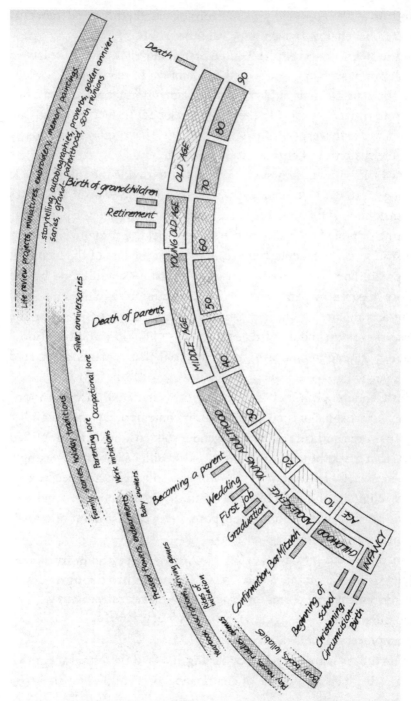

Figure 4. Chart by Allen Carroll

customary dance around the living room. The symbolic transition may involve only shifting a tassel from one side of a cap to another or blowing out the candles on a cake. Nonetheless, these informal rites define our movement through twenty-first-century American life.

Thinking about our life in this way can help us appreciate some of its subtle rhythms. According to Alan Jabbour, for instance, who studied traditional fiddlers in the southern United States, the fiddler's life follows a particular configuration. A child learns the instrument from his parents, or he plays it as a young man, but then he puts it away when he settles down to raise a family. When his children are grown, the fiddle becomes part of his life once again. Jabbour writes that although each of the fiddlers he interviewed had his own reasons for quitting, the pattern was unmistakable. By the time Jabbour had heard thirty different versions of the story, he began to realize that something bigger and more fundamental was going on: "I was not simply finding a few [older fiddlers] who still played. Rather I was learning that old age was precisely when one played the fiddle."[9] As Mary Hufford and Marjorie Hunt put it: "Fiddling, clogging, carving, and needlework . . . are not dying arts just because their practitioners are elderly. They are, in fact, the things that elderly people do."[10]

The movement from telling riddles as children to quoting proverbs as we grow older parallels the rhythms of the life cycle. "What happens once in a minute, twice in a moment, but not once in a thousand years?" my daughter once asked me. The answer to this children's riddle was not nearly as philosophical as the question: it was simply the letter *m*. At the Jewish Senior Center in Venice, California, where proverbs function as part of the standard social currency, the anthropologist Barbara Myerhoff recorded this poetic exchange:

"Learning is what makes us stay young forever," said Abe. "So that a Jew, a real Jew, is ageless."

"This is true," said Sophie. "My grandfather used to tell me, 'If you are ignorant, old age is a famine. If you are learned, it is a harvest.'"

"And what do you think my grandfather said?" asked Nathan in return. "I'll tell you. 'When the brain is green, it does no good, even if the hair is gray.'"[11]

Through each phase of life, poems and traditional sayings play a part in commemorating rites of passage.

Through each phase of life, poems and traditional sayings play a part in commemorating rites of passage. Their presence at key moments of the life cycle attests to the central role of poetry in our lives.

Among the best-loved poets of the world, the Lebanese American writer Kahlil Gibran was an important figure in the movement that transformed Arabic literature in the early twentieth century. His English-language collection of parables and poems, *The Prophet*, resonated profoundly among readers in the United States and abroad. At All Souls Unitarian Church in New York City, his beautiful poem "On Children" is used as part of the christening ceremony:

> Your children are not your children.
> They are the sons and daughters of Life's longing for itself.
> They come through you but not from you,
> And though they are with you yet they belong not to you.
>
> You may give them your love but not your thoughts,
> For they have their own thoughts.
> You may house their bodies but not their souls,
> For their souls dwell in the house of tomorrow,
>   which you cannot visit, not even in your dreams.
> You may strive to be like them, but seek not to make them
>   like you.
>
> For life goes not backward nor tarries with yesterday.
>
> You are the bows from which your children
> as living arrows are sent forth.[12]

Like the proverbs of old age, childhood has its own poetry, as the young play with newfound words that often address their common concerns. At their birthday parties they often recite parodies of the classic song: "Happy birthday to you / You belong in the zoo / You look like a monkey / And you smell like one too." In hand games like this one, played most often by girls aged eight to eleven, children from both white and black backgrounds trade lines back and forth as they clap in rapid rhythms:

Eenie meenie sissalini, u-um-bopchalini
Achi kachi Liberaci, I hate boys.
Saw you with your boyfriend.
How'd you know?
Looked out the window.
Nosey!
Ate a box of candy.
Greedy!
Didn't flush the toilet.
Nasty!
Jumped out the window.
Now I know you're really crazy!
Eenie meenie sissalini.[13]

Many couples quote poetry in their marriage ceremonies, such as this beautiful line by Rainer Maria Rilke from his book *Love and Other Difficulties*: "Once the realization is accepted that even between the closest human beings infinite distances continue to exist, a wonderful living side by side can grow, if they succeed in loving the distance between them which makes it possible for each to see the other whole against the sky."[14]

Another popular poem read at weddings is often referred to as the "Navajo Blessing" (or "Apache Blessing"):

Now you will feel no rain,
for each of you will be shelter for the other.

Now you will feel no cold,
for each of you will be warmth to the other.

Now there will be no loneliness,
for each of you will be companion to the other.

Now you are two persons,
but there is only one life before you.

May beauty surround you both in the
journey ahead and through all the years.

May happiness be your companion and your days
together be good and long upon the earth.

For generations, couples have reveled in what they imagined to be a Native American blessing. In fact, it was written for the 1947 western novel *Blood Brother*, by Elliott Arnold, and was popularized when it found its way into *Broken Arrow*, the 1950 film adaptation of the novel.

The Navajo concept of marriage is much larger. As folklorist Gerald Hausman explains, the ceremony "expresses the belief that good comes from the fecundity of Mother Earth, or as she is known in Navajo culture, Changing Woman. In the beginning, Changing Woman was found as a baby by First Man and First Woman. She matured quickly and at her first rite of passage as a woman, all earth creatures came to bless her. The chants and songs from this origin story are carried forth in traditional Navajo wedding ceremonies today." The wedding ceremony itself, Hausman continues, "is a kind of re-enactment of Changing Woman's power of regeneration. The holy people or *yei* bless the union of man and woman in marriage. In Navajo tradition, the Bluebird carries the gift of corn pollen on wing and feather and thus blesses the bride, who, herself, is a representative of Changing Woman, Mother Earth, the eternal flow of life and all the creatures who are a part of it."[15]

In his poem "The Joining," Hausman describes the couple's anticipation: "I wait for the day / that is blessed / with corn pollen. . . . / And now we will begin our life as one."[16] The Navaho poet J. R. Bluejay DeGroat offers this description in his poem "Bluebird Song":

> bluebird pollen we are blessed with
> bluebird pollen we have feasted with
> bluebird pollen touched our soul
> bluebird spirit world we dwell in
> bluebird song we sing
> in the house of the bird clan our life journeys
> forever we shall make our life together
>   in harmony[17]

Humorous poems are also written, especially for weddings, funerals, and notable birthdays, by family and friends. Though they mean little to those who don't know these people and who are not present at these celebrations, they are nevertheless an art form to be treasured by an audience of intimates. Author and librarian Ariel Zeitlin Cooke (no relation) wrote this poem for her mother's seventieth birthday. It has the rhythms and comic rhymes that often characterize poems written for family occasions:

The Ballad of Froma

Miss Froma Inselbuch was brought by the stork
To a hospital in New York, New York.
Her father and mother were Sam and Dora,
Both eminently qualified to dance the hora.

It was May 9, 1933,
And Europe was starting not to be free.
It was a chain of events that would later obsess her
But at the time no one knew she'd become a professor.

Soon Froma's star had risen.
Brooklyn, Rutgers, then to Princeton.
She analyzed the plays of Euripides
In a manner that was far from insipides.
She became known for dismissing tomfoolery
And also of course for spectacular jewelry.

Froma loves England, Froma loves France,
Traveling puts her in a happy trance.
It is not especially radical
For her to leave the country on sabbatical.

Now, Froma has always had a restless mind
And her interests wander over time.
She is impossible to exhaust
So she started to study the Holocaust.

The poem concludes, as many such poems do, with a toast:

In short, you can't keep a good woman down,
Or so Froma's fans have always found.
For leaping tall buildings with a single bound,
For plumbing tragedy to depths profound,
For achieving the impossible, she is renowned.
So this evening, let Froma Zeitlin be crowned,
Let congratulations and festivities abound![18]

At some point in middle age, the death of an elderly parent moves us closer to death ourselves, as we no longer have an older generation to serve as a buffer. "As long as you have a parent," my folklore professor Kenneth Goldstein once told me, "you are still a child." Even in late middle age and beyond, many of us feel that the death of our parents orphans us.

Retirement and birthdays and wedding anniversaries continue to mark our passage through old age, though the elderly tend to establish new customs and rituals to help them shape a satisfying, integrated life story. In the 1960s the psychiatrists Paul Rhudick and Arthur McMahon studied a group of Spanish-American War veterans whose average age was eighty-one, and observed that the most inveterate storytellers lived the longest.[19] "To experience the self as a stable, continuous being through time, across continents and epochs, despite dramatic physical changes," writes Barbara Myerhoff, "is especially important to the old, burdened with such vast and disparate memories."[20]

Poems and familiar catchphrases offer solace to the elderly and lighten the experience of growing older. "Old age is not for sissies" is one popular saying. The elderly joke about "organ recitals," and about the very nature of growing old. When she turned seventy, my good friend the storyteller Roslyn Bresnick-Perry ("Roz") was driving one day and noticed a long white hair growing out of her chin, reflected in the rearview mirror. "George," she said to her husband, "why didn't you tell me about this?"

"That's the strange thing about getting old," he said. "Nature has a funny way about it. As it's making you ugly, it's making me blind!"

Death itself brings poignant moments as the survivors look for and cling to last words. Roz Perry began her career telling tales she recalled from her life in an eastern European shtetl before she came to the United States. Later she told stories about New York, anecdotes like "My Sister on the Hood," about when her sister sat on the roof of her car to prevent it from getting towed in Midtown Manhattan. As she grew older and spent more time with seniors, she developed her "naughty bawdy tales" about senior sexcapades. In the days before her death, often in pain, Roz was still shaping stories that she would never be able to tell again, but that her family and friends would delight in after her death. Essentially, she left a new series—her deathbed stories. I chronicled this exchange, which took place at her deathbed, with Roz in hospice, fading in and out of consciousness:

You're still in the world, she says to us
I'm no longer part of the world

We circle her bed struggling to disagree
Her cousin bawling

Just then the phone rings

Her son says, *Roz, it's Jerry*

She holds up her index finger

Ah, she says, *the world is calling*

Another group of children and grandchildren gathered vigilantly around the hospital bed of their dying grandmother only to hear her say, "Children, a watched pot never boils."[21]

Many informal rites surrounding death ease the transition for friends and relatives, who assume the responsibility of reminiscing about the deceased. Kenneth Goldstein describes the stories that were told during the shivah, the seven-day formal Jewish mourning period, following the death of his father. Speechless grief gave way to stories of his father as a saint; later came stories of his father as an ordinary man, and finally, the tales of his father as a trickster, a shrewd and funny man, good and bad by turns. These last entered the family repertoire and maintain his father's spirit as a vital force in the life of the family. His story inspired these lines I jotted down years later, after a friend, Abby Watkins, who worked with me at the Smithsonian Folklife Festival, was killed in a car accident:

Gina bet against her in gin rummy,
Sarah summered with her as a child.

When she died, the stories
lay scattered
around her absence
like lost children.

So we gathered first the stories
of Abby as saint
then local sweetheart,
finally the trickster tales,

and we reconstructed Abby
at the storytelling wake[22]

Poems are often read at memorial services as well. Folklorist Deb Boykin told me some months ago that in her immediate family, Tennyson's "Crossing the Bar" is read at funerals. "I know that's hardly an original choice," she admitted. But during his college years, her father worked for a relative who owned a funeral home. "For the rest of his life, he'd tell stories about that experience, most of which were hilarious, despite the subject matter. He heard 'Crossing the Bar' read at someone's funeral and fell in love with the poem. He had it read at the funerals of my grandfather, grandmother, and one of my great aunts. When he died, in 1976, my mother had it read, and I asked that it be read at her funeral, three years ago. It's in the instructions for mine, and if my brothers don't want it, they better tell me before they go."

Alfred Lord Tennyson wrote "Crossing the Bar" in 1899. In it, he compares death to crossing a sandbar and reaching the sea that lies beyond death, to which each of us returns. Shortly before he died, Tennyson told his son Hallam to put "Crossing the Bar" at the end of all editions of his poems.

> Sunset and evening star,
>   And one clear call for me!
> And may there be no moaning of the bar,
>   When I put out to sea,
>
> But such a tide as moving seems asleep,
>   Too full for sound and foam,
> When that which drew from out the boundless deep
>   Turns again home.
>
> Twilight and evening bell,
>   And after that the dark!
> And may there be no sadness of farewell,
>   When I embark;
>
> For tho' from out our bourne of Time and Place
>   The flood may bear me far,
> I hope to see my Pilot face to face
>   When I have crost the bar.[23]

In the Boykin family, Deb said, there's a story that accompanies the reading of the poem. "My father had a multitude of friends who came from a multitude of backgrounds. One of his favorite haunts was Lamar's, a blue-collar bar just across the Alabama River in Montgomery County, which was a wet county. We lived on the other side of the river in what was then a dry county. As we were leaving the graveside, one of his drinking buddies from Lamar's came up to me and said, 'I liked that poetry and it just suited ol' Jake. He crossed every bar he ever came upon.'"

When Barbara Myerhoff, who had previously studied the Huichol Indians, embarked on her research project with elderly Jews, she realized that what she could learn from her work with the Huichol "was limited by the fact that I would never really be a Huichol Indian. But I would be a little old Jewish lady one day; thus it was essential for me to learn what the condition was like, in all its particulars."[24] Barbara Myerhoff died from cancer at the age of forty-nine and never did become that old lady.

The life cycle shapes the way we think about our own and others' lives—even if they are cut short. I wrote these lines about a wonderful and wise child who died of leukemia at the age of six, and who had remarkable insight into her brief years:[25]

> Liza Lister
> carefree little squirt
> diagnosed with leukemia at the age of four
> who in an act of will lived to be six—
> brave little girl, who asked to die on her mother's lap
> listening to her favorite lullaby,
> loved cows, milk by the quart
> concluded, "I've had a good life,
> only short"

In the book (and motion picture adaptation) *The Fault in Our Stars*, author John Green has his character Hazel, a sixteen-year-old dying of cancer, offer some intriguing thoughts on a short life while speculating on the nature of infinity. As she plans a eulogy for her boyfriend, also dying of cancer, she states: "There are infinite numbers between 0 and 1.

There's .1 and .12 and .112 and an infinite collection of others. Of course, there is a bigger infinite set of numbers between 0 and 2, or between 0 and a million. Some infinities are bigger than other infinities. . . . I cannot tell you how grateful I am for our little infinity. You gave me forever within the numbered days, and I'm grateful."[26]

A math blogger, Yen Duong, in her *Baking and Math* blog, disputes the mathematics behind this sweet sentiment, illustrating the proof that all infinities are, in fact, the same size. She ends up offering her own, mathematically sound way of looking at longer and shorter lives in relation to infinity: "Whether those different sorts of infinities apply to something like moments of time is unknown. What we do know is that if life has infinite moments, or infinite love, or infinite being, then a life twice as long still has exactly the same amount. Some infinities only look bigger than other infinities."[27]

Within the partly shared consciousness of a particular culture, the life cycle and its rites of passage make up "proto–life stories," a set of potential scripts that, as they are filled in over the years, gradually become our life's manuscript. We progress through the life cycle individually, but we are bound into communities by sharing in the life cycles of others.[28] By attending bar mitzvahs, weddings, and funerals, we rehearse our own future roles in and scripts for these ceremonies. Marriage and birth join us to one another's life cycles, just as death separates us. Metaphorical deaths and births happen as well; for example, when a baby is delivered, a mother, too, is born. Watching my wife, Amanda, as a young mother inspired these lines:

> Through the long hours of darkness
> Amanda keeps the family vigil,
> Keeping watch with one eye open
> On the sea of night
>
> And the beds are rocked to sleep on a swaying sea
> Like cradles
>
> Until she rises
> In the half sleep of newly born
>   mothers

Wafts across the shadowed room
Like an apparition on the waters
Cradling her baby like a quarter moon

Although the idea of the life cycle is essentially a belief system rooted in folk communities, its contours are often defined and underscored by corporate advertising and changing media and technology. For instance, before the advent of digital cameras, the advertising campaigns for Kodak film influenced and, perhaps, homogenized the way "the times of your life," as Kodak called them, were celebrated. So, too, Hallmark has made the greeting card a part of how occasions in the life cycle are commemorated, with predetermined categories of cards on the shelves. Online greeting card companies have also proliferated, and many Americans create online memorial pages for friends and family who have died.

Customs are usually celebrated in ethnic, family, religious, and community contexts, and sometimes force us to make choices that define our allegiance to a particular group. Buying a first car is a rite of passage emphasized particularly in American society. Folklorist Joan Gross wrote of one Hispanic girl: "Carmen Neris was given the choice. She could have a thousand dollars to use for a car or she could have a Sweet Fifteen Party (or *quinceañera*) for her birthday, but as the date approached she began to think that a car might be a better idea."[29] After her family talked with her, however, Carmen changed her mind and decided on the party. When two different life-cycle patterns were presented to her, she ultimately chose the one offered by her family and ethnic community, in which a *quinceañera* celebration is a custom marking status and transformation in a fashion different from a car.

We can also modify traditions to suit our own backgrounds. Before her senior prom, Tharima, a Bangladeshi American girl at Hamtramck High School in Michigan, conducted a survey of her classmates and realized that 65 percent of the girls were not going to be able to attend the event because of religious restrictions forbidding dating, dancing with boys, and appearing without a head scarf in front of males. In response, Tharima organized the first all-girls senior prom. Dancing to the playlist on Tharima's iPhone, close to one hundred young women let their hair down for the first time and partied the night away at their own prom in the decorated Hamtramck Knights of Columbus Hall.[30]

As we use rites of passage to mark our relationship with time and shape our lives according to prescribed patterns, we also determine which customs we wish to perpetuate for the next generation, which form the essence of tradition. By deciding to get married or to give our child a formal bar mitzvah or *quinceañera*, we tie ourselves to traditional customs; by deciding not to do these things, or by opting to alter or reformulate a customary event in some way (such as hosting a same-sex wedding ceremony or an all-girls prom), we tie ourselves to new and different ideas about community and tradition. Through its pattern of rites and customs, our culture establishes in the proto–life story an itinerary that we may decide to follow or from which we may diverge as we make decisions about our own lives, plan our futures, and reconstruct our pasts. Those proto–life stories also change over time. As John Sebastian of the Lovin' Spoonful sang, "Now I know that all I've learned my kid assumes / and all my deepest worries must be his cartoons."[31]

> **Through its pattern of rites and customs, our culture establishes in the proto–life story an itinerary that we may decide to follow or from which we may diverge as we make decisions about our own lives, plan our futures, and reconstruct our pasts.**

Generations ago, when a family was far more likely to operate as a single economic unit, the differences between occupational and family roles were diminished. Learning, earning, and growing up were all more closely intertwined, and because marriage was so important to a family's economic survival, the courtship of individuals was a far shorter, simpler process. Older adults lived in the family home, and most of them did not survive as long as people do today. Evidence suggests that many forms we now consider as children's classic folklore and literature— Grimm's fairy tales, American play-party songs, and African American children's games—were once shared by adults and children alike.

The social historian Tamara Hareven writes: "[Americans] discovered childhood in the first half of the nineteenth century and 'invented' adolescence toward the end of it. . . . However, despite the growing awareness of childhood, adolescence, and youth as pre-adult stages, no clear boundaries for adulthood in America emerged until much later, when interest in the 'middle years' as a distinct segment of adult life arose out of the need to differentiate the social and psychological problems of 'middle' from 'old' age."[32] With the human life span increasing, we are continuing to distinguish new phases of old age.

Although the proto–life story of each group is rooted in that group's history, the patterns that bind contemporaries to tradition are often not the same as those of their predecessors. Rather, every generation tends to find its own pathway through traditional customs. Our modern lives are more compartmentalized than those of our forebears; we have more identities and more fully developed life stages. In the United States, the four years of college become an often treasured phase of life in which students live away from their parents and can explore their interests and passions unencumbered. In many countries around the world, young people continue to live with their families until they marry, and college forces students to decide on a career right out of high school. In the United States, we tend to have more diverse bodies of folklore and folk customs and occasions to celebrate.

Ultimately, a responsibility for our society and for us as individuals is to foster, celebrate, mark, and nurture each stage of life. As we become activists in our own culture and in our own families, we have a stake in ensuring that different phases of the life cycle are clearly marked with memorable rites of passage. Folklorists, psychologists, and educators working with children and parents, social workers advising the elderly, and even funeral directors shaping the rituals of death need to be aware of how the nuances of the life cycle affect our communities and ourselves.

> **As we become activists in our own culture and in our own families, we have a stake in ensuring that different phases of the life cycle are clearly marked with memorable rites of passage.**

Perhaps folklorists are no different from others if they occasionally imagine their world as a devolution from a better age. And yet if we can create a society in which our apocryphal Solomon Grundy can play his heart out on Monday, raise hell on Tuesday, get a job on Wednesday, court all day Thursday, parent Friday, then retire, travel, and reminisce about it on Saturday—and if he finds traditional expressive material that is vital at every stage of his life—that really is not such a bad life for Solomon Grundy.

15

The Human Unit of Time

The Space between Memory and Legacy

Miss not the discourse of the elders.
—ECCLESIASTES

Margaret Mead devotes a chapter of her memoir *Blackberry Winter* to the joys of becoming a grandparent. Gazing at one's grandchild, she writes, makes it suddenly possible to "visualize that same child as a grandparent, and with the eyes of another generation . . . see other children, just as light-footed and vivid, as eager to learn and know and embrace the world, who must be taken into account—now."[1] Grandparenthood inspired Mead to consider the need for a human unit for marking time. Its span cannot be as short as a human lifetime, and yet it cannot rely on the scientist's notion of time stretching back millions of years to the Big Bang, or even the historian's conception of time spanning centuries of human tumult.

Mead mentions a friend who defined this human unit of time as "the space between a grandfather's memory of his own childhood and a grandson's knowledge of those memories as he heard about them."[2] This human time span, based on experiential reckoning rather than scientific exactitude, therefore stretches from our memories of ourselves as children to our grandparents' memories of their own childhoods, ultimately encompassing five generations. Elders bracket the human unit of time, with their memories on one side, their legacies on the other.

Folklorists echo Mead's notion when they speak of "a living cultural heritage," because we are often referring to traditions and histories passed on through living memory. We privilege stories passed down by

Elders bracket the human unit of time, with their memories on one side, their legacies on the other. word-of-mouth over historical episodes learned from books. A side effect of Google searches, Wikipedia, and many forms of twenty-first-century media has been the devaluing and undermining of the memories of our elders; we no longer need them as the chroniclers of our histories. Though we can access hard facts and information instantaneously, the memories and tales of the previous generations still matter; they are passed on firsthand as part of the poetry of everyday life, part of our own lived experience.

Certainly, death comes as an absolute finality, and the fact that we will be survived by children, grandchildren, nieces, and nephews may offer small comfort to many of us. Yet there is a do-si-do to the generations, a rhythm that is available for us to tune in to. Generational time is an aspect of the poetry of everyday life. When my grandfather died of a stroke, in 1965, my grandmother's sister Rose stood up at the family seder and said tearfully, "The captain is dead, but somehow the ship must sail on." In the years that followed, our family lost a whole generation of aunts and uncles. My cousin Richard echoed Rose's line at a seder a few months after my grandmother Bella, the last of her generation, died. "Now," he said, "the captain is dead and the whole crew is gone, but the ship must sail on." (Though I must say that when my aunt died—Aunt Elaine, who sustained us day after day with her phone calls and raucous humor—it felt as if the whole ship actually had gone down.) On occasions like this, when we need to come to terms with death, we often turn to memorable phrases spoken by generations before us, perhaps in an effort to sew a thread through our own history.

More than anyone else I have met, my friend the folklorist and folk artist Ruby Marcotte moves in that intergenerational dance. "I live in a little community of neighbors and family on West Mountain near Corinth, New York," she told me.

My grandmother Viola White-LaPier lived right across the road from where I was raised, and we had lots of meadows where we could pick berries—strawberries, blueberries, blackberries—and she loved to pick berries. There were rules that my grandmother had for picking berries: you had to wait for the dew to dry first. Then you had to wear long-sleeved shirts and long pants and you had to carry a galvanized tin pail on your belt so you could have two hands free to pick the berries. My grandmother weighed about one hundred pounds. She was about four foot eleven and always wore an apron. If we were picking blackberries, there was always both the low bush and the high bush. She would pick the low bush. "God made me short," she said, "so I could pick the low-bush berries."

I took my children to those very same meadows, and then along came the grandchildren and now the great-grandchildren. We walk in the same field. I tell them stories about my grandmother, and have them do the same things. You can imagine how cute it is when you have a teenage granddaughter and you tell her to get a belt and hang a pail on it. We then bring all the berries to the kitchen table, and, just like my grandmother did, if it's strawberry season we make strawberry shortcake, and if it's blackberry season we make a blackberry pie.

Like most of us, Ruby LaPier Marcotte does not live a stress-free life. "My life at times has not been easy," she told me, "but I'm a survivor and I get through the tough times. Because I continue to live on the same land that my grandfather settled over one hundred years ago, I can get away from everything in the same spaces as I did when I was a child. I can still go to the old barn, or sit on the big rock under the cherry tree—it is all connected. This place and these connections carry me back in time to my grandparents and forward to my children, grandchildren, and great-grandchildren. They pull me through."

As folklorists, my colleagues and I often present the work of elders and advocate for intergenerational exchange, encouraging young people to interview their grandparents, to stretch the measuring tape of time beyond their own lives—not an easy task for Americans, who continually embrace the present. According to Margaret Mead, a boy once told her that "long ago was before his grandfather's grandfather's time."[3] We need the human unit of time not only to extend the way we think about families and time but, in some cases, to limit it, to distinguish what happened in living memory from what happened "long ago," when an individual's human unit of time fades into the historical record. The human unit of time is not just about remembering but about forgetting, too.

The human unit of time might also be a useful tool for informing contemporary policy decisions that affect places and artworks that we care about. For instance, it could help shape copyright law. Corporate interests, in particular those led by Disney and by the Gershwin family, have continually argued for extensions of the copyright law and their own copyrights beyond their current terms, which, until recently, provided that copyright would endure for the life of the author plus fifty years, or seventy-five years for a work of corporate authorship. In fact, both Disney and the Gershwins have successfully hired lobbyists to ensure that Congress does not allow works produced after 1923 to go out of copyright, purportedly because that would mean that Mickey Mouse and *Porgy and Bess*, backed by their well-funded lobbying machines, would pass into the public domain and would cease to bring in as much revenue. Sometimes dubbed the Mickey Mouse Protection Act and passed in 1998, the new law ensures that Mickey won't go into the public domain until 2019, when we can expect another effort to extend the copyright.

Descendants of creative artists continue to receive royalties even if they are no longer connected to their ancestors in living memory, preventing art from returning to the public sphere. In many cases, this loophole has allowed the rich to stay rich just because they were born into a family with a successful ancestor. In the end, the "tax" that's paid on this policy is, for example, levied on schools and community groups who want to put on a Gershwin musical and have to pay dearly for the privilege. If the human unit of time were considered, these works would pass into the public domain much sooner. As Pete Seeger once told me, "The grandchildren should be able to find some other way to make a living, even if their grandfather did write 'How Much Is That Doggie in the Window?'"[4]

Similarly, historic preservation has often favored places of architectural rather than cultural distinction, because bricks and mortar can be preserved for hundreds of years. As history unfolds across centuries, certain community-based sites need to be landmarked or given designations that mark the contribution of a particular ethnic or labor group, or the dramatic contribution of an individual to our collective memory. The process of landmarking needs to be broadened to fulfill its mandate of preserving sites that are important not only to architectural history but to our historic, cultural, and aesthetic heritage as well.

The human unit of time can help us designate places that have fostered a sense of living memory. These designations might protect relevant sites for, say, a hundred years after some historical event occurred in that space (even though Mead's human unit of time is often a bit longer). The writer Jimmy Breslin poked fun at the name of Haggerty Park, on 201st Street and Jamaica Avenue in Hollis, Queens, quipping that there hadn't been a kid with the name and face of a Haggerty in that park in a quarter of a century. Perhaps it's time for the neighborhoods of Queens or the Bronx to be able to name their parks after local heroes—Fran Drescher, Sonia Sotomayor, Martin Scorsese, or 50 Cent—at least for a hundred-year time span.

The human unit of time can shape the way we preserve local establishments that continue to resonate for the cultural or ethnic groups that created them, even after the groups have moved away. On the Lower East Side, for instance, establishments like Yonah Schimmel's Knish Bakery, Katz's Delicatessen, and Russ and Daughters appetizing shop are still significant to New Yorkers, even though the neighborhood is no longer predominantly Jewish. Little Italy is no longer an Italian neighborhood, but Italians still flock to its restaurants and the annual Feast of San Gennaro. These places continue to flourish because Jews and Italians continue to patronize them, in some cases bringing their grandchildren to hear stories of the neighborhood from the older generations. A few generations hence, however, the need for preservation may no longer be felt so strongly in these neighborhoods, and the passing of a human unit of time can make way for a new group to reshape the neighborhood and its establishments in its own way.

Memory is the clock for this human unit of time. In the Jewish tradition, a male child was often called a *kaddish* by his father, referring to the prayer

Memory is the clock for this human unit of time.

that sons (and now daughters) are required to say for eleven months after the death of a parent. I recall the last words attributed to the writer Damon Runyon: "You can keep the things of bronze and stone and give me one man to remember me just once a year."

When Rosa Evans was born, around the year 1900, her grandmother Jane Wallace gave her a silver cup, and family lore quotes Jane's mother (my wife great-great-grandmother) telling her, "Arise, my daughter, and go to your daughter, for your daughter's daughter had a daughter." Amanda's family holds this cup—and its corresponding quote—as one of its precious possessions. As Amanda wrote in her study of her family's traditions, the quote and the cup are invoked to represent the five generations of their family in Darlington, South Carolina, and the multigenerational presence that continues there to this day. Although the saying is not unique to her family—and actually doesn't get the generation count quite right—it harbors meaning because it represents the closeness and longevity of their family ties, such that it would have been (and still is) possible for four generations to witness the birth of a fifth-generation child.[5] Amanda and I put these lines in a song about taking our daughter back to Amanda's parents' farm:

> I'll bring my daughter to Long Leaf Farm
> And perhaps my daughter's daughter
> Home is where the heart is
> And home is where I brought her
> We traveled seven hundred miles
> To swim in Black Creek water
> Black Creek's holy water.
>
> *Arise, my daughter,*
> *Go to your daughter,*
> *For your daughter's daughter*
> *Had a daughter*

And so it's possible for each of us to tune in to the poetics of generational time as it applies to our families.

Each group of our ancestors—from the Middle Ages back to the Stone Age—represents certain things to us. But in our hearts most of us want to be remembered by those who have a living connection to our lives. Life's task is to remember and be remembered. After our grandchildren have died, and after their grandchildren who remembered the stories their grandparents told about us have died, where will our memory live? If we're famous, someone may put our names on a street sign, but that's of less concern—especially after the first hundred years. Beyond that, we're history. We fade into the storied past. Let the dead bury the dead. As my dad used to say, "End of story."

16

Your Body as Symbol

Written in Ash

His death belongs to him like his wedding.
—Thomas Wolfe

Ironic, but one of the most intimate acts
of our body
is death

—Rabia, eighth-century Iraqi poet

Dead is dead, I know. Deader than a doorknob. Deader than a zebra in a lion's den. Dead is deeper than the deepest sleep. But no matter how dead I can envision myself to be—dead, dead, dead—I cannot imagine that I'll be even so much as okay with lying alone in a box in the cold, cold ground for all eternity, especially in winter, when the ground freezes. I suppose others can envision themselves as so dead that they won't care. I can't.

I tried to think my way around this dilemma. I came up with what I thought might be an ingenious solution. I suggested to my wife that we create a double coffin. I envisioned it in two sections, separated by a removable plank. Each section would have its own lid. If I died first, I would be placed in section A, awaiting Amanda. When she died, they would raise the coffin to place her in section B. (Since both sections would have lids, my decomposing body would *not* be visible to the funeral-goers.) Now, the coffin would not be designed as a regular box. The bottom would be angled like the bottom of a canoe. When the gravedigger unearthed me, he would place Amanda's body in section B, close the lid, and then pull up the plank dividing our sections—so the final act before reinterment would be the raising of the plank so we rolled together. What a plan!

The writer John Berger puts my idea more poetically:

What reconciles me to my own death more than anything else is the image of a place: a place where your bones and mine are buried, thrown, uncovered, together. They are strewn there pell-mell. One of your ribs leans against my skull. A metacarpal of my left hand lies inside your pelvis. (Against my broken ribs your breast like a flower.) The hundred bones of our feet are scattered like gravel. It is strange that this image of our proximity, concerning as it does mere phosphate of calcium, should bestow a sense of peace. Yet it does. With you I can imagine a place where to be phosphate of calcium is enough.[1]

When Peggy King-Jorde and her brother made their father's coffin, at his request, she felt she was creating a safe place that would embrace him. The coffin of C. B. King, a prominent black civil rights attorney who represented Martin Luther King Jr. (no relation), among others, reflected his modesty. "It was so much him," his daughter said. "His whole image of exiting this world was really about the elegance of simplicity—being simply buried in something that's crafted by your children."

The making of her father's coffin involved more than a hammer and nails. It was an event. Peggy's account reveals how the process took on a ceremonial richness that lured community members into it. Peggy was interviewed by folklorist Ilana Harlow, my collaborator on the book *Giving a Voice to Sorrow: Personal Responses to Death and Mourning.*

My father used to say to my four brothers and me, "I want you to build me a coffin." But death, at the time, was so far away for us. So we didn't think anything of it.

When my father died, his body was flown back to our home in Albany, Georgia. My brother and I sat in our family room and we drew sketches of the coffin on the back of an envelope for the shape, and the wood, and how we were going to do the handles—we wanted sisal rope handles. We designed it in a long rectangular shape, fairly deep, and we put in tongue-in-groove planks that interlocked with one another, and a flat top.

The funeral home that we were using was a new place. It wasn't this other, traditional funeral home that everybody always used to go to.

And the woman who was the funeral director was very supportive. We said, "We're not interested in buying a coffin; we want to build one."

And she said "Fine. I'll make one of my carpenters available. He has a truck, and he'll help you."

Then another friend of the family who made drapes and worked with fabric showed us an off-white, linen cloth for us to line the coffin. And we asked her to make just a small cushion to line the bottom and a small pillow.

My father was very prominent and everyone expected him to be in a very expensive coffin. So when word had it that his kids were making his coffin, people would come up on the back porch to see. It was a beautiful spring day. Everybody was sitting out on the banisters and there was lemonade. And on the sawhorses we had this coffin that we were crafting.

And it was funny: people would come up on this porch and they wouldn't talk about the coffin. They'd simply sit, especially a lot of the elderly people, they'd sit on the edge and they'd ask how everybody was doing and they'd almost ignore the coffin. Because, I think in a way, they were kind of amazed that it was actually happening.

The whole experience of being out on the porch was like a performance. People want to come as close as they can to certain events. Onlookers transcend and sort of transport themselves into a certain situation.

I have such a wonderful memory of crafting the coffin. I felt like I was creating this very safe environment for my father. And then after we completed it, our family enjoyed knowing that, okay, now we're ready to sort of let go. When I was working on the coffin, my focus was not much further beyond what was there, at that time and place, dealing with my brothers and other family members. I didn't expect to have that sense of satisfaction crafting a coffin.

Part of the ceremony at the graveside is that they lower the coffin a little just as kind of a gesture and then everybody leaves. Then the gravediggers get into doing the real burial. But as the coffin was being lowered, I was sitting next to my brother Leland and we realized that the coffin lid, which was designed with a little lip around the perimeter, was just a touch too big—so that if they lowered the coffin too much it was going to start lifting off. So there was a level of comedy. We thought, "Okay, all right, some design flaws." My father would have thought it was funny.

But still, at the burial I felt an enormous level of pride because there were so many compliments. I think that what people were seeing was the result of this collaboration among the children. A part of me went into the coffin. It's like any artist who feels there's part of them in something they've created. I felt that there was a part of each of us put into the coffin. That's what made it good and that's what made it a safe place.[2]

"I felt that there was a part of each of us put into the coffin. That's what made it good and that's what made it a safe place."

Like the King family, I understood that coffins are symbolic, but of course I was not offering to handcraft the double coffin I proposed. Amanda never rejected the possibility of that double coffin out of hand. But I can't say that she embraced it with all her heart, either. We did, however, collaborate on a bluegrass-style tune we called "Double Coffin":

> Make me a double coffin when I die, Babe,
> And I'll wait patiently for you
> Until your time is through
> I'll lie there tried and true
> Make me a double coffin when I die
>
> *Till then we'll just keep on on*
> *Wait for the other when we're gone*
> *It's not flesh rotting on the bone*
> *It's lying in the grave alone*
>
> Throw a bony arm across my shoulder, Babe
> Look right through my hollow eyes
> I'll feel your sweet surprise
> When you feel my skinny thighs
> Make me a double coffin when I die
>
> *Chorus*
>
> Make me a double coffin when I die, Babe,
> I'll come to terms with eternity
> Even when I cease to be
> I could use some company
> Make me a double coffin when I die

Somehow, writing the song seemed to get the double coffin notion out of my system.

Instead, I began to think about cremation. It did give me pause to consider that when Jesus or the Messiah or people from another planet arrive on earth and want to reconstitute and resuscitate everyone who has ever lived and died, they would have an easer time bringing the dead skeletons back to life than the cremated remains. But that, I reasoned, was a highly unlikely scenario.

Working on *Giving a Voice to Sorrow*, my coauthor, Ilana Harlow, also interviewed the undertaker and poet Thomas Lynch. He connected rising trends in cremation to an increasingly secular, increasingly mobile society:

> In thirty years we've gone from a country that cremates 3 percent of its dead to a country that cremates 30 percent of its dead. This is a radical shift and it's completely attached to the secularization of the culture. In most of Western religious thought, fire is punitive—when you were in trouble with God you burned in hell. In Eastern cultures, fire is purifying and releasing. It's not a question of what is done but how it's done. Our culture doesn't place any ceremonial value in cremation, whereas in Calcutta cremation is public and it's attended by a lot of symbolic and ritualized behavior. Fire is brought by the first-born child from the home to ignite the fire. But here cremation is often minimization, disappearance. So people never say, "Please cremate me"; they say, "Just cremate me." The emphasis is on the "just" part.
>
> When you cremate someone you end up with ashes, unlike when you bury them. How do we consider those remnants? Are they leftovers? Are they icons? Are they relics? What are they? Everybody gets to decide that for themselves.[3]

As cremation becomes more commonplace in America, creative ways of dispersing the ashes are on the rise. In my hometown of Hastings, New York, the hair salon Visual Difference is owned by a woman named Michelle Mosca. One day while Michelle was cutting my hair, we got into a conversation about her husband, who had recently passed away and was cremated. Her two young children, Lexi and Samantha, became despondent. Two months later, as Father's Day approached, Michelle came up with the idea of bringing them to Build-A-Bear at a nearby mall. One of the special moments when a child builds a bear is placing a tiny heart inside. Suddenly it occurred to Michelle that she could have the girls put a tiny urn with some of their father's ashes inside each bear. Lexi and Samantha dressed each of their bears. Lexi put hers in a Yankees uniform to remind her how much her dad loved watching baseball. Samantha dressed her bear up like SpongeBob because she used to watch that show together with her dad. They would snuggle with their bears at night, keeping their father close. "Someday," Michelle said, "they may take the urns out and do something else with them."

Dick Falk, a well known PR man who worked with Barbra Streisand in her early years, ran a side business of scattering people's ashes over Manhattan in the 1950s and 1960s. When New Yorkers requested this kind of aerial burial, he'd rent a Piper Cub and fly over the island of Manhattan. "I'm listed in the phone books as an undertaker, but actually I'm an 'overtaker'—I don't take people down. I take them up." He would pour the ashes from the crematorium's metal box or plain brown packaging to a more easily managed container. "Actually," he said, "I put them in an oatmeal box. Why? Because it fits." Ideal for easy pouring out of an airplane window.[4] I'm confident that this was no more legal then than it would be now.

Thomas Lynch continues:

It used to be that people would cremate their dead and then put the ashes in a columbarium or put them in a family plot. But now cremation makes the dead mobile. And it makes them divisible. You can't divide a body, but you can divide up the ashes. A son will say, "Dad liked to fish in the river; he'd liked to be scattered there." But Mom says, "Yeah, but I'd like to have Dad buried with me." And the daughter who lives in California says, "Yeah, but what about me?" So she'll take some in a locket, the son will scatter some up where he and his dad fished, and Mom will keep some at home to be buried with her when she dies. Those are creative responses to mortality.[5]

My mother, Shirley Zeitlin, was cremated when she passed away in 1999. She had been living with my dad in São Paulo. Given her druthers, she would probably have chosen to be buried in Roosevelt Cemetery, outside Philadelphia, near her parents, Harry and Bella, and her aunts and uncles. Jewish tradition adamantly opposes cremation. But my dad was a vehement atheist and eventually talked her into cremation. He didn't want his own ashes scattered anywhere: "Just leave them right there at the crematorium. No problem."

Surprisingly, at the rather minimal cremation service for my mom, the staff asked if the family wanted to play a favorite song of hers. My brother Bill recalled that she'd loved "Sunrise, Sunset" from *Fiddler on the Roof*. After the song played, an old friend of the family, Al Chadick, approached my dad. "Where are you thinking of putting her ashes?" he asked.

"Right where they lay, around the crematorium," my dad replied.

Al went on to explain to my father that when he moved from Japan to Brazil, he had opened a Japanese Buddhist cremation garden, called Kin-ka-kuji, outside São Paulo. As it happened, some of my parents' best friends, the Beamans and the Cooks, couples who had been part of a bridge group with them in the 1940s and 1950s, had had their ashes placed there as well. "I think Shirley would prefer to be in Kin-ka-kuji," Al told my father.

And so Mom's ashes were eventually placed inside a small pagoda overlooking a pond with carp and water lilies. The inside of the pagoda is lined with ornate drawers, and my mom's box of ashes was placed in a drawer next to those of her fellow bridge players.

When my dad died fourteen years later, we played three arias from the opera *Carmen* at the cremation ceremony and showed up at the offices of Kin-ka-kuji carrying his ashes in a tin box—only to discover that the cemetery had no record of my mom. It turned out that Al Chadick had donated a drawer to my dad but, as one of the cemetery's owners, hadn't bothered to inform the administration. So we asked the caretaker where the ashes of some of the bridge group members were stored; she looked up the records, and we located the correct pagoda. My mom was still there, and my dad is next to her now—along with a copy of the list Amanda, our kids, and I wrote, titled "Ninety-one Memories of Dad," one for each year of his life. We take some solace in the fact that in the next drawer lie the ashes of their old bridge group, and imagine that perhaps somewhere, some way, their game continues.

When I visited the cemetery with my two brothers on a trip to Brazil a few months ago, we brought along our lifelong friend Solomon Reuben, a devout Buddhist, whom we often referred to—along with myself and my brothers Mur and Bill—as the fourth musketeer. Sol had fallen on hard times and tried to commit suicide three times in the past year. A student of all religions, he had been reading a series of books about the Jewish religion at the time and, as we stood in front of the drawers that held my parents' ashes, donned a yarmulke and recited a kaddish as a Japanese couple in a different part of the temple was chanting in Japanese. We took his photograph smiling sweetly in front of the Japanese pagoda, perhaps with the foreknowledge that he'd wind up there. When he finally succeeded in killing himself less than a month later, we asked that his ashes be deposited in this lovely Buddhist cemetery, far more fitting for him than for my parents, a perfect resting place for my dear friend.

The poetry of everyday life is all about the use of symbols—in language and food and sex and place and story, in all of life's manifestations. The decisions we make about what to do with our own dead bodies symbolize how we have viewed our lives. We become our own memorabilia.

We become our own memorabilia.

All of us are charged with putting the bodies of our loved ones back into the cold, cold ground of Mother Earth. Unless we want to leave our decisions to others, we have to decide for ourselves how to dispose of our own remains. If I've chosen to live through symbols—and as a folklorist I figure that I have—then I should choose to die by them as well; I'll take that "creative approach to mortality." The Chinese poet Liu Xiaobo, imprisoned for his political beliefs, included these lovely lines in a letter to his wife: "Before you enter the grave / Don't forget to write me with your ashes / Do not forget to leave your address in the nether world."[6]

So, now that I have dismissed the impractical double coffin, my choice is to be cremated, with some of my ashes sprinkled into Amanda's coffin, which will rest in her family cemetery, outside Darlington, South Carolina. Some of my ashes will also be sprinkled on the grounds of my home, some on the beaches of Guarujá, in Brazil, where I spent my happiest childhood days, and some in the drawer with my parents and the old bridge group at Kin-ka-kuji. These choices will offer proof, if nothing else, of the power of symbol. Till then,

> I am the ashes
>
> just before the fire . . .
> jogging by the sea
> surfing on foam
> dancing on sand
>
> to the ocean's song
> the seagull's cry
>
> wrapped in water,
> soaked in wind
>
> till the ashes of my body
> scatter from the sky

As the poet Jeffrey Cyphers Wright tells us, "Inscribe the ashes."[7]

17

Intimations of Immortality

The Artist's Secular Sphere of Spirituality

No land on earth bears me.
Only my words bear me,
a bird born from me who builds a nest in my ruins . . .
—Mahmoud Darwish

I want to paint men and women with that something of the
eternal which the halo once used to symbolize and which we
try to convey by the actual radiance and vibration of our col-
oring.
—Vincent van Gogh

"I got me a sort of a one-man religion," Woody Guthrie wrote, "but it takes in everybody. My religion is so big, no matter who you are, you're in it, and no matter what you do, you can't get out of it."[1] I've never felt the strong pull of organized religion myself, simply because there is so much significance in the artfulness and plentitude of meaning tucked into everyday life. At the same time, I respect all religions for taking on the search for meaning. I believe in all the Gods.[2] As Joseph Campbell writes, "The way to become human is to learn to recognize the lineaments of God in all of the wonderful modulations of the face of man."[3] Even the nonbeliever (I believe) experiences moments of transcendence and grace—like, say, biting into one of Gus's pickles outside his shop on the Lower East Side—tempting even the most ardent atheist to doubt his faith.

Woody Guthrie never hesitated to espouse homespun philosophies about the nature of time and the universe: "I don't know what this stuff called time is made out of. Don't even know where it boils up and steams up from, don't even know where time rolls back to. . . . You could just take a handful of these things you call days and weeks, and things you say are months, and hold them in your hand like this, and blow them up into the air like a feather . . . you'd find me out there back in Oklahoma, out on my Grandma's farm paying a visit."[4]

As humans, we are graced with memories, and our challenge is to render our own memories vivid to ourselves and to those around us. "Memory," writes Jean Paul Sartre, "shows us the person we were with a fullness of being that imbues it with a kind of poetry."[5] We enshrine memory in story. Telling and retelling our memories as stories helps us remember them. We need, when our most vigorous days have passed, to "rest our souls on a memory," as the poet Carolyn Wells writes.[6]

Every preacher, every rabbi, everyone who gets up to speak at a funeral is charged with making the memory of the deceased palpable. Rabbi Edward Schecter of Temple Beth Shalom, in Hastings, New York, described his memorial services to me: "You know how you take fine crystal glass and plink it, and it should sound like a bell? That clear—that's how you want it to be. Sometimes I stay up all night thinking of the right story to make that pure sound."

Human memory speaks to the sense of past and present existing simultaneously. The anthropologist Barbara Myerhoff writes about the way the elderly use photographs and stories to render different phases of their lives synchronous, bringing their youth and old age together into a single, coherent entity, and finding themselves to have been the same person throughout their life cycle.[7]

When I sat at my father's bedside after a stroke rendered his speech slow and halting, he shared a number of stories I had never heard in all the years before. Yet at one point he grew exasperated and tired and said simply, "It's all forgettable." I wanted to tell him, *No! It's not forgettable.* In truth, the stories he told me that day were among his most unforgettable stories—about the war and his relationship with my mom, among other things. Life's task is the validation of memory, and the passing on of memories. As one tweet put it, "We never know the true value of a moment until it becomes a memory."[8]

When she was a little girl, my daughter, Eliza, once described to me a scene she saw at a funeral in a local cemetery: "It was just a small crowd standing together in a large field." She inspired this rumination on memory:

A Small Circle of Umbrellas at a Funeral in the Rain

Just a small circle of umbrellas
Is all the black I need

Only those who loved me
Half enough to cry

Just a small crowd
Huddled helplessly in a large field
Nothing but memory
To umbrella my soul.

In her memoir *L Is for Lion*, Annie Lanzillotto recalls trying to re-create her grandmother's signature biscotti recipe: "I am doing this for my own communion with my mother, grandmother, and great-grandmother. To repeat with my hands the circular motions on the rolling board that I saw GranmaRose make for years. My hands were engaged in a sacred act of remembering."[9] Time, perhaps, is a circle, not a line.

Many memories are carried in minute physical actions. As my wife, Amanda, says, "When a loaf of bread is in a plastic bag and you lose the twister, you kind of twist the top and fold it over itself—and every time I do that I think of my friend Carol Connor's mother, who taught me how to do that. It's the tiniest thing." I think about my grandfather Harry every time I tie my tie with a Windsor knot. Or as Flash Rosenberg said about her mother, afflicted with dementia, "We laugh together as mom 'helps' me cook. And when she expertly peels a hard-boiled egg, she is content to remember what it feels like to know to do things, even though she may forget she just peeled that egg."

Memory provides "intimations of immortality" for loved ones still alive to remember. I came across these beautiful lines by Henry Scott Holland (1847–1918), who was Regius Professor of Divinity at the University of Oxford, in the program at a memorial for a friend. For Holland, the power of memory is so strong that friends and family, though separated by the wall of death, continue to communicate with one another unchanged.

Death is nothing at all. It does not count. I have only slipped away into the next room. Nothing has happened. Everything remains exactly as it was. I am I, and you are you, and the old life that we lived so fondly together is untouched, unchanged. Whatever we were to each other, that we are still. Call me by the old familiar name. Speak of me in the easy way which you always used. Put no difference into your tone. Wear no forced air of solemnity or sorrow. Laugh as we always laughed at the little jokes that we enjoyed together. Play, smile, think of me, pray for me. Let my name be ever the household word that it always was. Let it be spoken without an effort, without the ghost of a shadow upon it. Life means all that it ever meant. It is the same as it ever was. There is absolute and unbroken continuity. What is this death but a negligible accident?

It's hard to hold each beautiful moment in our minds for even a second before our thoughts move on. Taking solace from memory is not easy. And of course, not all memories are positive. A person who was neglected or abused as a child may continue to project these memories onto the present, perpetuating dysfunctional patterns. Sometimes we need to break away from these memories in order to live fully and happily in the present. No one wants to be haunted by ghosts.

Life, a friend joked, is a sexually transmitted disease, with a 100 percent mortality rate. Yet we need memory and story to cope with—if not to transcend—our own impermanence. Carl Jung spoke about the importance of story, especially for someone facing death: "A categorical question is being put to him, and he is under an obligation to answer it. To this end he ought to have a myth about death, for reason shows him nothing but the dark pit into which he is descending."[10]

We need memory and story to cope with—if not to transcend—our own impermanence.

In *The Broken Connection: On Death and the Continuity of Life*, the psychiatrist Robert Jay Lifton conceives of five ways in which we seek out continuity as mortal beings: through our children and family, cycles of nature, theology, ecstasy and transcendence, and creative works.[11]

The first step in creating that myth is to talk about it. Talking about death is not easy, which is why this chapter has more poems than the others. Everyone needs some kind of philosophy or mythology in the face of aging and death. Death shapes our search for meaning in life. It's hard to imagine what would become of stories and memories if we didn't age and die. Perhaps if death didn't exist, we would have had to invent it. That is, perhaps, where Lifton's "creative works" come in.

When I was in the ninth grade, our class published a literary magazine called *The Inkwell*. My classmate Alex Pludwinski sought to explain life and death in two wonderful short poems:

Life
Is a mystery
Its purpose beyond us
Its pitfalls before us
It's amusing, and abusing
And confusing

Death
Is a mystery pondered by all
It even mystified Saul
Some fear it, others revere it
But why cry, my friend
It comes to us all

Alex's lines have stayed with me all these years, during which time I have sought to put my own thoughts and feelings about mortality into words. As a child on a visit to a snake farm near São Paulo, I watched a snake hypnotize a frog that sat helplessly in front of it, frozen in place until it was eaten. Years later, I jotted down this poem about death as an irrevocable fact:

Narrow Passage

like a frog hypnotized by a snake
I approach death

haunted by the narrow passage
my body's painful

squeeze into the
cold womb of
earth

cramming through
the rat hole of death
toward my un-birth

Though it's undeniably dark, I find the poem consoling simply because it expresses the horror of death in words. All we can do as human beings is try to think our way toward, around, or through death's final thud—to figure out a way to live with the idea of dying. Our art is that thought process made visible.

Viola Allo, a Cameroonian-born poet, echoes these themes in her beautiful poem "Bodies, Flowerbeds: A Villanelle." Here is an excerpt.

We soften death into poems and stories.
The art of writing is just a way of wailing
for the earth, carved up, sculpted by bodies . . .

A poem or a story is an etching of memories,
dignity in the fragile face of loss. Soothing
the earth, carved up, engraved with bodies,
we hum together beside a bed of flowers.[12]

The poet Thomas Lynch notes that "grief is the tax we pay on our attachments."

"The quest for symbolic immortality," Lifton suggests, "is an aspect of being human."[13] Beyond "symbolic immortality," the insights of contemporary science suggest to me that our existence may be eternal in other ways. In March 1955, Einstein heard that his close friend and frequent sounding board, Michele Besso, had passed away in his eighties, shortly before Einstein. Einstein wrote a letter to Besso's

> **"The distinction between past, present and future is only a stubbornly persistent illusion."**

sister, which he ended this way: "Now he has departed from this strange world a little ahead of me. That means nothing. People like us, who believe in physics, know that the distinction between past, present and future is only a stubbornly persistent illusion."[14]

When Viktor Frankl writes about the Holocaust in *Man's Search for Meaning*, he echoes a parallel sentiment:

> Those things which seem to take meaning away from human life include not only suffering but dying as well. I never tire of saying that the only really transitory aspects of life are the potentialities; but as soon as they are actualized, they are rendered realities at that very moment; they are saved and delivered into the past, wherein they are rescued and preserved from transitoriness. For, in the past, nothing is not irretrievably lost but everything irrevocably stored.[15]

In order not to take ourselves too seriously, I joke with my lifelong friend Sol Reuben, a therapist, that everyone is entitled to their own cracker-barrel philosophy, as long as they don't seek to impose it on others. We call this principle "crackerbarrelism." This leads us to debate, for instance, his Buddhist perspective, which views the universe as a symphony without a conductor, versus my own point of view, in which each individual conducts his own symphony.

Contemporary science suggests that time is a fourth dimension. We can easily picture the three dimensions of length, width, and depth. If we are meeting someone in an office building, for instance, we need to give these three dimensions: two horizontal and one vertical dimension (the street, the cross-street, and the floor of the building), but we also need to give the time of the meeting. If we miss the meeting, we can go back to the same place, but never at the exact time and date. We find it more difficult to envision time as a dimension that we're moving through much as we move through space, partly because, from our vantage point as human beings, we move through chronological time at a fixed pace in only one direction. If we can bend our minds to picture that fourth dimension the same way we picture the other three, and to imagine we move through time the same way we move through space, it's easier to envision an eternal quality to our lives. Memory takes us partway because it enables us to access the past, to take us back to things remembered.

Kurt Vonnegut goes further in his novel *Slaughterhouse-Five*, in which the protagonist, Billy Pilgrim, becomes "unstuck in time."[16]

Our perceptions of time are built into our language, with its present, past, and future tenses. I tried to capture my own sense of this conundrum in a few lines I called "Ghosts of Future Past":

> Once
> At the juncture
> Of anticipation and memory
>
> A gesture, a smile, a kiss . . .
>
> Though it seems long gone
> What happened, is.

Here is how I picture this. Imagine you are traveling on a train at night, passing by a village with a row of houses in which all the lights are on. In front of these houses is a row of evenly spaced trees. As your train whizzes past the trees, it appears as if the lights of the houses are flickering on and off, as the trees block and then reveal them. From our position moving through time and space, it appears that people are born, die, and disappear forever: they flare up, flicker, and are extinguished. But if we imagine their lives as the lights in these houses, there is a sense in which they continue to shine clearly even though it doesn't appear that way as we move past them. We perceive time only because we are conscious observers moving through it. Recent experiments in what scientists have termed quantum entanglement have confirmed that time is a phenomenon that exists for internal observers but is absent for external observers of the universe. "Nothing other than a conscious observer registers the flow of time."[17] We are all granted a permanent place on the continuum of time.

A life, then, is a little like a photograph slipped into the recesses of time, retained in the DNA of the time continuum.

As the poet Mary Oliver writes, "I look upon time as no more than an idea, / and I consider eternity as another possibility."[18] Not surprisingly, many of my friends are skeptical of this view, including the poet Tsaurah Litzky, who wrote in her poem "Sour Milk," "I struggle against my anger at life, the ultimate bad joke, with the worst punch line—eternal darkness." Not necessarily. I jotted down these lines to sum up our disagreement:

> She said, *Your life means nothing once you're dead*
>
> He said, *No, it's written down*
> *inscribed onto the cosmos*
> *scrawled in the margins of time*
>
> She said, *But inaccessible to humankind*
>
> *Yet permanent, still there*
> *like a book*, I said
>
> She replied,
> *A book nobody reads*

Of course, if everybody read everybody else's "life books," they wouldn't have time for much else. Tsaurah, on receiving this poem, responded with some additional lines:

> written down
> inscribed in the cosmos, Ha!
> where in the cosmos can
> I find inscribed the lives
> of my dear mother and father?
> what language will their lives
> be written in?

Perhaps our lives remain present just as they happened, Tsaurah, in the same language as life. Sorry to say, there is no way to access them, trapped as we are in the human condition.

Yet for me, there are, as Wordsworth put it so well, "intimations of immortality" not only in our creative lives and memories but in the art we create. In stories and jokes and poems and visual art we find the clearest manifestations of the secular eternal. Medicine show doc Fred Bloodgood, a purveyor of magnificent hyperboles, put it this way: "I'll say that when the last grand cataclysm of Earth's disintegration resounds with thunderous cacophony, as bursting stars and blazing fragments go hissing into uncharted stratosphere, the medicine show will still live in our hearts forever."[19] I feel that way about poetry and art: even if the planet comes to a crashing, cataclysmic end, and all our creative works are destroyed by ice or fire, these structures of meaning and feeling embodied in poems and art will still continue to exist somewhere out there in the ether.

Often art seems to develop an agency of its own, apart from its creator. Once the idea for a poem zaps across the synapses of my own mind, the work seems to develop an independent will. As my friend the poet Bob Holman puts it, "Let the poem be what it wants to be. That's poetry's essence." This speaks to the way any work of art begins, with a thought, observation, or insight about the world, or one's experience in it, but harbors its own structure of meaning and feeling that determines what it will be. That structure is what enables it to resonate beyond its creator; in some sense it continues to exist this way, as its own entity, into eternity. As the Hawaiian storyteller Nyla Fujii-Babb puts it: "You don't own [stories] . . . the stories don't belong to us. They're not ours. They are, of themselves, their own entity."[20]

A member of my poetry group, Leigh Harrison, shared a piece she calls "Poetry as Spiritual Practice," which speaks to the way poetry and, in a sense, all of our artistic creations have a life of their own. Here is an excerpt:

> I wrote a poem of mourning
> The words wept fitfully for me
> The tears became syllables of gold
> in a chain of grief
>
> I wrote a poem of acceptance
> Gave the lyric free rein to be
> Told the lines: *assume any form,*
> let them breathe peace deeply
>
> The poem meditated in familiar yoga positions,
> folding gracefully into its own silence

Art collapses time in such a way that you can think about a song or a poem, a play or a novel, in a single thought, just as you would glance at a painting: *Hamlet* and the *Mona Lisa* can, in this sense, hang side by side on the wall. In a letter to his father, Mozart explained how once he had completed a piece, he would "survey it like a fine picture, a beautiful statue, at a glance. Nor do I hear in my imagination the parts successively, but I hear them as it were, all at once."[21]

Poems and stories, written or told, seem to me to be units of meaning, like the atom or the molecule. Just as human cells do, they contain something like the DNA of their creators. When considered in this way, poems appear to push back the boundaries of mortality. They weave "the threads of temporality into the fabric of eternity," as the Jewish theologian Abraham Joshua Heschel writes.[22]

John Berger, philosophizing on the universe from a similar vantage point, expresses it this way:

> If poetry sometimes speaks of its own immortality, the claim is more far-reaching than that of the genius of a particular poet in a particular cultural history. Immortality here should be distinguished from posthumous fame. Poetry can speak of immortality because it abandons itself to language, in the belief that language embraces all experience, past, present, and future. . . .
>
> Poetry can repair no loss but it defies the space which separates. And it does this by its continual labor of reassembling what has been scattered. . . . Apart from reassembling by metaphor, poetry reunites by its reach. It equates the reach of a feeling with the reach of the universe.[23]

Are the ideas of poets and artists who address eternity parallel to the proofs of scientists? Are these poetic ideas about the nature of time actually etched onto the physical universe? Is it inconsistent to jump from Proust's conception of the "eternal now," or the Brazilian poet Vinicius de Moraes's wonderful line "infinite while it lasts," to Einstein's idea that "the distinction of past, present and future is only an illusion"? It's as if I were looking down a set of railroad tracks. On one track are the insights of scientists about the illusive nature of time; on the other are the thoughts and dreams of poets with their intimations of immortality. As I gaze into the distance, the two tracks seem to run together as if they were joined and ran on like that forever as they faded toward the horizon, proof that our lives are both poetic and eternal. But I have to admit that beyond the vanishing point of the horizon, the two tracks may continue to run on apart. Perhaps the "human unit of time" and generational memory that I wrote about earlier in the book are indeed the best we have to look forward to on this side of the grave.

On the seventh day, perhaps God didn't rest but instead, having already created planets and stars, trees, animals, and human beings, he or she lay back and spun the gossamer-thin structures of meaning. Perhaps weaving the warp and woof of sense and sensibility proved to be a good way to spend a day of rest. And perhaps as a result the universe became replete not only with Adam and Eve and their offspring, with the fish of the sea and the fowl of the air, but also with an impulse toward the poetry, music, and art that would one day fill the planet. Perhaps God created beauty on this day of rest. Perhaps that day of leisure was the day he or she chose to imagine, to dream. Perhaps on the seventh day God created our ability to perceive and enjoy the poetry of everyday life.

> On the seventh day, perhaps God didn't rest but instead, having already created planets and stars, trees, animals, and human beings, he or she lay back and spun the gossamer-thin structures of meaning.

My friend the writer Marc Kaminsky disagrees: "You see, Steve, on the third day, the Torah says, 'God caused to grow every tree that was pleasing to the sight and good for food.' So the aesthetics were already in play. Even when he first created light, he saw that it was 'Good.' So God created beauty from the start." Remarkably, it appears that the Divine Spirit not only put us on the earth but provided us with the consciousness to own it, express it, re-create it in our own image.

Although many believe in heaven and hell as part of a divinely created universe, for me they are among those structures of meaning that humans themselves conceived: grand religious ideas with endless artistic elaborations that enable those who believe in God—and those who don't—to imagine eternity. I can remember the moment in my childhood when I was about ten years old, sitting between my mother and father in the front seat of our Studebaker, when I had the realization that I could not believe in a creator who would form humankind in order to have someone to pray to Him or Her and use that act, in part, as the basis for whether or not to let a person into heaven. It's always been easier for me to imagine that humans received the capacity for artistic expression for the purpose of creating meaning, and that creating meaning—or finding the meaning already present in the universe—is our God-given task. To paraphrase the Jewish Talmud, you are not able to complete the act of creation, but you are not free to abstain from it either.

The harshest critic of my sometimes overly buoyant credos is Marc Kaminsky. Addressing me in the third person (as it is appropriate for the critic to do), Marc once wrote in the margins of an early draft of this chapter: "Zeitlin tightly equates spirit with the eternal, and the eternal as indestructible—a thoroughly Western conception. He conflates the experience of the eternal with its literalization as described in scientific concepts. Spirit can also be seen as Tao, as a force moving through the universe continually. For me Zeitlin's fallacy is to equate eternity with permanence (very Western). In the east in Taoism and Buddhism eternity is associated with impermanence, with Yin Yang alternations of creation and destruction moving through the endlessness of time." Ultimately, Marc rephrased my ideas in a way that made sense to him: "The artist's secular sphere of spirituality occurs at the intersection of time and timelessness. Our goal is not a denial of death, but to hold eternity and death in a single thought." The artist's secular sphere of spirituality has always been my home address.

Amen, Marc.

Part V POETRY IN YOU

18

God Is in the Details

Your Ur-Poem, Your Place Moments

One does not possess one's past as one possesses a thing one
can hold and turn in one's hand, inspecting every side of it. . . .
In order to possess it I must bind it to existence by a project.
—JEAN-PAUL SARTRE

All these places have their moments
—JOHN LENNON AND PAUL MCCARTNEY

Hovie Burgess, a renowned juggler, once told me that when he
teaches his classes in circus arts at New York University, he has students
say their names and then balance a pole on their index finger. From the
way the pole teeters and tips on each one's finger, he can remember
their names.

For my course called Writing New York Stories, which I taught for
more than ten years at Cooper Union, I developed my own approach to
remembering my students' names: I had everyone write, in class, a "list
poem" in which each line began "I am from . . ." The poem that spawned
this wonderful assignment is by Kentucky-born poet and children's
book writer George Ella Lyon. An excerpt:

> I am from clothespins,
> from Clorox and carbon-tetrachloride.
> I am from dirt under the back porch . . .
>
> I'm from fudge and eyeglasses,
>   from Imogene and Alafair.
> I'm from the know-it-alls
>   and the pass-it-ons,
> from Perk up! and Pipe down!

I'm from He restoreth my soul
　　with a cottonball lamb
　　and ten verses I can say myself.[1]

Exquisitely selected details and phrases reveal worlds about Lyon's rural family, their language, and their homespun religion. "My poem," she wrote to me, "started with a poem by Jo Carson, included in her book *Stories I Ain't Told Nobody Yet*, and *her* poem started with something she heard someone say, so it's all about handing something on. It's like sourdough starter."

"I am from . . ." poems are ur-poems: everyone has one in them, and if you don't write yours down, it remains locked in pure potentiality.

In their "I am from . . ." assignments, my students revealed their distinctive origins and backgrounds, evoked in resonant details. Before I gave this assignment, we went around the room and they all spoke a little about where they were from, how they made a living, and why they were taking the class. Then they wrote. When they read their poems aloud, the class was invariably astounded by how much more the poems revealed about each person than their initial introductions. "I am from . . ." poems are ur-poems: everyone has one in them, and if you don't write yours down, it remains locked in pure potentiality.

Alicia Vasquez, from Brooklyn, wrote:

I am from ducking bullets by the bedroom window with Mom in
　　1974 where a tree grows in Crown Heights, Brooklyn.
I am from controlling the flow of fire hydrant water through a can
　　of Chef Boyardee while dreaming of swimming in a real pool
　　one day.
I am from waiting for Mister Softee's beautiful symphony.
I am from listening to Cuban beats and salsa picante rhythms
　　on a transistor radio while camping out on someone
　　else's car.
I am from the old school when marshmallow shoes and bell-bottom
　　pants ruled the streets and Pro-Keds sneakers dangled from
　　wires above the block.

I am from the cheese line at Kings County Hospital and waiting on
line for a free summer meal.
I am from getting beat up in the girls' bathroom at Public School
221 when I was the only Spanish girl there.

From the suburbs, Caitlin Van Dusen wrote:

I am from early winter mornings waiting for the bus at the end of the
long driveway in the dark, gusts from the heater vent and the
rising, silvered world outside, the hiss and puff of my father's pipe,
curls of sweet smoke mixing with heated air, watching for the
reliable yellow lights to round the bend.

Ellia Bisker wrote about her Jewish upbringing:

I am from a bar or bat mitzvah every weekend and that awful naked
feeling of chilly pantyhose at thirteen, inexpert makeup, braces
for years and years before I was pretty.

A teacher whom my wife, Amanda, worked with in Louisiana described
her rural experience:

I am from the death scent of wild rabbit, dove, and quail in my
father's hunting vest.

Tracylyn John-Howell, a student from Tobago, wrote:

I am di Bake and Saltfish, Crab and Dumplin, Calaloo and Pong
Plantin
Coconut Jelly, Mango Chutney and Tamarine balls
all sold when the island have Boat Racin'.

Or from a student at the Yeshivah of Flatbush high school:

I am from technology
the microprocessor as a gateway to life.

From Stacy Morrison's fragile spirit:

I am from porcelain figurines . . . too close to the edge of the
table.

Some poems encapsulate family dramas. Richard Storm:

I am from my mother's chatter and my father's silence.

And Barbara Rothman, who ended her poem:

I am from longing. I am from loving. I am from leaving.

"I am from . . ." poems speak to the way we can dip into our own past tense to reveal how it has shaped who we are. We are grounded in our particularities. Folklore is always thought of as shared humor, shared stories, a common culture—but there is a folklore of one's own self as well, a knot of mythmaking lurking in our souls, threaded with details that the act of writing this particular poem can begin to unravel.

Many years ago our family visited the University of Mississippi on a tour of Delta blues sites and stumbled into a talk by Nikki Giovanni. Amanda remembers hearing her read her prose poem "What We Miss," which describes the rush of black mothers and aunts getting ready for church: "We miss the old fan oscillating and the grunt of the girdle resisting its chore, the smell of Dixie Peach waiting while the iron heats to do its touch-up . . . we will miss the click of heels on the sidewalk as they hurried off proud angry determined."[2] Like the "I am from . . ." exercise, the "What I miss . . ." prompt might be another way to jump-start your writing.

Now it's your turn. Take twenty minutes. Start every line with "I am from . . ." Do not edit yourself before the text is committed to paper. Finish writing first.

I am from . . . these words. God is in the details—so are you.

Place Moments

You are also steeped in particular places, places in time. "Unwittingly, I have turned into a student of light," writes *New York Times* reporter Somini Sengupta. "The August light that envelops the beaten-down old streets of Red Hook, I have learned, is more melancholy than the morning light during lilac season in the Brooklyn Botanic Garden. The sun sparkling on the crown of the Chrysler Building is whimsical, like a woman dressed for a party at high noon."[3]

Lawyer Stephanie Nilva described the way "on most days my city protects herself from the sun. But for those few days when the sun lines up with the crosstown streets, she rests like an ice cube in a glass to the west." One spring evening, City Lore's inveterate blogger, Caitlin Van Dusen, sought out "Manhattanhenge," a twice-yearly phenomenon that occurs when the setting sun aligns directly with the east–west street grid: "I had heard that the ideal spot for viewing Manhattanhenge was Tudor City Place, a tiny thoroughfare between First and Second Avenues whose virtually traffic-free overpass directly above Forty-Second Street offers an unobstructed view west across the island. At 8:17 p.m., the sun slid into full, blinding view, limning the edges of buildings and casting the Hyatt hotel flag, a fire escape, and even the Chrysler building's fierce plumage into shadow."[4]

Each semester I asked my students at Cooper Union to jot down their ten favorite places. I asked for "place moments," the way the places they selected existed for each of them at a particular moment in time. I also asked some wonderful folklorists and journalists to send us descriptions of their ten favorite places, homing in on the qualities that transform space into place. The writer Cara da Silva described not just the steeple of Trinity Church but "the way light plays on it at sunset; not just the Cloisters, but its medieval garden on a summer day, when, for the imaginative, the aroma of its plants can turn the clock back six hundred years."[5]

I asked for "place moments," the way the places they selected existed for each of them at a particular moment in time.

"There is a tree on East Seventieth Street between Park and Lexington Avenues rooted in front of a cream-colored Victorian mansion," wrote Susan Sorenson. "I always walk home via East Seventieth, stopping to remember being kissed beneath the tree one midnight when street noise gave way to an indigo air solely resplendent with windy sighs of springtime leaves."

"There is a tree on East Seventieth Street" could be the beginning of the first line of a novel. In fact, these place moments often read as if

Figure 5. Manhattanhenge. Photo by Caitlin Van Dusen.

each were a touchstone for a longer story about how the writer arrived at a particular place in time.

Robert J. Flynn wrote of "Kissena Park and the old Chinese ladies who do their tai chi ballet at dawn, listening to an inner music that cannot be resisted. Set against the ancient Asian flowering dogwoods in April, they bloom and bend to salute an inner spring."

And Jill Bressler recalled "the Coney Island boardwalk on a cold November day, when a bundled few seek their solace by the shore while they stroll silently down the wooden path, past concession stands and amusement rides that have been put to bed until summer. Once I listened to a man play his trumpet to the waves." I imagine a recurring image for a feature film.

I was first struck by the concept of "place moments" almost two decades ago, when folklorist Barbara Kirshenblatt-Gimblett shared with me a list of her favorite New York City places. She wrote of "watching bakers at the D&G Bakery slide loaves shaped by hand into a turn-of-the-century coal-fired brick oven in a tenement basement on Mulberry Street at midnight."[6]

Expansive place moments extend over time. My student Jacquelyn Coffee wrote about the years when she lived in the Chelsea Hotel: "The Victorian Gothic flophouse will always embody the pure essence of New York for me. Its status in my personal pantheon is insurmountable. It has no competitors because, you see, I pissed away the most bacchanalian ten years of my youth at the Chelsea in room 505. No excuses. No regrets (except for the cat)."

Even eras in New York assume the quality of place moments. In his memoir *Kafka Was the Rage*, Anatole Broyard writes about Greenwich Village after the Second World War. "Nineteen forty-six was a good time—perhaps the best time—in the twentieth century. The war was over, the Depression had ended, and everyone was rediscovering simple pleasures. A war is like an illness and when it's over you think you've never felt so well. . . Though much of the Village was shabby, I didn't mind. I thought all character was a form of shabbiness, a wearing away of surfaces. . . . I was twenty-six, and sadness was a stimulant, even an aphrodisiac."[7] You had to be exactly twenty-six in 1946 to fully appreciate the scene. The age and the era coincided. As singer-songwriter Jackson Browne sang, "In sixty-nine I was twenty one and I called the road my own."[8]

Details are what convey a sense of place, as do the layers of history and lore and perceptions that make up what philosopher Edward Casey calls "place memory."[9] Those moments, if they can be expressed in words—and perhaps even if they can't—are part of the poetry of everyday life. Writing about a place at a certain point in time, teasing out the details that defined the experience of being there then, is a way to practice writing about larger swatches of life that might eventually grow into a novel or work of nonfiction.

Personal experiences transform space into place. As expressive beings, we can create symmetry between places we have known and the interior spaces in our lives, and by writing, painting, create a scaffolding for the soul.

The value of places, perhaps, should be measured by the sum total of the place moments that take place within them and are committed to memory. The adventurer Beryl Markham writes about moving into a new house and that, sometimes, there are not enough lived experiences or place moments to make a site meaningful. "The walls of my house are without memories, or secrets, or laughter. Not enough of life has been breathed into them—their warmth is artificial; too few hands have turned the window latches, too few feet have trod the thresholds. The boards of the floor, self-conscious as youth or falsely proud as the newly rich, have not yet unlimbered enough to utter a single cordial creak. In time they will, but not for me."[10]

The places we care about are baskets that hold the perishable fruits of memory and experience. Take a notebook out to the places that you love, those places that are lush with low-hanging fruit. The moments when you encounter them mark the times when the experience is ripe for you. Savor them.

19

Breath on the Mirror

Finding Your Own Voice

Never using a stuntman,
I went through this life myself
—Harvey Shapiro

Who in the world am I? Ah, that's the great puzzle!
—C. S. Lewis

Ever since college, I have begun my days sitting in an armchair, writing poetry. Decades ago I tapped the keys of an old Olympia typewriter. Today I hold a laptop on my knees. I consider it a form of centering, looking into a different kind of mirror—not to comb my hair, but to remind myself of who I am. Writing gives me intrinsic pleasure; the hours I spend are their own reward.

In old film noirs, the cops often hold a mirror to the mouth of crime victims to find out whether they are still breathing. My own breath on the mirror lets me know I am. Nevertheless, sitting down to write each day is not always easy or pleasant. One of my students, Anna Zucker, wrote about sitting in front of a computer, as I do, but was less effusive about the results:

> There is a computer resting precariously on an unsanded wooden board, itself fitting precariously over two broken filing cabinets. The contraption serves as the writer's desk. Surrounding the sticky keyboard are seven half-full cups of cold, fermenting coffee, eleven almost-empty glasses of evaporating water, and one jar of peanut butter with a spoon. These serve as the writer's sustenance. There is a small gray kitten napping on a pile of unlaundered clothing spread out over the sofa, periodically waking to rub its head on something hard.

This is the writer's muse. There are three short sentences typed in small black letters on the ugly, glaring white screen of the monitor—that would be the writer's work.

The aim of my creative writing class is always for the students to develop one or more pieces in which they can express and discern their own distinctive voice, to encourage each of them to cast a true reflection of himself or herself onto the page. Students experiment with fiction and nonfiction, poetry and prose. Some of my students write songs; others develop one-person shows. The students learn that even if they are writing about something far outside themselves, it is still a reflection of who they are and how they interpret what they see. A portrait will always resemble the painter as well as the sitter. Painting, writing, even taking a photograph of what you are seeing in the world around you is a way of internalizing it, making it your own.

In my class, students are asked to write about an experience in the New York City subway. Jim Pignetti, who was in my very first class, responded with an essay that immediately established his distinctive voice:

Applause . . . Applause . . . (well, imagined applause) . . . Flawlessly executed . . . Very well done . . . Excellent . . . Excellent.
There was no applause . . . I imagined applause. Later . . . Now I imagine applause . . .
The inky dark. A kind of creamy inky dark. Different from other darks that one feels in the subways of New York. A blend of soot and dirt, and the eternal grindings spewed by the screeching and clanking of metal wheels on metal track. The glow of numberless incandescent light bulbs resolutely resisted by hard ceramic tiles, everything annoying in their repetition. Brooklyn in February.
This was the G train, the crosstown G local, Brooklyn to Queens, never touching the elite sub-soils of the great isle of Manahatta . . . returning home from night classes at Pratt Institute, with the sad sequence of stations: Willoughby, Bedford, Lorimer, Greenpoint, Courthouse Square, Queens Plaza, Steinway . . .
Across from me, seated by the door, another student, female, attractive, unknown to me, but, like me, diligent . . . going home to Mom, or Hubby . . . but at this moment, we're a pair, both of us clad in our standard New York armor . . . more secure in our partnership,

our eyes never meeting . . . informally mated in this metal box, zipping along . . . united in our fears and aspirations . . . whether acknowledged or not.

I don't remember which station—one of the stations in the creamy dark—one of the stations in the monotonous succession of stations in the dark. . . . the doors open . . . no one gets off . . . no one gets on . . . the doors linger for a few seconds. I'm looking at my partner. I'm reviewing the cut of her armor, the flare of her calf, the rise of her breast, the gold necklace resting there . . . I'm imagining the scent that lies behind her ear and floats in the little hairs at the border of scalp and skin. . . . I'm lost in a sensuous reverie, entangled in an erotic etching cut into her breastplate.

Suddenly! At the very second the doors begin to close—as if orchestrated—as if practiced a thousand times, perfected nightly at this very spot . . .

A gasp sounds from her throat, her hand flies up to her neck, her elbow a perfect hinge! Her necklace has disappeared! It's gone! Vanished! Otherwise she does not move . . . the doors close. The train jerks into movement . . . I observe. There's nothing to do . . . the train accelerates into the creamy darkness.

The thief's hand reached in, timed with the closing of the doors . . . totally unseen. He snared the necklace with an obviously fine hand from beyond the door, calculating its exact location. He levied not a scratch.

The train rattles on . . . my jaw gapes. Into the creamy, inky dark. There was no applause.

Jim directs a company called Metalmen, which specializes in distributing specialized metals to scientists and manufacturers. He went on to found the poetry group Brevitas with me and became a frequently anthologized poet. I've always thought that Jim writes in a distinctive masculine tone that mirrors, perhaps, the way he bends and cuts aluminum and steel in his factory.

Another student of mine, Donald Semenza, grew up in the mob-run Italian social clubs on the Lower East Side. He speaks tough-guy New York City English but has a smile that reveals his kind, gentle nature. His poem, called "The Line," captures his voice perfectly:

Back then it was the line
The line was everything back then

We walked up the line
Waited for the bookmaker to get off the line
To give us the line
5½ – 6½ – pick-em – 8½ – 9½
We put our money on the line
We bet the games with the red line
The blue line, the foul line, the goal line, the 50 yard line, the
    finish line
We spoke the line back then
Our line had all the answers
It was the wise guys' line not the wise man's line . . .
We watched Mantle, Mays and Snyder spray line drives between
    the lines
There was no place for Euclid's geometric lines
Shakespeare's poetic lines
Mozart's lyrical lines
Picasso's abstract lines
We had Sinatra lines
So Deep In My Heart, Witchcraft, That Wicked Witchcraft
Nat Cole lines
Mona Lisa, Mona Lisa –Slam, Bam, Alakazam
We stood on line, not in line
With the date, the girl, the chick, the babe
We watched Bogart deliver his lines
The stuff dreams are made of . . .
We fed the date, the girl, the chick, the babe
The line
Fed the boss the line
Wound up on the unemployment line
Finally some of us crossed the line
We left the subculture
We became citizens
We strive to improve our line of thinking
Sucking up information on line not in line
We read the editorial lines
The New York Times, The Wall Street Journal . . .
Wait
I hear it
It's haunting me
It's Yogi's line

It's déjà vu all over again
5½ – 6½ – pick-em – 8½ – 9½
How about that

As my students endeavor to find their own voice, I often share the work of famous writers whose voice is embedded in their sentence structure and is immediately recognizable; for instance, the first lines from Joan Didion's classic essay "Goodbye to All That": "When I first saw New York I was twenty, and it was summertime, and I got off a DC-7 at the old Idlewild temporary terminal in a new dress which had seemed very smart in Sacramento but seemed less smart already, even in the old Idlewild temporary terminal, and the warm air smelled of mildew and some instinct, programmed by all the movies I had ever seen and all the songs I had ever read about New York, informed me that I would never be quite the same again."[1] In the way she strings this sentence together, Didion captures all the nervousness and hopefulness of a young adult on her first big journey.

As another example of fine writing that, like Didion's essay, speaks to the theme of self-discovery, I frequently offer this example, from the first chapter of Edith Wharton's autobiography, *A Backward Glance*. She describes walking with her father down Fifth Avenue, past low brownstones broken up by fenced-in plots where cows were still pastured:

On Sundays after church the fashionable of various denominations paraded there on foot, in gathered satin bonnets and tall hats; but at other times [Fifth Avenue] presented long stretches of empty pavement, so that the little girl, advancing at her father's side, was able to see at a considerable distance the approach of another pair of legs, not as long but considerably stockier than her father's. The little girl was so very little that she never got much higher than the knees in her survey of grown-up people, and would not have known, if her father had not told her, that the approaching legs belonged to his cousin Henry. The news was very interesting, because in attendance on Cousin Henry was a small person, no bigger than herself, who must obviously be Cousin Henry's little boy Daniel, and therefore somehow belong to the little girl. So when the tall legs and the stocky ones halted for a talk, which took place somewhere high up in the air, and the small Daniel and Edith found themselves face to face close to the pavement, the little girl peered with interest at the little boy through the white woolen mist over her face. The little boy, who was very round and rosy, looked back with equal interest; and suddenly he put out a chubby hand, lifted the little girl's veil, and boldly planted a kiss on her cheek. It was the first time—and the little girl found it very pleasant.

This is my earliest definite memory of anything happening to me; and it will be seen that I was wakened to conscious life by the two tremendous forces of love and vanity.[2]

To convey her preconscious girlhood self, Wharton begins this passage in the third person and moves to the first person as she discovers her newfound consciousness. The passage, which tells a coming-of-age story in just a few lines, never fails to amaze and inspire my students.

I also share with them Antigua-born Jamaica Kincaid's short story "Life in the City: Putting Myself Together." I point out her sexy last paragraph, which captures the wackiness of uninhibited youth—and its fleetingness:

One year, I created a Halloween costume for myself by buying a dozen and a half bananas made of plastic (the sort used in some homes as a centerpiece for the dining table), stringing them together so that they made a skirt of sorts, and then tying the whole thing around my waist. I wore nothing underneath, had nothing to cover the rest of my body except an old fur coat that I had bought in an old-fur-coat store for thirty dollars. When I arrived at the party, of course, I removed the coat. The hair on the other parts of my body was not the same color as the hair on my head. I wore no hat to conceal this; it was not a detail that concerned me. And the evening passed, joining the other long evenings that were so exhausting to fill. What did I want? Did I know? I was twenty-five, I was twenty-six, I was twenty-seven, I was twenty-eight. At thirty, I was married.[3]

I tell my students to follow their passions and study what they care about, formally or informally, till they internalize the subject and can use this vantage point to express themselves. I decided to study folklore on a lark, but over the years I internalized the subject matter till I got to the point where I didn't write only *about* folklore; I wrote *from* it, and it gradually helped to shape my perspective on the world. In my classes, I work with the students individually to determine what each one's passions might be. Writing about or doing a project about people or places is a way of communing with them, making them a part of you.

People who write often do it because they are driven to: it's where their minds want to go. My creative writing teacher in grad school once told me that he far preferred my short stories to my poems. But that wasn't where my mind wanted to go. After his class, I never wrote another short story, but my poems, which I felt were the truest expression of myself, became a lifelong avocation. Writing enables me to tease out the meanings in the world around me, to see what's behind things. It enlarges me.[4] As Brenda Ueland says in *If You Want to Write: A Book about Art, Independence and Spirit*, "By painting the sky, Van Gogh was really able to see it and adore it better than if he had just looked at it."[5]

I also encourage my students to look for moments when their own life stories intersect with a larger history. One student developed a story about jumping over a fence one night at her boarding school circa 1964 and escaping to see a Beatles concert. Jiří Boudník, a student from the former Czechoslovakia, and who initially didn't speak English, wrote about meeting an American girl for the first time and summoning the only words he knew: "I love you yeah yeah yeah." The associations of both stories with the Beatles made them resonate for the class.

Creative inspiration, for me, is about being in the zone. When I seek to understand my own creative process, it has to do with the way I lock experience into poetic form. Generally, two ideas from disparate occurrences collide to spark an idea for a poem, a story, or a song. Something has to happen outside your head for anything to happen inside.[6] In order for disparate ideas to meet in this way, the brain has to be in a place where it can experience and conceive of new things. Often my best ideas are spawned when I'm traveling or meeting new people.

When Amanda and I re-created a historic mid-twentieth-century American tent show some years ago for the American Talkers program at the Smithsonian Folklife Festival, among the acts was a troupe of old-time magicians who created the illusion of sawing a woman in half.

A few years later, when Benh and Eliza were born, both by cesarean section, my memory of their sawing the woman in two collided in my mind with their births, and then again years later with a question Benh asked me as a young boy. From the collision of images, a poem was born:

When they sawed Amanda in half
And pulled a rabbit from the hat

The magician said,
"It's a boy, it's a beautiful boy,"

Who five years later asked his dad,
"If it's a trick,
Is there no such thing as magic?

Only tricksters, no magicians?"
And can it be that life
Is all we know of miracles?

I see this crashing together of two disparate ideas in the work of other writers as well. The poet Billy Collins includes an inscription from an article about printing at the start of his wonderful poem "Flock": "It has been calculated that each copy of the Gutenberg Bible . . . required the skins of 300 sheep."

I can see them squeezed into the holding pen
behind the stone building
where the printing press is housed,

all of them squirming around
to find a little room
and looking so much alike

it would be nearly impossible
to count them,
and there is no telling

which one will carry the news
that the Lord is a shepherd,
one of the few things they already know.[7]

In this masterly short poem, I can imagine his eureka moment when a stray line with an obscure fact from an article relating to the Gutenberg

Bible came together with "the Lord is my shepherd" and an image of sheep. By taking disparate images and creating a poem that seamlessly weaves them together, the poet, perhaps, repairs a small tear in the universe.

Other artists talk about many different ways that inspiration comes to them. Tom Waits told an interviewer that some songs come as a dream through a straw, while others are like pieces of gum you find on the bottom of chairs and put together to make something.[8]

No need to be afraid of yourself when you write, I tell my students. Do it freely and recklessly. You can put on your makeup and fix your hair later, but you need to cast the true reflection first. Make sure that whatever's in you pours out onto the page before you start to judge what you see. And don't feel that you need to have your whole piece thought through before you start. Writing has been compared to driving at night: you don't need to be able to see too far beyond the road right in front of you.

"Tell all the truth but tell it slant," Emily Dickinson wrote. Let the quirkiness of your mind spill out onto the page. Most of us do not have minds as quirky and offbeat as e.e. cummings, Bob Dylan, or Emily herself had. But surprise yourself with what's inside. Tease it out. As Robert Frost once said, "No surprise for the writer, no surprise for the reader." Set down incongruous scenes or images and then, as you edit, try to figure out what holds them together.

In the twentieth century, poets moved toward free verse and away from rhythm and rhyme. More recently, songwriters and rap artists have moved away from perfect rhymes toward off rhymes or away from rhyme altogether. Regardless of the trends, write to your own aesthetic.

Regardless of the trends, write to your own aesthetic.

The editing process can also help you find your voice. Once you have something on paper, you need to free the angel from the stone. Cut away the things that are not written in your own voice or that haven't come out of what you truly know. I once described editing as a kind of "striptease":

Strip the poem down to bare essentials
Tease it into being

Discard the falsies and the bustier
Let the fake fur fall to floor
Strip off all that's crude

Let the words bump and grind
Not even pasties and a G-string
When you're through

The poem stripped, stands nude
You stand naked
Brood

I've always considered myself lucky to enjoy reading and rereading my own work. In 2002, soon after I published a volume of poetry, my friend Marge Hahn approached me and said, "Steve, I can't believe it. I was on the subway and I saw someone sitting at the other end of the car reading a book—and it was your book of poetry. I was amazed. That's so great, I thought. Some random person on the subway is reading Steve's book. Then I noticed it was you!" I feel as if, like many a poet, I will be revising my poems on my deathbed.

Writing has enabled me to look into the deeper parts of myself. It's enabled me to create a mythical self, a self outside myself that I can gaze at as if it were a cloud of breath visible on a cold day. "And there was a new voice," the poet Mary Oliver writes,

which you slowly
recognized as your own,
that kept you company
as you strode deeper and deeper
into the world[9]

The scribbled page and the painted canvas, your creations, act as both a window and a mirror. They reflect your own self back to you, but they are also the window through which others can see and appreciate your deepest self.[10] My friend Audrey Kindred who teaches at the Ethics For Children program at New York Society for Ethical Culture sees them, too, as reflector that bounces between what she calls "the infinite inner and the infinite outer"—in other words, self and universe. Using a children's book I wrote decades ago, *The Four Corners of the Sky*, she tells her students about ancient cosmologies in order for them to contemplate their own cosmologies. In my book I describe the Desana Indians of the Amazon who believe the brain is split in two halves, with the divide consisting of two entwined snakes, a dark-colored female anaconda and a brightly colored male rainbow boa. Their sky, too, is divided in half, with the Milky Way appearing as a white band in the sky splitting the two hemispheres; the brain is thus the mirror image of the universe. "Create your own cosmology," Audrey tells her students. As one of Audrey's young students closed his eyes to envision his own cosmology, he described his experience as entering "the solar system of my mind."

Julius Sokolsky, whom Amanda and I interviewed for our book *City Play*, was about ten years old when traffic lights were being installed in the Bronx. There was a short period when the light posts were up but the electricity hadn't yet been turned on. Julius and his friends came up with the idea of taking a mirror and reflecting the sun onto the stoplights to "light up" the red or green lights. During these precious few days, they made the neighborhood cars stop and go with giddy delight.[11]

As Julius did with his mirror, perhaps you can use the "mirror" of the written page or the canvas to move the cars of fortune and fame as you will. If you're talented and lucky, people will respond to your work and you will be able to offer your vision to the world, and perhaps even earn your living from it.

But sending your work into the world requires a different mind-set, which I discuss in the next chapter. The first task is to keep writing—and eventually editing—until it feels like an expression of your true self. When will you be certain? When you see your breath on the mirror.

20

The Best Stories versus My Story

Shepherding the Word into the World

You can lead a horse to water but you can't make it drink.
—TRADITIONAL SAYING

As a student at Rhode Island School of Design, my daughter, Eliza, took spoons, nails, and coins—an array of small metal objects—and laid them on the train tracks that run through Providence. She hid in the bushes a few hundred yards away and waited for the oncoming train to press them into shape. Then she rescued the now flat metal amulets from the tracks. The pieces were later fitted into a scouting manual from the 1930s, found at a used-book store, Riverrun, in our hometown of Hastings, New York. She carved niches in the worn, stuck-together pages for each of the flattened pieces of metal. She then assembled a remarkable art book with these embedded amulets. Amanda and I were smitten with this amazing altered art book. "Eliza," we told her, "this is such a great idea. You should make more of these books and sell them. You should do an exhibit."

"You know what my idea is for this?" she said. "My idea is to take the book and put it back on the shelf of the used-book store where I got it, and hope that someday someone will come along, pick that book off the shelf, and just discover it."

My own work as a folklorist has much in common with my daughter's altered book. In my quest to spend my life doing something that strives toward the unique and beautiful, I have produced or coproduced a series of documentaries on (among other topics) the traveling medicine shows of the 1920s and 1930s, girls' hand-clapping games, the Erie Canal, an ancient African epic, and family home movies. These out-of-the-way subjects were never destined for the mainstream. My hope is that, over time, there will always be individuals who become intrigued or fascinated by these subjects, and that they will find their way to these films.

Not long ago a woman came into my office to talk about the issues street performers were having with the authorities in Rome. She goes by the name of Ann Taps, and she sings old favorites like "Stormy Weather" and "The Sunny Side of the Street" on the Piazza Navona in Rome with her dog, Ginger, and sets out a hat with a sign that says "*Grazie.*" At age sixty, she is exhilarated each day that she can dance. "There are much better dancers and much better singers, but no one does what I do." She was visiting me as she prepared to have some serious surgery on her feet. She showed me the X-rays, which were a surrealistic, almost beautiful array of twisted and cracked toes from so many years of dancing on concrete. She was fully prepared for whatever might happen. "They can't take that away," she sang to me, referring to her dancing days. She left me with a beautiful image for life itself—an aging artist dancing on broken feet.

Not all artists approach their art in quite this philosophical way. Among the students in my class at Cooper Union was a gentleman who drove to class in a Cadillac from north Jersey. He had to bring the Cadillac because, as he explained to the class, his daughter had recently wrecked his Mercedes. The pieces he wrote for the course chronicled breaking arms and legs to collect debts for his friends in one of the long-standing Italian mobs. The violence matched that in the novels of Mario Puzo and the *Godfather* films, but with little of the artfulness.

The class that semester was being taught in the clock tower at Cooper Union, which looks out over Astor Place. One evening, on the balcony during one of the breaks, he cornered me below the clock and asked, "Steve, is there any money in this for me?" I stammered a bit. Then I told him that, in fact, I could not promise that his book would make him rich. In fact, I couldn't promise him that his book would make any money at all. He never appeared in class again.

Another student, a talented writer, once showed me his novel and told me that it was as good as anything F. Scott Fitzgerald ever wrote. The class always created a space apart, with a thin membrane covering and insulating us. Students felt safe and appreciated inside the bubble, even in the face of strong criticism. Overall, the students were amazed by one another's talents, and this student in particular wrote some wonderful pieces. But in real life, I can only smile when I wonder about the comparison. After a long dormant spell, he had started to write again at age sixty, and he did not have any connections to the literary world. Publishing is not what it was in the 1920s, and even if he had been every bit as good as Fitzgerald, it wouldn't have guaranteed him success. Perhaps he would have benefited from the wise words of Rabbi Zusya, an early Hasidic luminary, who, shortly before he died, remarked: "In the world to come I shall not be asked: 'Why were you not Moses?' I shall be asked: 'Why were you not Zusya?'"

In my class, I watch students struggle to maintain their passion for writing in the face of an outside world that doesn't seem to care about their heartfelt expression. They ask me, "How can I afford to spend my time writing if it brings no material rewards and can't help me make a living?"

For me, it comes down to the compartmentalization of body and soul. The soul needs the sustenance that writing and all forms of creativity can bring. The soul doesn't care about fame or money. The body needs to figure out how to make a living, acquire the necessary creature comforts, and find its way in the world. It is rare to be able to sustain the body on the pure expression of the soul. It's wonderful if you can do it and make your living working so close to the heart. Throughout almost all of history, however, even the most well-known writers and artists have had other jobs.

Keep in mind that the things you have to do for a living will always tend to fill all the time you have. That's why it may be helpful to claim a set hour right at the beginning or the end of the day for yourself and your deepest work. Then everything else will fit into the time you still have available.

When I moved to New York City and started City Lore, in 1986, I had the opportunity to work with the radio producer David Isay; City Lore served as his nonprofit sponsor. Dave helped bring the stories of ordinary people to public radio, and, after winning a MacArthur

Fellowship, he founded StoryCorps, now the world's largest oral history project. At the time, a number of individuals were developing "booths" to collect stories, but they never quite succeeded, as these early booths required that people talk directly to a video camera. The brilliance of Isay's StoryCorps concept was threefold: first, it allowed anyone and everyone the opportunity to tell their stories and become part of a permanent record; second, it carefully curated the best of these stories for radio; and third, it created an interviewing process that was person-to-person, asking people to bring to the booth their loved ones, friends, or anyone they knew who had an interesting story, and share a conversation, with the help of a facilitator.

Although a populist at heart, Dave Isay is decidedly conscious of what makes "the best stories." In the years leading up to the founding of Story-Corps, City Lore hired a cultural specialist to locate stories for the *American Talkers* series that we co-sponsored with Dave. She worked for six months and suggested probably fifty stories; not one met Dave's standards for the radio. StoryCorps struck a balance between participation and curatorship, giving a wide swath of Americans a chance to tell their stories and also to hear some of the finest stories on the radio.

At City Lore, we created City of Memory, a dynamic, participatory online story map of the city. The site features highlights of City Lore's extensive documentation, invites viewers to post their own stories, and enables us to work closely with communities to place themselves "on the map." The project was a collaboration between City Lore and new-media designer Jake Barton, principal at the design firm Local Projects. As we brainstormed about the project, Jake casually suggested an idea that became our mantra. He said that visitors to the site would be interested in only two things: *What are the best stories?* and *What is my story?* Of course, these questions are not particular to Internet culture; they mark a dilemma faced by every aspiring artist. Ultimately, the question becomes *Is my story one of the best stories?* There's only one way to find out: tell it and put it out there in the world.

The tension between the two questions presents an immense challenge for any creative person. People who are interested in expressing their inner self in writing, film, or visual art have a deep appreciation for the great masters of their form. They want to be blown away by the best stories without abandoning or losing faith in the importance of their own story. Your own story, needless to say, is the story that *only you* can tell. Is it one of the best stories? Possibly so. But even if it isn't, it needs to be told.

In 1999 I helped to create the first People's Poetry Gathering, co-sponsored by City Lore and Poets House. The New York City event brought together literary and folk poets alike; the cast included cowboy and hobo poets, U.S. poet laureates, poetry slammers, Mexican and Puerto Rican musicians who improvised poems on the spot, and others. The first day of the event was designed for high school students, and the poet Ed Hirsch, who would later become president of the Guggenheim Foundation, was asked to speak about his work. "There's no need for you to write the poems that I have already written or that Elizabeth Bishop has written or that Pablo Neruda has written," he told the students. "You need to write the poems that only you can write. But if you never learn it from other poetry, you're doomed to fall into this vast cauldron of poetry that all sounds alike. Oddly enough, the way you are delivered to your own feelings in poetry is to learn how to do it from other poets. And then applying it, using it, taking it to your own experience and your own life."[1]

You learn from other artists—and you borrow and steal as well. In the 1987 catalogue for her first big museum show, the abstract painter Elizabeth Murray wrote: "Everything has been done a million times. Sometimes you use it and it's yours; another time you do it and it's still theirs."[2] How can you tell that it's yours? How can you *make* it yours?

I'm reminded of the schism that always existed between the two iconic folklorists Pete Seeger and Alan Lomax. Lomax, it's been said, wanted to collect the best stories and put them on the radio; Pete Seeger just wanted to get everybody singing. My task—and certainly I'm not alone in this—is to get everybody to express their inner selves.

Only fools believe that this will flood the world with bad art. I've heard literary critics rail against populist programs that spawn what they call "bad poetry." Participation in poetry—even if it's "bad poetry"—creates an audience for poetry. It inspires good poetry by allowing poetry to be judged by a larger audience, not only by a small circle of English professors in an ivory tower who create critical theories and poems that feed off each other.

In 2002 Alaka Wali served as the principal investigator of a two-year ethnographic study of collaborative "informal arts" groups in the Chicago metropolitan region. The team looked at writing groups, painting circles, choirs, and other informal networks in which people congregate around a shared interest. They discovered that the collective pursuit of informal arts enables people to come together across the often intransigent boundaries of race, ethnicity, and geography. The study suggests that these groups create a "metaphorical space of informality" with few barriers to participation, affirmation, and mentoring.[3] They allow everyone to tell "their story" and cull the "best stories" from their collective efforts.

Many of my strongest bonds and deepest friendships have come with those with whom I've collaborated in creative ways. I've often quipped that shared creativity creates a bond as powerful as sex. Although my wife was raised in rural South Carolina and I'm from a Philadelphia Jewish family and was raised in Brazil, we have always shared a love of folk and traditional music. That's what inspired us separately to study folklore and what ultimately brought us together. One afternoon, Amanda took her dusty Gibson guitar from its case. The *Rise Up Singing* songbook lay on the table, and I attempted to coax her into playing some old favorite tunes. But our beloved cat, the late, fat, overfed Homebone, black with patches of white, invoked the muses. Suddenly Amanda was improvising a silly song about the cat ("I just love my chicken, and I love my chicken man"). No sooner sung than the song inspired other songs, and I recognized that my wife knows me so well that she's able to compose the perfect melodies for my versified ramblings. With Amanda writing the melodies and working with me on the lyrics, this has become a decade-long collaboration.

As a college music major, Amanda used to slip through the back door of the practice studios and onto the auditorium balcony to listen to the gorgeous music of the faculty orchestra rehearsals. At home, I often lie low and listen as Amanda experiments with melodies for the songs we write, composing in her head and humming variations. The sweet strains of newly formed melodies arising out of the ether are among the most beautiful sounds I know. Shared creativity is and continues to be a powerful bond between us. After all, my first connection to music came in kindergarten, when I failed the talent test and, rather than receiving a drum or a triangle, I was handed two sticks to hit together. Amanda has given me a new way to get closer to music. As we put it in one of our songs, "Between the rhythm and the melody, / that's where I want to be. / Close to music."

To move from the ridiculous to the sublime, I was reminded of Amanda's and my musical collaborations when I read Keith Richards's description, in his book *Life*, of how he works with Mick Jagger: "We always come up with something when we're alone together. There's an electromagnetic spark between us. There always has been. That's what we look forward to and that's what helps turn folks on. . . . There's a marked difference between Mick and me alone and Mick and me when there's somebody else—anybody else—in the room. It could just be the housemaid, the chef, anybody. It becomes totally different. . . . I pull things out of him; he pulls things out of me."[4] Later in the book, he writes about the frustration of knowing that the two of them are far better together than apart.

Sharing work with family and friends, even when you're not collaborating, carries its own rewards—and is one way of getting your story out into the world. There is something wonderful for me about intimacy that develops from sharing my art and appreciating my friends' artistry: it adds a dimension to the ways I can understand and know someone, and be known by them. Some of my friends have made careers from their creative selves, and others work at their art for quieter reasons, yet seeing their art and knowing the person who created it enables me to behold a greater depth in both.

It's as if someone's true spirit were a combination of the individual and his art. The friendships I've made are deepened through sharing collages, paintings, graffiti, folk art, poems, short stories, and songs. The arts are one of the ways we reveal ourselves to one another.

Not long after I started teaching creative writing at Cooper Union, I started an online poetry circle called Brevitas with my former student Jim Pignetti. This was how Jim described the group: "One or two short poems—fourteen lines, max—circulate via email on the first and fifteenth of the month, to every other member of the group. Responses are in private, or silence." Although we encourage the responses to take a positive tone, our fellow writers don't hesitate to tinker with our poems, offering editing suggestions or rewrites that have elevated all of our work. Richard Storm, one of our early members, and the editor of our annual anthologies, waxed poetic (appropriately) about Brevitas:

> On the first and fifteenth of each month, Brevitas poets fill my in-box with whimsy, heartbreak, and delight, all acutely observed in fourteen lines or less. Because the price for receiving these nuggets is to contribute my own, I troll for poetry as I wander through my days. What's happening around me? Can I distill it into a brief verbal photograph? Can I translate a vivid, complex emotion into a few lines? Because of Brevitas, everything is a potential poem and everyone a potential poet. Because of Brevitas, poetry waits for me . . . on every next block, around the corner, in every stranger's face.

Richard even wrote a poem about the search:

> Between poems I cast about for the next.
> I sift the world, it's all grist:
> the dead eyes of a stranger yelling into her phone—
> that naked young man in the third-floor window
> swigging wine from a bottle—
> the big green butterfly wings of
> wind-tossed leaves in the sun—
> a woman walking her resented stepchild the dog—
> the male couple nose-to-nose screaming at each other
> in whispers—snapshots to send, stories to tell.
> Even when my net returns empty, the search
> connects me—my numbed urban soul revives.

More than fifty poets have participated in the monthly poetry exchange. No doubt there are English teachers who could take our anthologies, published each year in tandem with the Brevitas festival, and rank the poets from best to worst. Yet every one of those poets writes from the vantage point of a sentient human being who is trying to figure out the world and their place within it in a distinctive, meaningful form.

Without a writers' group like Brevitas, trying to get honest opinions about your stories can be challenging. When you show a piece to a friend, you may need to interpret the coded response. "I liked it" might mean that, in fact, she didn't like it, or that she didn't even read or listen to it. If she says, "I loved it," there's a better chance that she liked it. (You can judge by the person sometimes.) But the best sign that someone engaged with your work is when she answers with something specific about it—"I love the way you did this . . ."—especially if it's something from beyond the first page. My favorite is when she quotes your own lines back to you.

As my brother Bill put it, "If you're going to be in the arts, you have to be something of a show-off." The writer Dan Harmon put it another way: "Find your voice, shout it from the rooftops, and keep doing it until the people who are looking for you find you."[5]

Dreams of fame and fortune never seem far from many of my students' minds when they put pen to paper. I can remember walking down a New York City street with Al Lewis, who played the grandpa on the TV show *The Munsters*, when a passing stranger put up his hand, gave Al a high five, and walked on. Nothing needed to be said. I asked Al if he liked being famous. "Of course," he said. "Everybody loves you. Who can complain? Did you think I was going to say it was like a ball and chain?"

Although it must be a thrill to be adored by the masses, most of us are far more concerned with winning the admiration of those close to us. "They cheered your great performance / encores again and then again," Amanda and I once wrote. "But the big bouquet of roses / is from an audience of family and friends."

It helps to be philosophical about failure and success. My friend, a sideshow talker, stood on the bally platform and said to his audiences: "My name is John Bradshaw. You may have seen me in the movies." Then he paused. "I sit in the back."

You don't want success to go to your head. As Mayer Kirshenblatt put it when, in his later years, his paintings were the centerpiece of a traveling exhibit, "I guess I need a bigger hat." Or as Herman Glick wrote after he won a major short story contest, "Now that my social status has been elevated from gabby old coot to raconteur, I waddle a little prouder in the marketplace."

Author Brenda Ueland remarks: "I understood that writing was this: an impulse to share with other people a feeling or truth that I myself had. Not to preach to them, but to give it to them if they cared to hear it. If they did not—fine. They did not need to listen. That was all right too. And I would never fall into those two extremes (both lies) of saying: 'I have nothing to say and am of no importance and have no gift'; or 'The public doesn't want good stuff.'"[6]

Artists like Stephen King and Steven Spielberg are clearly crafting pieces that are close to their hearts, and yet they also have their finger on society's pulse. Perhaps what is in your heart to write or paint will strike a chord in a thousand other hearts, but we have to remember that it's rare for a singular voice to do that.

My friend Annie Lanzillotto and I joked that we feel like peddlers, pushing a pushcart of books and songs and poems up a steep hill. We're doing all the work. What does it take to make this pushcart fly? What does it take for people buy these books on their own without our personal marketing efforts? But wings are hard to come by.

If creation is your primary directive, create. If your primary goal is to be read, you may need to shepherd your work into the world. Although it has nothing to do with creation, you need to get to a point where you set aside your writer self and become your own editor, fund-raiser, agent, or publisher—a process that might take not days or weeks but years. Make a *sustained* effort: don't give up, and don't take no for an answer. Go back to those who reject your

> **You need to get to a point where you set aside your writer self and become your own editor, fund-raiser, agent, or publisher.**

work and ask how you can make it better, then rework a piece a hundred times if you have to. Let others read it—and listen to their opinions. If you ask for criticism, God knows, you will receive it—perhaps even more than you bargained for. But you'll discover critiques that can elevate your work. One of the readers for Cornell University Press submitted a twenty-three-page critique of this book. I incorporated most of the suggestions. Believe me, it's a better book for it.

When my son, Benh, submitted his short film *Glory at Sea* to the South by Southwest Film Festival, he received a rejection that read something like "Thank you so much for submitting your film. We love it and wish we could use it, but it's too long for our short film format." My son was completely dejected. I looked at the letter and said to him, "Benh, this is not a rejection; it's an acceptance! They said they loved the film." He then wrote them back, saying, in effect, "Thank you for accepting the film. We are hard at work to make it shorter to fit your format." My son and his team never did cut it to the necessary length, but they made some changes and the film was eventually shown at the festival and won a prize that helped to propel his career. If a rejection says anything other than a flat "no," there may be an opportunity to restart the conversation.

You may also want to immerse yourself in the creative world you are seeking to enter. Attending poetry readings or art openings, reading trade periodicals, and making personal connections facilitate the process. Try to learn as much as you can about what is published or exhibited by the magazines or galleries that interest you. Try to engage editors in dialogues about your work and about what excites their own interest. All of the arts are judged subjectively, and the process of getting work out into the world often depends on a person-to-person interchange. It is far more difficult to get pieces published if they are sent in cold.

By watching friends and family, I have learned that it helps to be young and part of a coterie of friends who have different roles in a given field: writers, editors, painters, critics, gallery owners, patrons, and those who might also be trying to reinvent their fields. "Establishments" are constantly looking for young and creative people who can revolutionize and reinvigorate art forms and ultimately sell work to a public that is always interested in what's new and groundbreaking. Although it's difficult to break into a field from the outside at any age, it is possible.

Amanda's great-aunt died a few weeks before her 110th birthday. She had been a writer all her life, and had published a few novels. Her obituary quoted her saying that she dated her writing career to her first rejection: from the *Farmer's Almanac*, when she was seventeen. I loved that she dated her writing career not from her first acceptance but from her first rejection. The vicissitudes of acceptances and rejections in the highly subjective fields of the arts can lead to superstitious behaviors. From 1973 to 1977, long before he became the *New Yorker*'s cartoon editor, Bob Mankoff submitted two thousand cartoons to the magazine.

He wallpapered his bathroom with the rejection letters. I never save a rejection but throw it out immediately, before it can taint the atmosphere.

Finding a trade publisher, a record label, or a gallery to distribute your artwork can jump-start your career, and, despite the changes in these industries, that route remains the most lucrative and effective. Self-publishing, however, is often a viable option. George Bernard Shaw, Anaïs Nin, Virginia Wolff, e. e. cummings, William Blake, Edgar Allan Poe, Rudyard Kipling, Henry David Thoreau, Benjamin Franklin, and Walt Whitman were all self-published. Self-publishing is not the same as vanity publishing, for which you pay a steep fee to have a commercial venture publish and market your book. Publishing your own work as a do-it-yourself project has some distinct advantages. After all, the chief marketing representative for the book is likely to be you no matter who publishes it—and if you sell many copies of a self-published book, trade publishers are more likely to express interest. In addition, as a self-published author you will have total control of your product. Commercial publishers usually have the prerogative to decide the cover of your book, the paper it's printed on, often even the title. As a friend once quipped, no matter where you start out in American culture, you always end up in sales.

No matter where you start out in American culture, you always end up in sales.

I'm inspired by Marjorie Eliot, who lives in the Sugar Hill neighborhood, in New York. When her son died, at the age of thirty, in 1992, she found herself going crazy.

> Phil died on a Sunday, and every Sunday I would scream— understandably. I would have my little nervous breakdown every Sunday leading up to his birthday, July 18. I can remember thinking, I'm not getting through this. . . . So I desperately wanted to find a way to celebrate him. It was a Sunday when he passed and I wondered, How am I going to celebrate that anniversary? Then I had the idea of playing music in his honor. He loved music and I had played for him when he was sick. Now I would play in order to remember him.[7]

Every Sunday since that day, Marjorie has presented a concert at her home, at 555 Edgecombe Avenue, inviting well-known jazz musicians to play with her. She has never missed a Sunday. Her music and, more recently, her plays attract audiences from all over the world, who crowd into her tiny living room. Marjorie struggles to pay the rent each month, yet she touches thousands of New Yorkers and visitors from around the world. "I don't see it as sacrificing to do it," she said. "I see it as my life depends on it. I have to do it." When I attended one of her concerts a few years ago, she told the crowd assembled, "The majesty within us is larger than any of us, so I can trumpet this and not blow my own horn."

The arts offer many ways to make your own contribution to the poetry of everyday life. Why have a creative life? Possible answers include to collaborate with others; to have a public presence; to find intimacy with friends and family; to deepen self-knowledge; to create narratives or a personal mythology. I once imagined a mythical gateway where our lives were judged:

> Through an opening in the barbed wire
> a sinister checkpoint
> defines a ravaged dreamscape
>
> heart in hand
> I present my Carta de Identidad
> to the uniformed policeman
>
> sheaf of crumpled papers
> chronicle of consciousness
> proof of existence
>
> *I am not here to judge,*
>
> he scoffs
>
> *then bear witness*
>
> he sighs
>
> scribbler, pass by

Yes, the scribbler made it through.

And if you find yourself in the Riverrun bookstore and happen to pull an old scout manual from the shelf, with flattened spoons and coins embedded in it, you'll make my daughter a very happy girl.

Part VI POETRY IN STONE

21

The Grease Lamp's Flicker and Flare

Dark Caves Illuminate

We have learned nothing in ten thousand years.
—ATTRIBUTED TO PICASSO AFTER VISITING
THE CAVE PAINTINGS AT LASCAUX

Here's where it starts. Between ten thousand and forty thousand years ago, our ancestors, the first *Homo sapiens*, armed with supplies of iron oxide and magnesium, ventured into the hollows of caves and painted their visions on the walls. They crushed the minerals into a pulverized pigment and moistened them with animal fat, water, or bone marrow. Their grease lamps flickered and flared on the hollow handheld stone slabs they used as palettes. They used the contours of the rock to accentuate the muscles and movements of the beasts they painted. Often, these early artists crawled into the caves on their bellies and painted lying on their backs. Long before the first stirrings of art in Babylonia and in the civilizations along Nile, art was alive in France, at Lascaux and Rouffignac and Font de Gaume, caves in and around the foothills of the Pyrenees and the valley of the Vézère River.

In recent times, the bones of reindeer and fish have been discovered inside the caves. But the images on the walls do not depict these creatures, which were hunted for food. The painted animals are larger, grander: bison, aurochs, horses, and wild stags. This realization led researchers to speculate that the caves had been a site of sanctuary, not of habitation. The paintings are from a time when the sacred had to be invented out of whole cloth rather than adapted or stitched together from beliefs and practices from a previous era.

In September 2011 my family and I traveled to the caves in France. Before we left, I wrote a letter to the French authorities (translated into perfect French) requesting a tour of the original Lascaux cave, which has been closed to the public since 1963. I noted that I was a folklorist married to a folklorist. I said I had a daughter who's a visual artist and a son whose film *Beasts of the Southern Wild*, then in progress, was replete with images of prehistoric aurochs that live in a little girl's imagination. This was, therefore, a necessary pilgrimage for our entire family. The French authorities summarily dismissed our request.

We were not dissuaded, determined to experience the origins of human consciousness and art. Numerous original caves apart from Lascaux are still open to the public. With a copy of Greg Curtis's marvelous book *The Cave Painters: Probing the Mysteries of the World's First Artists* as our guide, we prepared for our journey by reading the theories of anthropologists, priests, and art historians.[1] We discovered how these early humans developed their own sense of perspective eons prior to the Renaissance. We learned of the priest and anthropologist Henri Breuil, who believed the cave paintings might have been used as talismans for fertility or hunting. In the late nineteenth and early twentieth centuries, he hunkered down inside the caves and traced and sketched the images to share with the outside world.

We read about Max Raphael, the Marxist art historian who sought meaning in the paintings by exploring the relationships among the painted beasts, and who suggested that the different animal groupings represented clans—the horse clan, the bison or deer clan. Raphael believed that the superimposition of animals represented weddings, alliances, and battles. He surmised that art emerged from a propitious moment in prehistory when humans began distinguishing themselves from the zoological world. The era of cave painting defined a tipping point at which humans went from being dominated by to dominating animals. The grand epics emblazoned on the cave walls, he said, may represent a Garden of Eden narrative expressing the guilt, regret, and triumph of humans banished forever from the animal kingdom.

From Curtis's book, we also learned about Annette Laming-Emperaire, the French anthropologist and archaeologist who set out to "unlock the secrets of this first Treatise on Nature" and convinced the scholarly world that the paintings were not "primitive" but rather the expressions of an advanced civilization, akin to those of the Egyptians or the Greeks.[2] South African anthropologist David Lewis-Williams and French curator and cave administrator Jean Clottes argued that the paintings and their accompanying symbols were the hallucinogenic expressions of shamanistic trance behavior.[3]

When we finally arrived at the replica of the Lascaux cave and I entered the "Hall of Bulls," my eyes overflowed with tears. I was overwhelmed by the power of the artistic impulse, the will to express beauty and grandeur. I was moved to tears, too, at Pech Merle, the massive underground cathedral where thousands of pink stalactites pour down like frozen rain, and stalactites, stalagmites, and stone discs emerge from crevices, forming ridges along the rock, sometimes vertical, other times horizontal, suggesting a divine creator's incomprehensible writing. Here the cave dwellers painted magnificent spotted horses, a powerful human response to this hallowed space.

"Why the cavemen came in here, we have no idea," the French guide said to us. We laughed. Why wouldn't any human being be drawn to the beauty of these rock formations? It occurred to me then why we had made this pilgrimage: I needed to pay homage to these astonishing early humans who had grasped that the meaning of life is entwined with our ability to express it. As Eliza suggested, the work expressed the grandeur of humanity. It made her proud to be a human being.

I needed to pay homage to these astonishing early humans who had grasped that the meaning of life is entwined with our ability to express it.

The cave paintings embody the earliest humans' realization that they could draw lines with pigment and magically depict the figure of an animal. They must have marveled at the mystical way a natural line of the rock wall could mimic a bison's back, an aurochs's tail, a stag's antlers; I imagine that they must have been blown away by the discovery that they could express the world around them in a new form. Their images reminded me of Socrates and Plato's "Form of the Good," the archetypes of a more perfect and pure world that inform our journey.

As Stanley Kunitz writes: "Listen! We make a world! I hear the sound / Of Matter pouring through eternal forms."[4] Their images were part of the real world, and yet a visionary rendering of that world. We now take that magic for granted. Yet the transcendent enchantment of art remains.

The four of us wished we could have entered the caves with a grease lamp—as the cave painters had—and watched the paintings flicker and flare, move and sway, disappear and reveal themselves momentarily in all their grandeur. We longed to see what the paintings looked like illuminated by the tiny flames that threw light and shadow against portions of the cave, like an ancient motion picture, presaging the magic lantern and the film projector. I was reminded, too, of the intrepid graffiti artists who ventured into the Amtrak tunnel under the West Side Highway and sprayed their art under the large iron grates, creating underground masterpieces illuminated by streaks of sunlight pouring through.

I imagine that the cave dwellers, their pupils dilating, gazed with humility and awe at the sacred aurochs and bison painted by the masters among them, and that the experience was enhanced during ceremonies, as some anthropologists have speculated, by the sounds of early music. Scientists can carbon-date the pigments, but the art also holds something of the artists' spiritual imprint, which we can still appreciate today.

I was left imagining that each of our souls is akin to that flickering, wavering light dancing upon the stone pallettes of the cave painters. A tiny lamp burns in each of us, flickering as we move through the cave of our experience, illuminating the bones of reindeer and fish, the small images of our daily lives. Our peak moments, however, are like the huge painted images—the aurochs, bison, and bulls—that appear suddenly before us in the flare of our lamps. In these transcendent moments, we witness the grand ideas that shape our path.

In modern times, we are far removed from the cave painters' world of ceremony. Our climactic experiences are often defined by an electrical charge that suffuses our synapses and our being: a burst of laughter, the epiphany of creating or seeing a work of art, the heat of sexual fulfillment. But it remains up to us to find ways to give expression to those moments. The cave paintings, to me, represent a behest from our ancestors to record our own experiences on the page, canvas, stage, or screen so that others might discover them. Only a few of the many painted caves have been preserved; shifting landmasses and water seepage have destroyed most of them, just as most—but not all—of our artistic works are destined to remain undiscovered. Some survive.

The cave paintings, to me, represent a behest from our ancestors to record our own experiences on the page, canvas, stage, or screen so that others might discover them.

In at least a dozen ancient caves, painters created images by placing their palm against the cave wall and blowing paint over and around it, leaving the negative space emblazoned on the stone when they lifted their hand. "Hi fives from tens of thousands of years ago," wrote the poet Evie Ivy.[5] The handprints are like a signature, telling us, *This is my creation.* Beyond that, they seem to remind us: *Even when I am as lifeless as the cave painters' hands on the wall, even when my life is apparent only as a silhouette, as negative space defined by the effect I had on others who then affected others, the colors around it will continue to define a shape that is distinctly mine, visible to those who discover it in their own grease lamp's flicker and flare.*

22

Lion's Gate

Myths as Metaphors

Mythology is not a lie, mythology is poetry, it is metaphorical. . . . It is beyond words, beyond images, beyond that
bounding rim of the Buddhist Wheel of Becoming. Mythology
pitches the mind beyond that rim, to what can be known but
not told.

—JOSEPH CAMPBELL

Wandering through the Garden of Eden, looking for the Temple
of Love, Victoria and I strayed from the beaten path. Visiting from New
Orleans, Victoria is a friend of my daughter's, closer to my age than
hers. She was staying with our family in Westchester while she attended
an art opening in Manhattan that included her work. She had a few
hours to kill before her flight. Since she is a naturalist, I decided to take
her to one of my favorite places in all of New York State: Untermyer
Gardens, in Yonkers, just north of the Bronx.

In 1899 Samuel Untermyer purchased what was then the Greystone
Estate, and in 1915 he hired William Welles Bosworth, an École des
Beaux-Arts–trained architect and landscape designer, to create the
"greatest gardens in the world." The centerpiece at Untermyer is the
Walled Garden, inspired by the Indo-Persian gardens of the ancient
world, which, in turn, were inspired by descriptions of the Garden of
Eden. The biblical Eden includes four rivers (the Pishon, the Gihon, the
Tigris, and the Euphrates) and two great trees (the Tree of the Knowledge of Good and Evil and the Tree of Life). The Walled Garden is
divided into quadrants, with four long rectangular pools representing
the four rivers. Victoria and I walked between the two majestic trees at
the entrance and marveled at the pools, resplendent with water lilies

and other references to Greek and Islamic mythologies. If an apple had been hanging from one of the trees, I am sure Victoria would have picked it.

Once we'd seen the Tree of Knowledge and wandered through the Walled Garden, I asked Victoria if she wanted to see the Temple of Love, which I had visited once before. It's a fanciful rock structure, once an elaborate fountain, with three stone bridges topped with a tiny temple, where John Lennon had a now-famous photograph taken, and where the Son of Sam serial killer is said to have performed dark rituals back in the 1970s, when the park was in disrepair.

Following a less-than-clear map, we made our way along seemingly endless winding pathways till we crossed a brook. Victoria mentioned that the ions in the water were charged in a way that should improve our moods, which was a good thing, since after wandering for another fifteen minutes, we crossed right back over the same brook from the

Figure 6. Walled Garden ("Garden of Eden"), Untermyer Gardens, Yonkers, N.Y. Photo by Jonathan Wallen.

other direction. Victoria was increasingly nervous about missing her flight. We were hot and sweaty and needed to get back to the Garden of Eden, past the Tree of Life, to where our car was parked.

Suddenly, we came upon the heavily vandalized sculpture of a lion and a headless horse, set apart to form an opening or passage with overgrown bushes behind it. The gateway seemed uninviting, like the entrance to a cave that, if we entered it, we would never find our way out of. From the brochure we learned that the piece was tentatively attributed to Edward Clark Potter, the sculptor responsible for the famous lions Patience and Fortitude, which guard the main branch of the New York Public Library. We wondered who had stolen the horse's stone head. Looking at the map, we realized that the path we had been following would not, in fact, have led us to the Temple of Love.

The path back to the Walled Garden looked to be just south of the Lion's Gate. We searched the underbrush and saw what looked like a pathway.

Figure 7. Lion's Gate, Untermyer Gardens, Yonkers, N.Y. Photo by Jonathan Wallen.

We started up it—and ran smack into a wall of brambles. Definitely not a path. We studied the map once more. Aha! The path was on the other side of the gate. We started up the path again—till the trail disappeared. It's said that not all those who wander are lost. But we were truly lost.

Perhaps when you're lost, you're also searching, seeking. In the same way that Untermyer and Bosworth grew a garden by mythologizing a place, we can start to "grow a soul," as anthropologist Barbara Myerhoff once put it, by mythologizing our lives—using myths to explore and illuminate the inner landscape through which we journey, and in which we are, inevitably, often lost.[1]

The trek through the gardens invites us to consider our inner journeys where ancient myths entwine with our own life stories. Many religions make reference to the idea of a place of innocence like the Garden of Eden at the beginning of humankind and a heaven or paradise after death. The hero's journey—the sinner's journey, the seeker's journey—unfurls between the two realms. In the Sumerian tale of Enki and Ninhursag, the city of Dilmun is a paradise for the immortals where death and illness are unknown. In Greek mythology, the garden of the Hesperides resembles the biblical Garden.

Western myths suggest that an Eden existed at the beginning of time, and that we might return to such a glorious place in heaven. Even if we don't believe in either, we can recognize that they represent a world not as it is, but as it should or could be and that our minds are capable of imagining.

The Garden of Eden that Victoria and I were striving to return to on our pedestrian heroes' journey might be seen as a metaphor for a golden age that all of us seek to discover in our own lives. In the opening scene of Martin Scorsese's biographical documentary *No Direction Home*, Bob Dylan says: "I was born very far from where I'm supposed to be—so I'm on my way home."[2] We are the protagonists of our own life story. We are all Ulysses on our long journeys to get back to where we once belonged. This journey often includes a spiral down from grace, a fall from innocence.

> **We are the protagonists of our own life story.**

We often create our own golden ages, and document and recall them through stories and photographs. Susan Sontag, in her collection of essays *On Photography*, notes that the camera has the unique ability to "freeze moments in a life or a society" so that they are salvaged from "the relentless melt of time. . . . Through photography each family constructs a portrait of itself, a kit of images that bears witness to its connectedness."[3] On a trip back from his home in Brazil to visit his new grandson, my father told my wife, Amanda, "Remember these years when your children are little. They are the best years." He documented those years of my own childhood with his Rolleiflex camera.

Perhaps, as the poet Patrick Phillips suggests, the golden ages that we imagine in our personal pasts are what heaven might be like. His poem "Heaven" describes such a place:

It will be the past
and we'll live there together.

Not as it was to *live*
but as it is remembered.

It will be the past.
We'll all go back together.

Everyone we ever loved,
and lost, and must remember.

It will be the past.
And it will last forever.[4]

When I was a graduate student in folklore, I was assigned to write an intellectual biography of a folklore scholar. To the consternation of my professor, I chose Joseph Campbell. Campbell's wide-ranging work compares disparate mythologies, and my professors considered him suspect. He was neither a folklorist, nor an ethnographer, nor an anthropologist, and they didn't care for his politics, either.[5]

Nonetheless, Campbell was gracious and kind during my interview. He told me he had hoped to become a folklorist until the *Journal of American Folklore* rejected his extended essay "Flight of the Wild Gander," and he decided to take a different path. He explained how his students at Sarah Lawrence College had been receptive to his classes on mythology because they could apply these ancient stories to their own lives. He also explained how he saw his writings about mythology as his art.

Just before I left his apartment after the interview, Campbell told me two Native American proverbs. One was about a boy who, fleeing a threatening beast, comes upon a huge chasm that he thinks he cannot possibly leap across. But he jumps and, miraculously, makes it to the other side. The other was simply this phrase: "If birds do their droppings on you, don't even bother to brush them off."

As I was finishing my paper, I asked my girlfriend, Rosemary, if she thought my professor would catch the reference to Campbell if I ended it with the proverb that he quoted to me as I left: "If birds do their droppings on you . . ." She said, "Oh, no, he'll never catch that. It's much too subtle." Sure enough, I got my paper back with the comment "I know you will think this is just birds doing their droppings on you." A "B–."

Regardless of my professor's skepticism about comparative mythology, ancient myths continue to shape contemporary culture through comic books, films, and other media and through the metaphors they provide. I was inspired to become a folklore student by reading Campbell's *Hero with a Thousand Faces* and the wonderful book by Otto Rank *The Myth of the Birth of the Hero*, originally published in 1909.

In his book Rank discusses the commonalities in ancient myths. The standard saga itself, he writes,

> may be formulated according to the following scheme: The hero is the child of most distinguished parents, usually the son of a king. His origin is preceded by difficulties, such as . . . prolonged barrenness, or secret intercourse of the parents due to external prohibition or obstacles. During or before the pregnancy, there is a prophecy, in the form of a dream or oracle, cautioning against his birth, and usually threatening danger to the father (or his representative). As a rule, he is surrendered to the water, in a box. He is then saved by animals, or by lowly people (shepherds), and is suckled by a female animal or by a humble woman. After he has grown up, he finds his distinguished parents, in a highly versatile fashion. . . . Finally he achieves rank and honors.[6]

As an example, he cites the story of Moses, in which, when Pharaoh commands all sons born to Hebrews to be drowned, Moses's mother hides her newborn son for three months. She then takes him to "an ark of bulrushes, and daubed it with slime and with pitch, and put the child therein; and she laid it in the flags by the river's brink in the bulrushes."[7] Rank observed the same patterns in the legends of Romulus and Remus, Perseus, Gilgamesh, Hercules, and Tristan.

When I first entered graduate school, I had endless conversations about this common strain in mythology with my friend and fellow folklorist Jack Santino. Jack, who loves comics, was fascinated by the way another legend followed Rank's trajectory:

> What's amazing is that Superman follows a similar pattern. He's from a superhuman race, definitely from distinguished parents, who live on the planet Krypton. The planet was about to blow up—something unstable at its core. Jor-El, Superman's father, knew this but no one believed him. So he sent his baby son off into space in a rocket ship. Instead of being sent away in a basket, he's sent away in a spaceship. Perfect parallel. He's raised by farmers and at a young age shows his remarkable characteristics, like lifting a car.
>
> Superman was created by Jerry Siegel and artist Joe Shuster, high school students living in Cleveland, Ohio, in 1933. As two Jewish boys, it seems likely they knew about the Moses story.
>
> In some ways, Superman is also the ultimate immigrant, who has to "pass" to get along in society—as Clark Kent, a WASP. And I always loved that he had the Superman costume underneath his clothes—as if to say we're truly special, and that at certain moments you emerge as the real person that you are, the person that the rest of the world doesn't see.

In *The Hero with a Thousand Faces*, Joseph Campbell also writes about the patterns in ancient mythology: "A hero ventures forth from the world of common day into a region of supernatural wonder: fabulous forces are there encountered and a decisive victory is won: the hero comes back from this mysterious adventure with the power to bestow boons on his fellow man."[8]

He offers as examples Prometheus, who ascends to the heavens to steal fire from the gods, and Jason, who proceeds through the Clashing

Rocks and the Sea of Marvels, tricks the dragon who guards the Golden Fleece, and returns with the fleece to reclaim the throne.

Folklorists and anthropologists understand that each of these mythologies described by Campbell and the cultures that created them are vastly different from one another, and in some ways incomparable. The more one knows about any one of these cultures, the more apparent this becomes. They are as different as each and every individual is unlike any other. Yet both perspectives can be valuable: "we are all one" and "we are all unique"; "our myths and stories have common patterns but are wholly different." Both perspectives are present in humanity's great art and grand creations. (An old joke: What did the Dalai Lama say to the hot dog vendor? "Make me one with everything.")

When I sent a copy of this essay to Victoria following our escapade in the gardens, she said, "I'm happy to be part of the folklore." These ancient myths and epic tales resonate not just in our popular culture but as metaphors in our own lives. As Joseph Campbell writes, "The latest incarnation of Oedipus, the continued romance of Beauty and the Beast, stand this afternoon on the corner of Forty Second Street and Fifth Avenue, waiting for the traffic light to change."[9]

> **These ancient myths and epic tales resonate not just in our popular culture but as metaphors in our own lives.**

On the wall opposite my bed hangs a painting by a surrealistic painter and street artist named Décio Fereira that I purchased while visiting my family in São Paulo some years ago. Based on the Amazonian legend of the woods nymph Curupira and his dog, Papamel, it depicts a boy on a boat afloat on a blue-green sea. He wears a green jester's cap with feathers and holds a flute. A brown dog is carved into the prow of the boat, and an actual black dog faces the stern of the small vessel. The real and the carved dogs signify for me the dichotomy between life and art. The boy with the feathery cap sits between the dogs of life and art, and I see the boy as a reflection of myself—my avatar, or my mythological self—and I gaze at him just before I go to sleep just as

Figure 8. Painting by Décio Fereira, São Paulo.

regularly as I read and write poetry in the morning. I imagine that before I fall asleep the boy begins to play his flute—which for some reason sounds a lot like Bob Dylan's harmonica.

"My worlds on canvas," writes Décio Fereira, "are musicians and their instruments—piano, guitar, flute, violin and drums. What do they play? Schumann, Tchaikovsky or Gershwin? Concert, rhapsody, jazz? I don't know, really, but I want you to listen to it . . . to imagine, to fly over an elephant, like a bird. Feel the colours, rhythms, forms and silent interludes. Your dreams create images in blue, green songs, adagio, presto. Well, sometimes in my life I don't understand anything—that's the time to make a painting because in this moment I love my work and my work loves me, too."[10]

Décio Fereira's painted, mythic image provides enormous comfort, a personal mythology, which I sought to express in these lines:

> framed on my bedroom wall
> a boy on a boat in the universe
>
> wandering a blue-green world
> fading into water
> conscious of the sea
>
> from the space beneath my eyelids
> the two of us embark
>
> through shipwrecked waters
> rainbow-colored eels
> towards a darkness darker than the dark

Leigh Melander grew up reading children's books about mythology with large, colorful illustrations, and then playing Greek gods with her sisters. She would be Artemis and her sisters Demeter and Persephone. When she grew up she received a doctorate in cultural mythology and psychology, and is the "founding fomenter" of the Imaginal Institute and of the Spillian retreat center in the Catskills. In her "Wisdom Workshops," she asks participants to tell their own story and then connect it to a larger story, often a myth. People imagine that they are living their own life story alone, as a lost soul tumbling through the universe; she asks them what pieces of their story resonate with larger stories. "What stories are your own stories nesting in? In a sense," Leigh says, "we are telling our own stories but our stories are also telling us."[11]

If a man or woman in her workshops talks about the Garden of Eden myth, about a golden age of innocence that they've experienced, she encourages them to use it as a metaphor. What were the qualities, she asks them, that made it feel that way? "Are you content to live in the mythology that we've been rejected from the Garden? Are you able to get back to it? How do you reclaim it so that you're not just on the long

Figure 9. Lion's Gate, Untermyer Gardens, Yonkers, N.Y. Photo by Jonathan Wallen.

Bataan Death March? I try to tell the participants that they are living in these beautiful stories—some of them are painful as hell—but they are enlarged by them."

"We've got to get ourselves back to the garden," I told Victoria, quoting Joni Mitchell. Flummoxed, struggling to get back to the Garden of Eden, Victoria and I stood between the carved lion and the headless horse. "Oh my god," I told Victoria. "Perhaps the pathway is through the Lion's Gate." I was reminded of *Indiana Jones and the Last Crusade*, in which Indy has to traverse a treacherous cave to find the Holy Grail.

"What does the grail look like? Is it a thing? Is it very plain or intricately jeweled? Where is your journey taking you as you look for it—and who is coming with you? Are there gatekeeper figures with whom you can choose to engage?" Those are the questions Leigh, who also uses the grail quest of the Arthurian legends in her workshops, might ask.

In the film, the necessary clue for Indiana Jones to advance is the phrase "Only the penitent man shall pass." We felt penitent, Victoria and I, or perhaps just brave, but we were also swept up in the mythologies invoked by the gardens. A eureka moment—we would penetrate the Lion's Gate. Not to the left of it, not to the right of it, but straight through. Would it be another dead end or the pathway to paradise? With trepidation, summoning fortitude, between the lion and the headless horse, we chanced it.

Suddenly, just a small steep climb ahead, we could see the long set of stairs that led back up. I took Victoria's hand to help her up the hill. We laughed our way back to the garden.

Now it's up to you, pilgrims, to stray from your own beaten paths and visit Untermyer Gardens. It's a mythic landscape to wander through, and an inspiration to journey inward, and to imagine yourself as the hero of your own life story. It may be in Yonkers, but it's as close as you'll get to the Garden of Eden.

23

Rock and Word

Building a Stone Wall as a Lesson in Poetry

Digo da pedra, "E uma pedra."
(Of the stone I say, "It's a stone.")
—Fernando Pessoa

Death left some lives without design, but they were rebuilt
again, as lives and stones are, into other patterns.
—Beryl Markham

Before work each day, I brew a cup of coffee, sit in my favorite armchair, open my laptop, and begin work on my poems. Yet when I turned
fifty, I felt the need for a new avocation. I decided to forgo my morning
writing ritual for a bit and to spend the early part of my days building a
stone wall by hand in the backyard. My wife had recently completed a
project on the stonemasons of Westchester County. Perhaps I was trying
to prove to her that I could do something productive with my hands
(not something I'm known for in the family), or that I could muster the
machismo of the local masons for my own backyard masterpiece.

Besides, I reasoned, poems are just a few coded scratches on papyrus,
or dots on an electronic screen. A stone has weight and mass and exists
as a tangible object. My poems had kept me seated at my computer;
finding stones for the wall necessitated a journey.

Ultimately the journey brought me back to poetry. Searching for
stones took me into crooked streams and vacant lots near our home and
down to the rock beaches that run along the train tracks in north Yonkers. It took me back to a childhood spent foraging in vacant lots. I once
again became Steve Zeitlin, master of creek beds. The rock-strewn lots
triggered memories of the way the bottoms of my feet took on the shape

of the uneven stones; I recalled the way my body assumed the form of boulders as I clambered over them, the way a small rock rested in my hands.

The experience of writing a poem embodies some of this same joy: the words take your shape as you wander through creek beds of syllables, with your own life rolling over them. I discovered the thrill of unearthing the right rock for a particular spot in the wall just as I would sometimes come upon the perfect word or line for a poem. Stones, like words, are everywhere; the trick to building a dry stone wall is to find stones that fit perfectly into one another and form a structure that won't collapse under its own weight. It bears only a passing resemblance to a wet stone wall held together by concrete, which is more like a song whose music holds the lyrics together.

I marveled at the way a stone wall—made of one of the heaviest objects on the planet—nevertheless has a lightness and delicacy in the way the stones touch and balance. The best poems—made of the lightest things on the planet (words)—demonstrate a sturdiness, with the words coupled so perfectly that one cannot be removed without the whole structure crumbling. In my own poems, I strive to balance sound, humor, feeling, and thought to support one another.

To take two stones from two different places—each shaped by different winds, erosions, waters, landslides, and earthquakes—and to find that they fit together in a way that nature could hardly have intended: that's the thrill. Words, like stones, are taken for granted, the story of each one shaped by the currents of history or language. Lines bubble up from the unconscious like lava; ideas from deep inside the mind surface and can be stacked one on the other.

Soon after I finished my motley fifteen-foot wall, I paid a pilgrimage to artist Andrew Goldsworthy's 2,278-foot stone wall, at the Storm King Art Center, about an hour north of our hometown of Hastings, New York. The five-foot-high wall was built with the help of five master stonemasons from England and Scotland, masons who (unlike me) knew how to split a rock along the grain, the way a good poet knows where to break a line.

I discovered Goldsworthy's grand epic poem rolling across the countryside, at one point dipping down into a pond and appearing to rise out of it on the other side. Goldsworthy's wall curves around the trees it passes, so that it seems alternately to fence them in and embrace them. "One of the narratives of this work," writes Robert Louis Chianese in *American Scientist*, "evokes a fairy tale wall that wanted to end a life of straight lines and square corners." Like a poem, perhaps, "it tired also of its job of separating and boxing things in."[1] He playfully titled it *Wall That Went for a Walk*.

Equally grand, though not made from human hands, are the beautiful cascading stone-cold cliffs of the Palisades, across the Hudson River from my hometown. My house does not have a river view, but each morning at the train station I marvel at the fjord-like basalt rock face. The sheer cliffs appear to have been carved by a glacier that moved with the grace of a sculptor's hand. In autumn, the reds and yellows of the trees set against the stone are like bursts of evanescent poetry and art against the immutable face of death.

Ursula K. Le Guin writes of discovering a twelfth-century church in Wales with the words "Tolfin was here" inscribed in runes on a stone wall outside. The words, which represent perhaps the minimal human tale, carry this message: "Life is short, the material was intractable, someone was here."[2] My stone wall was an exercise not in writing on but in composing with stone. From nature's wondrous shapes, I labored to create a functional work of art in my backyard. Life is short; the material is intractable. Undaunted, I continue to build walls of rocks and words on the unyielding landscape. How else to get blood from a stone?

"Life is short, the material was intractable, someone was here."

FOR FURTHER READING

Berger, John. *And Our Faces, My Heart, Brief as Photos.* New York: Vintage Books, 1984.

Campbell, Joseph. *The Hero with a Thousand Faces.* New York: Pantheon Books, 1949.

Caton, Stephen. *"Peaks of Yemen I Summon": Poetry as Cultural Practice in a North Yemeni Tribe.* Berkeley: University of California Press, 1990.

Curtis, Gregory. *The Cave Painters: Probing the Mysteries of the World's First Artists.* New York: Knopf, 2006.

de Caro, Frank. *Stories of Our Lives: Memory, History, Narrative.* Logan, Ut.: Utah State University Press, 2013.

Dissanayake, Ellen. *Art and Intimacy: How the Arts Began.* Seattle: University of Washington Press, 2000.

Glassie, Henry. *Passing the Time in Ballymenone.* Bloomington: Indiana University Press, 1995.

Goldberg, Natalie. *Writing Down the Bones: Freeing the Writer Within.* Boston: Shambhala, 1986.

Hufford, Mary, Marjorie Hunt, and Steve Zeitlin. *The Grand Generation: Memory, Mastery, Legacy.* Washington, D.C.: Smithsonian Institution, 1987.

Hutton, Julia. *Good Sex: Real Stories from Real People.* San Francisco: Cleis Press, 1995.

Isay, Dave, ed. *Listening Is an Act of Love: A Celebration of American Life from the StoryCorps Project.* New York: Penguin Books, 2007.

Jackson, Bruce. *The Story Is True: The Art and Meaning of Telling Stories.* Philadelphia: Temple University Press, 2007.

Kaminsky, Marc. *What's Inside You, It Shines Out of You.* New York: Horizon Press, 1974.

Kugelmass, Jack. *Miracle on Intervale Avenue.* New York: Schocken, 1987.

Lanzillotto, Annie Rachele. *L Is for Lion: An Italian Bronx Butch Freedom Memoir.* Albany, N.Y.: SUNY Press, 2013.

Lederman, Leon, and Dick Teresi. *The God Particle: If the Universe Is the Answer, What Is the Question?* New York: Houghton Mifflin, 1993.

Lyon, George Ella. *Where I'm From: Where Poems Come From.* Spring, Tx.: Absey and Co., 1999.

Mead, Margaret. *Blackberry Winter: My Earlier Years.* New York: William Morrow and Company, 1972.

Myerhoff, Barbara. *Number Our Days.* New York: E. P. Dutton, 1979.

——. *Stories as Equipment for Living: Last Talks and Tales of Barbara Myerhoff,* ed. Marc Kaminsky and Deena Metzger. Ann Arbor: University of Michigan Press, 2007.

——. Ed. Marc Kaminsky. *Remembered Lives: The Work of Ritual, Storytelling, and Growing Older.* Ann Arbor: University of Michigan Press, 1992.

Rank, Otto. *The Myth of the Birth of the Hero.* New York: Vintage Books, 1959.

Rosen, Kim. *Saved by a Poem: The Transformative Power of Words.* Carlsbad, Calif.: Hay House, 2009.

Ueland, Brenda. *If You Want to Write: A Book about Art, Independence and Spirit.* Floyd, Va.: Sublime Books, 2014.

Zeitlin, Steve, and Ilana Harlow. *Giving a Voice to Sorrow: Personal Responses to Death and Mourning.* New York: Berkley Publishing Group, 2001.

NOTES

Introduction

1. This was told to me by the writer Marc Kaminsky, loosely paraphrasing a quote by Samuel Beckett.

2. Owen Barfield, *Poetic Diction: A Study in Meaning* (Oxford: Barfield Press, 2010), 19.

3. See Amanda Dargan and Steve Zeitlin, *City Play* (New Brunswick: Rutgers University Press, 1990), 10.

4. Steven Smith, "Secrets," *Blind Zone* (Toronto: Aya Press, 1986), 60.

5. Mary Hufford, *American Folklife: A Commonwealth of Cultures* (Washington, D.C.: Library of Congress, American Folklife Center, 1991), 1.

6. Dell Hymes, "Folklore's Nature and the Sun's Myth," *Journal of American Folklore* 88, no. 350 (October–December 1975): 346.

7. See Marc Kaminsky, *What's Inside You It Shines Out of You* (New York: Horizon Press, 1974).

8. Marc Kaminsky, introduction to *Remembered Lives: The Work of Ritual, Storytelling, and Growing Older* by Barbara Myerhoff (Ann Arbor: University of Michigan Press, 1992), 12.

9. Thanks to my friend and cultural activist Julie Tay for this insight.

10. "Artify" is a word used by the writer Ellen Dissanayake and told to me in conversation.

11. Ralph Waldo Emerson, "The Poet" (1844), in *Essays and Poems by Ralph Waldo Emerson* (New York: Barnes & Noble, 2004), 222, 223.

12. Percy Bysshe Shelley, "A Defence of Poetry" (1821), in *A Defence of Poetry and Other Essays* (Middletown, DE: CreateSpace Independent Publishing Platform, 2014), 34, 35.

13. Thanks to Jerome Rothenberg for this insight.

14. Najwa Adra, unpublished manuscript, 2015.

15. Ibid.

16. Rachel Arons, "A Mythical Bayou's All-Too-Real Peril: The Making of 'Beasts of the Southern Wild,'" *New York Times,* June 8, 2012.

17. Daniel Taylor, *The Healing Power of Stories* (New York: Doubleday, 1996), 1.

18. Roald Dahl, *The Minpins* (New York: Puffin Books, 1991), 48.

1. Kindred Spirits

1. Tony Butler, interview by Steve Zeitlin, *The Next Big Thing*, WNYC, October 26, 2002.

2. See Margaret Morton, *The Tunnel: The Underground Homeless of New York City (Architecture of Despair)* (New Haven: Yale University Press, 1995).

3. Albert Einstein, *Ideas and Opinions* (New York: Dell Publishing Company, 1954), 60.

4. Thanks to Jack Tchen for these insights, told to me in conversation.

5. *The Grand Generation*, a film by Marjorie Hunt, Paul Wagner, and Steve Zeitlin, streaming on folkstreams.net 1993.

6. See Jack Kugelmass, *The Miracle of Intervale Avenue: The Story of a Jewish Congregation in the South Bronx* (New York: Columbia University Press, 1986).

7. *The Grand Generation*, directed by Paul Wagner, Marjorie Hunt, and Steve Zeitlin, 1993. See www.folkstreams.net.

8. Dave Isay and Harvey Wang, *Holding On: Dreamers, Visionaries, Eccentrics and Other American Heroes* (New York: W.W. Norton & Co, 1996), 191, 192.

9. See Amanda Dargan, *Vitonka Medicine Show Program*, ed. Glen Hinson and Brooks McNamara, American Place Theatre, 1983, available on folkstreams.net. See *Free Show Tonight*.

10. Fred Bloodgood's geek show pitch appears on Amanda Dargan and Steve Zeitlin, eds., *American Talkers: The Art of the Pitchman*, a cassette issued by Global Village Music, 2007, available through iTunes.

11. Annie Lanzillotto, *L Is for Lion: An Italian Bronx Butch Freedom Memoir* (Albany: SUNY Press, 2013), 33, 35.

12. Marci Reaven and Steve Zeitlin, *Hidden New York: A Guide to Places That Matter* (New Brunswick: Rutgers University Press, 2007) 93.

13. Lanzillotto, *L Is for Lion*, 33.

14. *The Grand Generation* documentary.

15. Saxon White Kessinger, "Indispensable Man" (1959), originally published in *The Nutmegger Poetry Club* under the name Saxon Uberuaga. It has also been published in *Boots* (Spring 1993), *The Country Courier* (1996), *Rhyme Time* (Winter 2000), and *Golden Times* (August 2003).

16. *Style Wars*, a film by Tony Silver and Henry Chalfant (MVD Distributors, 1983).

17. See Brooks McNamara, *Step Right Up* (1975; repr., New York: Doubleday, 1995).

18. Anna Mae Noell, *The History of Noell's Ark Gorilla Show* (Tarpon Springs, Fla.: Noell's Ark Publisher, 1979).

19. David Pitts, "Rosina Tucker—A Century of Commitment: Civil Rights, Union Activist Recounts 100 Years of Struggle, Progress," IIP Digital, February 8, 1996. http://iipdigital.usembassy.gov/st/english/article/2005/06/20050606092525pssnik wad0.0264551.html#axzz40eZ1IU3T.

20. *The Grand Generation* documentary.

21. Thanks to Marc Kaminsky for this observation, originally told at the memorial for the Yiddish folklorist Ruth Rubin (1906–2000).

2. Intimacy in Language

1. Anand Prahad (Dennis W. Foley), "Getting the Butter from the Duck: Proverbs and Proverbial Expressions in an Afro-American Family," in *A Celebration of American*

Family Folklore: Tales and Traditions from the Smithsonian's Collection, ed. Steven Zeitlin, Amy Kotkin, and Holly Cutting Baker (New York: Pantheon, 1982), 236, 237.

2. "Thank god for guts and gristle" and "Too tired to tuck" are from Claudia Fugar. See ibid., 146–61.

3. From J. Jaffe, B. Beebe, S. Feldstein, C. L. Crown, and M. D. Jasnow, "Rhythms of Dialogue in Infancy: Coordinated Timing in Development," *Monographs of the Society for Research in Child Development* 66, no. 2 (2001): 1–132.

4. Ellen Dissanayake, *Art and Intimacy: How the Arts Began* (Seattle: University of Washington Press, 2000), 3–10.

5. Ibid., 30, 16.

6. A later version of this essay appeared September 16, 2015, in the online journal *narrative.ly*.

3. Laughter for Dessert

1. See *Make 'Em Laugh: The Funny Business of America*, directed by Michael Kantor, Ghost Light Films and Thirteen/WNET New York, 2009.

2. Ibid.

3. Ibid.

4. "Bronx Beat," *Saturday Night Live*, NBC, season 32, episode 10, January 13, 2007.

5. George Eells, *The Life That Late He Led: A Biography of Cole Porter* (London: W. H. Allen, 1967), 155.

4. The Poetry of Ping-Pong

1. Mihaly Csikszentmihalyi, *Beyond Boredom and Anxiety: Experiencing Flow in Work and Play* (San Francisco: Jossey Bass, 1975), 36.

2. David Gonzalez, "Old King Pong May Be Down, but Not Out," *New York Times*, October 14, 1998.

3. Jerome Charyn, *Sizzling Chops and Devilish Spins: Ping-Pong and the Art of Staying Alive* (New York: Four Walls, Eight Windows, 2001), 48–49.

4. José Miguel Wisnik, "Where Prose Turned to Poetry," *New York Times*, June 16, 2014.

5. Beppe Severgnini, "Never Boring, Always Beautiful," *New York Times*, June 16, 2014.

6. Steve Zeitlin and Amanda Dargan, *City Play* (New Brunswick: Rutgers University Press, 1990), 79.

7. Joseph Wallace, *Diamond Ruby* (New York: Simon & Schuster, 2010), 429.

5. Days of Chess and Backgammon

1. For this and the other quotations in the discussion that follows, see Steve Zeitlin and Marci Reaven, *Hidden New York* (New Brunswick: Rutgers University Press, 2006), 116–23.

2. From Maurice Ashley, "Slaying King George," *Moth Radio Hour*, July 9, 2013. The *Moth Radio Hour* is produced by artistic director Catherine Burns and Jay Allison at Atlantic Public Media, and presented by PRX, the Public Radio Exchange.

6. Inventing a Language for Love

1. This story was first told to me at a conference on Jewish humor at the Yiddish Book Center by Moshe Waldoks.

2. Julia Hutton, *Good Sex: Real Stories from Real People* (San Francisco: Cleis Press, 1995), 13.

3. Ray Charles, "What I'd Say" (Atlantic Records, 1959).

4. Forugh Farrokhzad, "Inaugurating the Garden," in *Sin: Selected Poems of Forugh Farrokhzad*, trans. Sholeh Wolpe (Fayetteville: University of Arkansas Press, 2010), 67.

5. See Ronald A. Veenker, "Forbidden Fruit: Ancient Near Eastern Sexual Metaphors," *Hebrew Union College Annual* 70–71 (1999–2000): 57, 58.

6. *The Collected Poems of Emily Dickinson*, ed. Mabel Loomis Todd, 1856–1932 (Boston: Little, Brown and Co., 1914), 3.

7. Hutton, *Good Sex*, 10, 107, 124.

8. Stephanie Summerville, *Moth Radio Hour*, October 14, 2014, produced by Catherine Burns and Jay Allison, PRX.

9. Florence King, *Southern Ladies and Gentlemen* (New York: St. Martin's Press, 1975), 38–39.

10. T. S. Eliot, "Little Gidding," pt. V, from *Four Quartets* (1943).

11. Alan Dundes, "Structural Typology in North American Indian Folktales," *Southwestern Journal of Anthropology* 19, no. 1 (Spring 1963): 121–30.

12. Mark Baker, *Sex Lives: A Sexual Self Portrait of America* (New York: Pocket Books, 1994), 159–60.

13. Gregory Bateson, "A Theory of Play and Fantasy," *Psychiatric Research Reports* 2 (December 1955), reprinted in *Steps to an Ecology of Mind* (New York: Ballantine, 1972), 177–93.

14. Hutton, *Good Sex*, 137–38.

15. Ibid., 15–17.

16. See Brian Sutton Smith, *A History of Children's Play: The New Zealand Playground, 1840–1950* (Philadelphia: University of Pennsylvania Press, 1981), 297, 14.

7. Poetry on the Porch

1. Eugenio Montale, *The Second Life of Art*, trans. Jonathan Galassi (New York: Ecco Press, 1977), 22.

8. All My Trials

1. Jalal al-Din Rumi, "The Guest House," in *The Essential Rumi*, new expanded ed., trans. Coleman Barks (New York: HarperCollins, 2004), 109.

2. Karen Finley, "The Black Sheep," in *A Different Kind of Intimacy: The Collected Writings of Karen Finley* (Berkeley: Thunder's Mouth Press, 2000), 67.

3. Harold Scheub, *The Poem in the Story: Music, Poetry, and Narrative* (Madison: University of Wisconsin Press, 2002), 23.

9. The AIDS Poets

1. See Lila Zeiger, "A Prom and a Yearbook," in *Giving a Voice to Sorrow*, ed. Ilana Harlow and Steve Zeitlin (New York: Penguin Putnam, 2001), 144–53.

2. Ibid., 73–77.

3. From an interview with Steve Zeitlin, August 21, 1995.

4. Zeiger, "A Prom and a Yearbook," 153.

10. Oh Did You See the Ashes Come Thickly Falling Down?

A version of this essay appeared in Jack Santino, ed., *Spontaneous Shrines and the Public Memorialization of Death* (New York: Palgrave Macmillan, 2006), 57–98. The essay grows out of City Lore's research and documentation in the days, weeks, and months that followed September 11, as well as the exhibition *Missing: Streetscape of a City in Mourning*, which ran from March 8 to July 7, 2002, at the New-York Historical Society. It was funded by a discretionary chairman's grant from the National Endowment for the Humanities, William Ferris, director. For research, interpretation, and poetic turn of phrase, I am deeply indebted to my two co-curators and partners in the project, Marci Reaven and Martha Cooper, to field researcher Elena Martínez, to intern Joseph Dobkin, and to co-curator of the People's Poetry Gathering, poet and poetry activist Bob Holman. The title quote was found by Steve Zeitlin on September 25, 2001, on a handwritten scrap of paper pinned up near the entrance to the subway at Union Square.

1. From a photograph taken by C. Mills, City Lore Archives.

2. Dan Barry, "From a World Lost, Ephemeral Notes Bear Witness to the Unspeakable," *New York Times*, September 25, 2001.

3. Jordan Schuster, interview with Steve Zeitlin, November 2001.

4. Taken from a sheet of butcher block paper set down by Jordan Schuster on the day of the tragedy.

5. From a photograph by Martha Cooper, September 13, 2001, City Lore Archives.

6. From a photograph by Martha Cooper, September 14, 2001, City Lore Archives.

7. From a photograph by Martha Cooper, September 17, 2001, City Lore Archives.

8. I thank exhibit co-curator and my colleague at City Lore Marci Reaven for this insight.

9. Drawn from City Lore photographer Martha Cooper's observations and images.

10. Amy Waldman, "Posters of the Missing Now Speak of Losses," *New York Times*, September 29, 2001.

11. See Edward T. Linenthal, *The Unfinished Bombing: Oklahoma City in American Memory* (Oxford: Oxford University Press, 2003).

12. John Urry, "Social Relations, Space and Time," in *Social Relations and Spatial Structures*, ed. Derek Gregory and John Urry (New York: St. Martin's Press, 1985), 30, quoted in David Chidester and Edward T. Linenthal, eds., *American Sacred Space* (Bloomington: Indiana University Press, 1995), 18.

13. Michel Foucault, "Space, Knowledge, and Power," in *The Foucault Reader*, ed. Paul Rabinow (New York: Pantheon, 1984), 252.

14. Chidester and Linenthal, *American Sacred Space*, 15–16.

15. Thanks to Joseph Dobkin for assisting with this research.

16. Ubiquitous after September 11, these are the lyrics from a song by Mary Frye, composed in 1932.

17. Transcribed by Steve Zeitlin at Grand Central Terminal's memorial wall in New York, September 15, 2001.

18. See Mircea Eliade, *The Sacred and the Profane: The Nature of Religion* (New York: Harcourt Brace Jovanovich, 1987), and *The Myth of the Eternal Return* (Princeton: Princeton University Press, 1971).

19. Ilana Harlow and Steve Zeitin, "How Much of the City's Grief Should We Preserve?" *Newsday*, October 14, 2001.

11. *The POEMobile Dreams of Peace*

1. Martin Espada, "The Owl and the Lightning, Brooklyn, New York," in *Alabanza: New and Selected Poems, 1982–2002* (New York: W. W. Norton & Company, 2004), 120.

2. Bob Holman, *Sing This One Back to Me* (Minneapolis: Coffee House Press, 2013), 30.

3. From an informal communication with Bob Holman waxing poetic over a POEMobile presentation on July 15, 2011.

4. Denize Lauture, "Neg Ak Fank Powet Nou," in *Denizens of Hope*, ed. Jack Hirschman (Berkeley: CC Marimbo, 2013), 46, 47.

5. From "Interview with Iranian Poet Farideh Hassanzadeh: Iranian poet Farideh Hassanzadeh talks about war, loss, and the politics of poetry" by Melissa Tuckey and John Feffer on June 12, 2007 on the website Foreign Policy in Focus, fpif.org/interview_with_iranian_poet_farideh_hassanzadeh/. The line has been translated in different ways. A version of the poem called "The Bird Shall One Day Die" appears in Forugh Farrokhzad in *Sin: Selected Poems of Forugh Farrokhzad*, ed. and trans. Sholeh Wolpeh (Fayetteville: The University of Arkansas Press, 2007), 111.

6. Yevgeny Yevtushenko, *The Collected Poems, 1952–1990*, ed. Albert C. Todd with the author and James Ragan (New York: Henry Holt and Company, 1991), 149.

7. Steven C. Caton, *Peaks of Yemen I Summon: Poetry as Cultural Practice in a North Yemeni Tribe* (Los Angeles: University of California Press, 1993), 168, 169, 174.

8. Robyn Creswell and Bernard Haykel, "Battle Lines: Want to Understand the Jihadis? Read Their Poetry," *The New Yorker*, June 8, 2015, http://www.newyorker.com/magazine/2015/06/08/battle-lines-jihad-creswell-and-haykel.

9. Ibid.

10. Annie Lanzillotto, "Catching a Fly Ball in Incoming Traffic," in *Schistsong* (New York: Bordighera Press, 2013), 60.

12. *Free Market Flavor*

1. Written by Bob Hershon as an "I Am" poem, a "New York City Epic," produced by City Lore and the Bowery Poetry Club for the People's Poetry Gathering in 2006. The project was written up and the poem reprinted in "They Sing the City Poetic," *New York Times*, April 30, 2006. Reprinted from *Goldfish and Rose* © 2013 by Robert Hershon, by permission of Hanging Loose Press.

2. Mark Kurlansky, *Cod: The Biography of a Fish That Changed the World* (New York: Penguin Group, 1997), and *Salt: A World History* (New York: Penguin Group, 2002).

13. *The Poetry in Science*

1. Michio Kaku, *Hyperspace: A Scientific Odyssey through Parallel Universes, Time Warps, and the Tenth Dimension* (New York: Random House, 1995); Gary Zukav,

Dancing Wu Li Masters: An Overview of the New Physics (New York: HarperOne, 2001), 82.

2. John A. Wheeler and Kenneth Ford, *Geons, Black Holes, and Quantum Foam: A Life in Physics* (New York: W. W. Norton and Company, 2000), quoted in Dennis Overbye, "John A. Wheeler, Physicist Who Coined the Term 'Black Hole,' Is Dead at 96," *New York Times*, April 14, 2008.

3. See, for instance, John P. Briggs and F. David Peat, *Looking Glass Universe: The Emerging Science of Wholeness* (New York: Simon & Schuster, 1984), 66.

4. Brian Greene, *The Enchanted Universe: Superstrings, Hidden Dimensions, and the Quest for the Ultimate Theory* (New York: Vintage Books, 2000). For the books by Kako and Zukav, see note 1.

5. Edwin A. Abbott, *Flatland: A Romance of Many Dimensions* (1884; repr., New York: Dover Publications, 1992).

6. Leon Lederman and Dick Teresi, *The God Particle: If the Universe Is the Answer, What Is the Question?* (Boston: Houghton Mifflin, 1993).

7. Ibid., xi, 24.

8. Ibid., 142.

9. *Particle Fever*, directed by Mark Levinson (Anthos Media, 2013).

10. Lederman and Teresi, *The God Particle*, 142.

11. Briggs and Peat, *Looking Glass Universe*, 272.

12. Brian Thomas Swimme and Mary Evelyn Tucker, *Journey of the Universe: Conversations* (New Haven: Yale University Press, 2011) 2–3.

13. David Loy, *The World Is Made of Stories* (Somerville, Mass: Wisdom Press, 2010), 3.

14. Lederman and Teresi, *The God Particle*, 410.

15. Graham Farmelo, *It Must Be Beautiful: Great Equations of Modern Science* (London: Granta Books, 2002), ix–xvi.

16. Lederman and Teresi, *The God Particle*, 14.

14. Navigating Transitions

I thank Mary Hufford and Marjorie Hunt, my two collaborators on *The Grand Generation*, for many of their insights which are reflected in this essay. Some of the ideas were also developed for the Conference on American Folk Custom at the Library of Congress, October 3–5, 1980.

1. For variants of "Solomon Grundy," see Iona Opie and Peter Opie, eds., *The Oxford Dictionary of Nursery Rhymes* (Oxford: Oxford University Press, 1951), 392–93.

2. See John 21:18 (New Revised Standard Edition).

3. Tony Heriza, Robert Lee, and Jean Tsien, *Singing to Remember*, documentary film distributed by the Asian American Arts Center, New York, 1991.

4. William Shakespeare, *As You Like It*, Act II, Scene VII, in *The Complete Works of William Shakespeare*, William Albis Wright, ed. (New York: Doubleday and Co., Inc., 1936), 677.

5. Arnold van Gennep, *The Rites of Passage*, trans. Monika B. Vizedom and Gabrielle L. Caffee (Chicago: University of Chicago Press, 1960), 30.

6. Victor Turner, *The Forest of Symbols: Aspects of Ndembu Ritual* (Ithaca: Cornell University Press, 1967), 93.

7. Erik H. Erikson, *Childhood and Society* (New York: W. W. Norton, 1963).

8. Chart by Allen Carroll from Hufford, Hunt, and Zeitlin, *The Grand Generation*, 20.

9. Alan Jabbour, "Creativity and Aging: Some Thoughts from a Folk Cultural Perspective," in *Perspectives on Aging: Exploding the Myth*, ed. Priscilla W. Johnston (Cambridge, Mass.: Ballinger Publishing Company, 1981), 144.

10. Mary Hufford and Marjorie Hunt, in Hufford, Hunt, and Zeitlin, *The Grand Generation*, 27.

11. Barbara Myerhoff, *Number Our Days: A Triumph of Continuity and Culture among Jewish Old People in an Urban Ghetto* (New York: E. P. Dutton, 1979), 94.

12. Kahlil Gibran, "On Children," *The Prophet* (1923; repr., Mumbai: Jaico Publishing House, 2013), 17.

13. See *Let's Get the Rhythm: The Life and Times of Miss Mary Mack*, documentary film directed by Irene Chagall, coproduced by City Lore, distributed by Women Make Movies, 2015.

14. Rainer Maria Rilke, *Love and Other Difficulties*, trans. John L. Mood (New York: W. W. Norton, 1975), 28–29.

15. From a personal communication with Gerald Hausman. See also Gerald Hausman, *Meditations with the Navajo: Prayers, Songs, and Stories of Healing and Harmony* (Rochester, Vt.: Bear & Company/Inner Traditions, 2001).

16. From a personal communication with Gerald Hausman.

17. J. R. Bluejay DeGroat, "Bluebird Song," from a privately printed booklet, *Whimpering Chant*.

18. From a personal email communication with Ariel Zeitlin Cooke.

19. Arthur W. McMahon and Paul J. Rhudick, "Reminiscing: Adaptational Significance in the Aged," *Archives of General Psychiatry* 10 (1964): 222, 98; see also Harriet Wyre and Jacqueline Churilla, "Looking Inward, Looking Backward: Reminiscence and the Life Review," *Frontiers: A Journal of Women's Studies* 2 (1977): 98–106.

20. Myerhoff, *Number Our Days*, 108.

21. Allen Klein, *The Courage to Laugh: Humor, Hope, and Healing in the Face of Death and Dying* (New York: Penguin Putnam, 1998), 29, 30.

22. The title and last line were inspired by Kelly S. Taylor's essay, "The Storytelling Wake: Performance in the Absence of Established Ritual," *Southern Folklore* 50, no. 2 (1993): 99–111.

23. Alfred Lord Tennyson, "Crossing the Bar," in *One Hundred and One Famous Poems*, ed. Roy J. Cook (Chicago: Reilly & Lee, 1958), 142.

24. Myerhoff, *Number Our Days*, 19.

25. See the interview conducted by Ilana Harlow in Ilana Harlow and Steve Zeitlin, eds., *Giving a Voice to Sorrow: Personal Responses to Death and Mourning* (New York: Penguin Putnam, 2001), 120–35.

26. John Green, *The Fault in Our Stars* (New York: Penguin Books, 2014), 260.

27. Evelyn Lamb, "Some Infinities Are Bigger Than Other Infinities, and Some Are Just the Same Size," scientificamerican.com, July 10, 2014.

28. See Hufford, Hunt, and Zeitlin, *The Grand Generation*.

29. Joan Gross, "Las Princessa for a Day: Sweet Sixteens in Philadelphia," *Works in Progress Newsletter of the Philadelphia Folklore Project* 2, no. 1 (Fall 1988).

30. Patricia Leigh Brown, "This Prom Has Everything, Except for Boys," *New York Times*, May 1, 2012.

31. John Sebastian, "Younger Generation," *Everything Playing* (Kama Sutra, 1967).

32. Tamara Hareven, "The Last Stage: Historical Adulthood and Old Age," *Daedalus* 105, no. 4 (1976), 15.

15. The Human Unit of Time

1. Margaret Mead, *Blackberry Winter* (New York: William Morrow and Company, 1972), 311.

2. Ibid.

3. Ibid.

4. Steve Zeitlin, "Strangling Culture with a Copyright Law," *New York Times*, April 25, 1998.

5. Mary Hufford, Marjorie Hunt, and Steve Zeitlin, *The Grand Generation: Memory, Mastery, Legacy* (Washington, D.C.: Smithsonian Institution Traveling Exhibition Service and Office of Folklife Programs in association with University of Washington Press, 1987), 108.

16. Your Body as Symbol

1. John Berger, *And Our Faces, My Heart, Brief as Photos* (New York: Vintage Books, 1984), 101.

2. See the interview conducted by Ilana Harlow in Ilana Harlow and Steve Zeitlin, eds., *Giving a Voice to Sorrow* (New York: Penguin Putnam, 2001), 6–7.

3. See the interview conducted by Ilana Harlow, ibid.

4. Dave Isay and Harvey Wang, 89.

5. Harlow and Zeitlin, *Giving a Voice to Sorrow*, 165–70.

6. Liu Xiaobo, "The Poet in an Unknown Prison," trans. Liao Tienchi, *New York Review of Books*, May 28, 2009.

7. Jeffrey Cyphers Wright, "Full of Bad Ideas," in *Brevitas 12* (New York: First Street Press, 2015), 99.

17. Intimations of Immortality

1. *Ribbon of Highway Endless Skyway: Tribute to Woody Guthrie* (Music Road Records, 2008).

2. Thanks to folklorist Jack Santino for this wonderful turn of phrase.

3. Joseph Campbell, *The Hero with a Thousand Faces*, Bollingen series 17 (1949; repr., Princeton: Princeton University Press, 1968), 390.

4. *Ribbon of Highway.*

5. Quoted in *The Grand Generation* documentary, produced and directed by Paul Wagner, Marjorie Hunt and Steve Zeitlin, 1993. See www.folkstreams.net.

6. Thanks to Carolyn Wells who used the line "rest my soul on a memory" from her unpublished poem, "Prato," shared with our poetry group, Brevitas.

7. Barbara Myerhoff, *Number Our Days: Culture and Community among Elderly Jews in an American Ghetto* (New York: E. P. Dutton, 1979).

8. Tweeted by Iman Bowie about her husband, the pop icon David Bowie, before he passed away January 11, 2016.

9. Annie Lanzillotto, *L Is for Lion: An Italian Bronx Butch Freedom Memoir* (Albany: SUNY University Press, 2013), 308.

10. Carl Jung, *Memories, Dreams, Reflections* (New York: Pantheon Books, 1963), quoted in Robert Jay Lifton, *The Broken Connection: On Death and the Continuity of Life* (Washington, D.C.: American Psychiatric Press, 1979), 15.

11. Lifton, *The Broken Connection*, 18.

12. Viola Allo, "Bodies, Flowerbeds" in the chapbook, *Bird from Africa*, included in *Eight New-Generation African Poets: A Chapbook Box Set* (Brooklyn, N.Y.: Akashic Books and the African Poetry Book Fund, 2015), 16.

13. Lifton, *The Broken Connection*, 18.

14. Letter from Einstein, March 1955, to the family of his lifelong friend Michele Besso after learning of his death, quoted in Freeman Dyson, "A Distant Mirror," chap. 17 of *Disturbing the Universe* (New York: Basic Books, 1979), 193.

15. Viktor E. Frankl, *Man's Search for Meaning* (Boston: Beacon Press, 1959, 2006), 120.

16. See Kurt Vonnegut, *Slaughterhouse-Five* (New York: Dell Publishing, 1991).

17. "A Matter of Time," *Scientific American* 23, no. 4 (Autumn 2014): 13.

18. Mary Oliver, "When Death Comes," in *New and Selected Poems* (Boston: Beacon Press, 1992), 10.

19. *Free Show Tonight*, a documentary by Paul Wagner and Steve Zeitlin (1982), streamed on Folkstreams.net.

20. Transcribed by Milbre Burch from archival recordings for The Storytelling Project of the Cotsen Children's Library.

21. Brenda Ueland, *If You Want to Write: A Book about Art, Independence and Spirit* (Thousand Oaks, Calif.: BN Publishing, 2010), 142.

22. Abraham Joshua Heschel, *Moral Grandeur and Spiritual Audacity: Essays* (New York: Farrar, Straus and Giroux, 1997), 378.

23. John Berger, *And Our Faces, My Heart, Brief as Photos* (New York: Vintage Books, 1984), 22, 96–97.

18. God Is in the Details

1. George Ella Lyon, *Where I'm From: Where Poems Come From* (Spring, Tx.: Absey and Co., 1999), 3.

2. Nikki Giovanni, *Quilting the Black-Eyed Pea: Poems and Not Quite Poems* (New York: HarperCollins, 2002), 10.

3. Somini Sengupta, "My City: Plotting Your Winter Days to Gather the Light," *New York Times*, January 14, 2000.

4. Caitlin Van Dusen, Sense & the City blog, Blogspot, June 2, 2009.

5. Cara da Silva, "My New York," *City Lore Magazine*, vol. 6, 1997–1998, 22.

6. Barbara Kirshenblatt-Gimblett, "My New York," *City Lore Magazine*, vol. 5, 1995–1996, 22.

7. Anatole Broyard, *Kafka Was the Rage: A Greenwich Village Memoir* (New York: C. Southern Books, 1993).

8. Jackson Browne, "Running on Empty" (Asylum Records, 1977).

9. See Edward Casey, *Getting Back into Place: Toward a Renewed Understanding of the Place-World* (Bloomington: Indiana University Press, 1993).

10. Beryl Markham, *West with the Night* (New York: Farrar Strauss and Giroux, 1942, 1983), 242.

19. Breath on the Mirror

1. Joan Didion, "Goodbye to All That," in *Slouching Towards Bethlehem* (New York: Farrar, Straus & Giroux, 1968).

2. Edith Wharton, "The Background," in *Writing New York: A Literary Anthology*, ed. Philip Lopate (New York: Library of America, 2008), 581, 582.

3. Jamaica Kincaid, "Life in the City: Putting Myself Together," *The New Yorker*, February 20, 1994, 101.

4. Thanks to my friend the poet David Brown for this insight.

5. Brenda Ueland, *If You Want to Write: A Book about Art, Independence and Spirit* (Thousand Oaks, Calif.: BN Publishing, 2010), 25.

6. Paraphrased from a quip by the folksinger-storyteller Bruce "Utah" Phillips at Lena's Café in Saratoga Springs, New York.

7. Billy Collins, "Flock," in *Aimless Love: New and Selected Poems* (New York: Random House, 2013), 57.

8. Tom Waits, interview by Elizabeth Gilbert, from Radiolab, hosted by Jad Abumradl, Radiolab, produced by WNYC Studios; http://www.radiolab.org/story/117294-me-myself-and-muse/.

9. Mary Oliver, "When Death Comes," in *New and Selected Poems* (Boston: Beacon Press, 1992), 114.

10. Thanks to my friend Ariel Zeitlin Cooke (no relation) for this turn of phrase.

11. Julius Sokolsky, quoted in Amanda Dargan and Steve Zeitlin, *City Play* (New Brunswick: Rutgers University Press, 1992), 136.

20. The Best Stories versus My Story

1. Steve Zeitlin and Nick Doob, *The People's Poetry Gathering* (City Lore Films, 2001).

2. Roberta Smith, "Elizabeth Murray, 66, Artist of Vivid Forms, Dies," *New York Times*, August 13, 2007.

3. Alaka Wali, Rebeca Severson, and Mario Longoni, "Informal Arts: Finding Cohesion, Capacity and Other Cultural Benefits in Unexpected Places," Research Report to the Chicago Center for Arts Policy at Columbia College, 2002.

4. Keith Richards, *Life* (New York: Little, Brown and Company, 2010), 478.

5. Dan Harmon, quoted in Austin Kleon, *Show Your Work: 10 Ways to Share Your Creativity and Get Discovered* (New York: Workman Publishing, 2014), 20.

6. Brenda Ueland, *If You Want to Write: A Book about Art, Independence and Spirit* (Thousand Oaks, Calif.: BN Publishing, 2010), 26.

7. Ilana Harlow and Steve Zeitlin, *Giving a Voice to Sorrow: Personal Responses to Death and Mourning* (New York: Viking Penguin, 2001), 180.

21. The Grease Lamp's Flicker and Flare

1. Gregory Curtis, *The Cave Painters: Probing the Mysteries of the World's First Artists* (New York: Anchor Books, 2006).

2. Ibid., 145.

3. Ibid., 219–27.

4. Stanley Kunitz, "Among the Gods," in *Selected Poems* (Boston: Atlantic–Little, Brown, 1958), 7.

5. Evie Ivy, "Symbol for the Now," in *Brevitas 11* (New York: First Street Press, 2014), 28.

22. Lion's Gate

1. Barbara Myerhoff, *Number Our Days: Culture and Community among Elderly Jews in an American Ghetto* (New York: Simon & Schuster, 1968).

2. *No Direction Home*, directed by Martin Scorsese (Paramount Pictures, 2005).

3. Susan Sontag, *On Photography* (New York: Farrar, Straus & Giroux, 1977), 15, 81.

4. Patrick Phillips, *Boy: Poems* (Athens: University of Georgia Press, 2008), 50.

5. See, for example, Richard Bernstein, "After Death, a Writer Is Accused of Anti-Semitism," *New York Times*, November 6, 1989, which offers little evidence to back up the accusation of anti-Semitism.

6. Otto Rank, *The Myth of the Birth of the Hero* (New York: Vintage Books, 1959), 61.

7. Ibid., 13.

8. Joseph Campbell, *The Hero with a Thousand Faces* (Bollingen Series XVII, Princeton: Princeton University Press, 1949), 30.

9. Ibid., 4.

10. Décio Ferreira, International Fine Arts website, http://www.fine-arts-interna tional.com/Décio-Ferreira.htm.

11. From a personal conversation with Leigh Melander.

23. Rock and Word

1. Robert Louis Chianese, *American Scientist* 10, no. 3 (May–June 2013): 1.

2. Quoted in Barbara Myerhoff, *Stories as Equipment for Living: Last Talks and Tales of Barbara Myerhoff*, ed. Marc Kaminsky and Deena Metzger (Ann Arbor: University of Michigan Press, 2007), 17.

PERMISSIONS

Several chapters in this book began as entries for my column "Downstate" in *Voices: Journal of the New York Folklore Society*. These were: "Chop Slam: The Inner Life of Ping Pong," vol. 26, Fall–Winter 2000; "The Human Unit of Time," vol. 28, Fall–Winter 2002; "Scientists as Storytellers," vol. 29, Fall–Winter 2003; "Rock and Word," vol. 30, Fall–Winter 2004; "Of Clothespins and Cottonball Lambs," vol. 32, Fall–Winter 2006; "Free Market Flavor," vol. 35, Spring–Summer 2009; "Is Sex Play," vol. 35, Fall–Winter 2009; "Place Moments," vol. 37 Spring–Summer 2011; "Poetry on the Porch," vol. 37, Fall–Winter 2011; "The Humor Pill," vol. 38, Fall–Winter 2012; "Kindred Spirits," vol. 39, Spring–Summer 2013; "The POEMobile Dreams of Peace," vol. 40, Spring–Summer 2014; "Lion's Gate," vol. 40, Fall–Winter 2014; and "High Banter," vol. 41, Spring–Summer 2015. Thank you to the Society's director, Ellen McHale. Used with permission.

A version of "Free Market Flavor" was reprinted in *The New York Folklife Reader: Diverse Voices*, ed. Elizabeth Tucker and Ellen McHale (University Press of Mississippi, 2013), 242–45; used by permission from the University Press of Mississippi. My essay "Rock and Word" and four of my poems, "Margaret," "Cat," "The Storytelling Wake," and "Once Upon a Time," were anthologized in *The Folklore Muse: Poetry, Fiction, and Other Reflections by Folklorists* (Logan, Ut.: Utah State University Press, 2008). A version of "Oh Did You See the Ashes Come Thickly Falling Down: September 11th Street Poems" appeared in Jack Santino, ed., *Spontaneous Shrines and the Public Memorialization of Death* (New York: Palgrave Macmillan, 2006), 57–98; reprinted with permission from Palgrave MacMillan.

"Flock" appears from *The Trouble with Poetry: And Other Poems* by Billy Collins, copyright © 2005 by Billy Collins, used by permission of Random House, an imprint and division of Penguin Random House LLC; all rights reserved. Bob Holman's poem "Song" is reprinted from *Sing This One Back to Me* (Minneapolis: Coffee House Press, 2013); used with permission. Excerpt of three lines from "What We Miss" from *Quilting the Black-Eyed Pea* © 2002 by Nikki Giovanni is reprinted by permission of HarperCollins Publishers. Forugh Farrokhzad's "Inaugurating the Garden" from *Sin: Selected Poems of Forugh Farrokkhzad*, translated by Sholeh Wolpé, copyright © 2007 by Sholeh Wolpé, is reprinted with the permission of The Permissions Company, Inc., on behalf of the University of Arkansas Press. "On Children" is from *The Prophet* by